102 CONTENT STRATEGIES FOR ENGLISH LANGUAGE LEARNERS

TEACHING FOR ACADEMIC SUCCESS IN GRADES 3–12

Jodi Reiss

Florida International University (Retired)

PEARSON

Merrill
Prentice Hall

Upper Saddle River, New Jersey
Columbus, Ohio

Library of Congress Cataloging-in-Publication Data

Reiss, Jodi.
  102 content strategies for English language learners: teaching for academic
success in grades 3–12 / Jodi Reiss.
    p. cm.
  Includes bibliographical references.
  ISBN 0–13–221819–4
  1. English language–Study and teaching (Elementary)–Foreign speakers.
2. Education, Bilingual. I. Title. II. Title: One hundred two content strategies
for English language learners.
  PE1128.A2R4545 2008
  428.2'4–dc22   2006032312

Vice President and Executive Publisher: Jeffery W. Johnston
Executive Editor: Debra A. Stollenwerk
Development Editor: Daniel J. Richcreek
Production Editor: Alexandrina Benedicto Wolf
Production Coordination: Techbooks
Design Coordinator: Diane C. Lorenzo
Cover Designer: Candace Rowley
Cover Image: Jupiter Images
Production Manager: Susan W. Hannahs
Director of Marketing: David Gesell
Senior Marketing Manager: Darcy Betts Prybella
Marketing Coordinator: Brian Mounts

This book was set in Garamond by Techbooks. It was printed and bound by Bind-Rite Graphics.
The cover was printed by Phoenix Color Corp.

Pearson Education Ltd.   Pearson Education Australia Pty. Limited
Pearson Education Singapore Pte. Ltd.   Pearson Education North Asia Ltd.
Pearson Education Canada, Ltd.   Pearson Educación de Mexico, S.A. de C.V.
Pearson Education—Japan   Pearson Education Malaysia Pte. Ltd.

10 9 8 7 6 5 4 3 2 1
ISBN-13: 978-0-13-221819-1
ISBN-10: 0-13-221819-4

This book, *102 Content Strategies for English Language Learners: Teaching for Academic Success in Grades 3-12,* is dedicated to those who teach content to English language learners. It is written in the belief that mainstream teachers, as much as English language development teachers, have much to contribute to the academic success of these students.

QUICK REFERENCE

CHAPTER 11

CHAPTER 12

ABOUT THE AUTHOR

Photo: Ron Elkind

JODI REISS   Before retiring from Florida International University in Miami, Jodi Reiss served as the director of the TESOL masters' program. In her nine years there, she developed, adapted, and taught a variety of graduate and undergraduate TESOL courses. Her three favorites were Methods of TESOL, Assessment for English Language Learners, and the final seminar in the masters' program, in which her teachers directed their full attention toward observing, analyzing and reflecting upon their own teaching attitudes and behaviors. This unique course, developed by Ms. Reiss, consistently earned the highest student praise.

In her many years as an educator, Ms. Reiss taught students at every level of instruction. In her earliest experiences as a sixth-grade teacher, she discovered that she most enjoyed classes and programs that encouraged curricular innovation and development. She still does.

Since her retirement, Ms. Reiss has written several books for teachers on strategies for teaching content to English language learners. In conjunction with these books, she conducts teacher workshops and presentations for school districts throughout the United States. Although no longer in the classroom, her clearly written books and popular workshops have allowed her to continue to provide information and inspiration to teachers of English language learners.

BRIEF CONTENTS

CONTENTS

 **PREFACE**

Purpose of This Book

Teaching content to students who are in the process of learning English is a challenge, both for teachers whose expertise lies in subjects such as math, science, and social studies and for those who teach English either as a new language or as language arts and literature. I have written this book for all of them.

This is a reader-friendly resource book that presents content teaching strategies built on a foundation of second-language acquisition theory. I had two goals in writing this book. The first was to balance theory and application—to provide readers with a wealth of practical instructional and assessment strategies for teaching content to English language learners along with the theoretical understanding to make informed pedagogical decisions about when, how, and with whom to use which strategies. For this reason, the strategies are presented in a two-part format. The concept of strategy is discussed first; practical application is then presented.

The second goal involved the adage "Nothing succeeds like success." Teachers care about their students' success. I wanted to write a book that offered teachers practical, adaptable strategies to help English language learners experience academic success in content classrooms. For these students and their teachers, even the beginnings of success can be their own reward.

Organization

This book is divided into three parts. Part I presents the foundations that inform the strategies.

- Chapter 1 provides an overview of select theories and principles of second-language acquisition that form the theoretical basis for the strategies. The end of the chapter unifies the separate theories into an application called *Theory to Application: Guidelines for Practice.*
- Chapter 2 aims to develop teacher awareness of the deep roots of culture that may lead to cross-cultural misunderstandings. The chapter examines culture as a potential determinant of English language learners' classroom behavior patterns and presents details of specific cultural considerations for teaching math, science, social studies, and language arts.

Part II takes readers through sets of strategies that follow the logical pattern of developmental steps in the instructional process.

- Chapter 3 looks at state standards in relation to English language learners and offers strategies for making sound curricular choices.
- Chapter 4 presents first a general overview of learning strategies and then learning strategies for English language learners. It looks at the need to incorporate learning strategies into daily instruction and provides strategies to explicitly teach them to students.

- Chapter 5 deals with the relationship between background knowledge and learning and then presents strategies to build and activate background knowledge for English language learners.

- Chapter 6 analyzes teacher talk and offers strategies to facilitate comprehension for English language learners during periods of oral instruction.

- Chapter 7 examines traditional question-and-answer patterns in the classroom and presents strategies to increase the quality and quantity of participation for all students.

- Chapters 8 and 9 focus on facilitating English language learners' comprehension of the textbook. Chapter 8 details vocabulary strategies, and Chapter 9 describes reading strategies.

- Chapter 10 presents strategies for activities and assignments that reinforce conceptual learning for students at varying stages of English language development.

Part III covers assessment practices as they relate to English language learners.

- Chapter 11 examines the difficulties of traditional essay and multiple-choice tests for English language learners and presents strategies for modifying classroom tests and creating alternative testing formats. The chapter ends with a section on grading, advocating the need to evaluate English language learners in ways that promote academic success.

- Chapter 12 focuses on the topic of accountability and high-stakes tests. The chapter offers strategies to prepare English language learners for high-stakes tests and then examines test accommodation strategies to maximize students' performance potential at every level of English language development.

Features

Theory to Application: Guidelines for Practice appears at the beginning of each chapter. As the successive steps in the instructional process are examined, appropriate guidelines are selected from the full listing in Chapter 1 to tie the strategies to their theoretical foundations.

The strategy chapters (Chapters 3–12) follow an organized and practical format. Each chapter contains these sections:

- An introductory examination of the needs and difficulties that English language learners may encounter with the lesson segment under consideration.
- *The Objective* succinctly states the goal toward which teachers must strive in leading English language learners toward academic success.
- *The Rationale* explains the reasoning underlying each objective.
- Each *Strategy* provides a set of practical and widely adaptable techniques that teachers can use to help English language learners experience success within the objective. Each strategy is presented in two sections. (Strategies are listed on pp. v–vii.)
- The *In Concept* section introduces the strategy and explains *why* the strategy will be advantageous to English language learners.
- The *In Practice* section details *how* to use the strategy, showing through graphic illustration and clear explanation, often with examples, specific techniques for classroom application.
- The *In Summary* segment ends each chapter with concluding thoughts, pointers, and suggestions.

Post-reading questions and a resource section end each chapter. The *Questions for Discussion* include reflective, research, and observational activities to extend and apply students' conceptual understanding of the strategies and the theories that inform them. The listings in *References and Resources* include reference citations, informative articles and books on the topic, and helpful Web sites.

Appendix I contains additional teacher resources—books and Web sites that are excellent sources of information for teaching content to English language learners. Their scope is simply too broad to have been included in the reference section of any single chapter. The Glossary lists commonly encountered acronyms relating to all aspects of English language development, including, but not limited to, those used in this book.

ACKNOWLEDGMENTS

I owe much to the prospective and practicing teachers who filled my university classes. Many of the strategies in this book were developed in a spirit of mutual cooperation and collaboration to meet specific challenges they faced. I must also thank them for the many times they asked, "When are you going to write a book?"

I am grateful to my editors, Debbie Stollenwerk and Dan Richcreek, for their guidance and insightful input. Special thanks go to Heath Lynn Silberfeld for her amazing copy editing skills.

I am also appreciative of the reviewers for their incredibly thorough critiques and detailed suggestions: John McAndrew, Kutztown University of Pennsylvania; Imelda Basurto, California State University, Fresno; Juanita N. Benioni, Utah Valley State College; George C. Bunch, University of California, Santa Cruz; Sandy Cmajdalka, University of Houston–Downtown; Dana L. Grisham, San Diego State University; Linda Holley Mohr, Texas A&M University; Oneyda M. Paneque, Barry University; and W. Robert Walker, Northern Arizona University, Yuma. Their efforts made this a much better book.

And finally, I thank my family who, during those months of intense concentration, willingly excused me from my normal life. They, and I, continue to delight in my return.

TEN QUESTIONS

1. Is this book primarily for teachers of English language learners?

No, it is for every teacher with English language learners in their classes. It is for middle and high school teachers of math, science, social studies, and language arts who want to find ways to teach their content to students who are in the process of learning English. And it is for English language development (ELD) teachers who need to teach their students the language skills they need for academic success. In actuality, both groups teach language *and* content: Content teachers use language to teach content, and ELD teachers use content to teach language.

2. Is this book primarily for middle and high school teachers?

No. Although my original intent was to write a book of strategies for secondary school content teachers, many of the strategies presented here can be used by elementary school teachers of third grade or higher.

English language learners in the primary grades have the advantage of learning to read and write English at the same time as their native English-speaking peers. It is in third grade, however, that a shift occurs—from learning to read to reading to learn.

As an upper elementary school teacher, you will find a number of strategies in this book that are appropriate for your students and your content. As content complexity increases with each successive grade, more strategies can be successfully incorporated into classroom instruction.

3. Is this book for practicing teachers?

Yes, it is for practicing teachers *and* for preservice teachers.

For the preservice teacher, I hope this book will inspire you with new and exciting ideas. From your first day in the classroom, you will have a wide range of creative strategies to meet your students' needs.

For the practicing teacher, I hope this book will offer innovative approaches to the content you teach. You may find in it some strategies that you use regularly and some that you recall knowing once but have long ago forgotten. Mostly, I hope you discover inspiring new strategies that give you many *Aha!* moments.

4. Do I have to be in a teacher training program to benefit from this book?

No, not really. Although this book is written as a text for teacher training courses, it can certainly be used by those whose coursework is complete. The strategies are formatted in a manner that facilitates comprehension for all readers.

5. Will reading this book give me new ideas about ways to teach content to my English language learners?

Yes, and I'd be very disappointed if it did not! My goal is to share with you a multitude of solutions that work with the English language learners in your classes. You should find strategies in this text that expand your repertoire of approaches to instruction and assessment, as well as strategies that enrich your daily activities of teaching in ways that will be more effective for your language-learning students.

6. Do I have to change the way I teach to incorporate the strategies in this book?

No. I know that today's teachers already face enough challenges to their time and resources. The purpose of this book is to provide you with practical, easy-to-incorporate ideas that fit right in with the techniques and activities you currently use in your class-room. You do not have to change the way you teach at all; the strategies are designed to offer you versatile options. Choose the ones that fit your content, your teaching style, and your students.

7. Will reading this book give me new ideas about ways to assess what my English language learners really know about the content I teach?

Again, yes, I certainly hope so! I believe that teachers use traditional forms of classroom assessment simply because that's what they've always used. The strategies for classroom assessment in this book offer interesting alternatives to multiple-choice and essay tests. I hope they inspire you to try new approaches to assessing the achievement of your English language learners.

8. Do I need to know a lot of specialized jargon to understand this book?

No. By design, this book is user-friendly. The writing is light on jargon and technical ter-minology.

9. Do I need to know a lot about second-language acquisition theory to read this book?

No. The more you know, of course, the better your knowledge base will be. However, out of the vast body of research and theory that constitutes the field of second-language acquisition, I have selected and included here those that most strongly inform these strategies. Chapter 1 first explains the need for some basic theo-retical background and then the pertinent theories and principles. The final pages of that chapter put everything together into a cohesive whole that forms the foundation upon which all the strategies are based. Understanding the theoretical foundation is essential to making the choices that work best for you, your students, and the content you teach.

10. Will reading this book make me a better teacher?

Reading it will *not* make you a better teacher; *using* the strategies in the book will.

Let me start by saying that I believe that those who choose teaching as a profession do so because they enjoy it. (We *know* they don't do it for the money!) They strive to be the very best they can be. They love finding solutions to issues they face in the classroom.

The strategies in this book offer you many creative solutions. Using them helps you to become a more accomplished professional. Successful teachers are happy teachers. It is my hope that these strategies will add to your pleasure in teaching. I wish you great success!

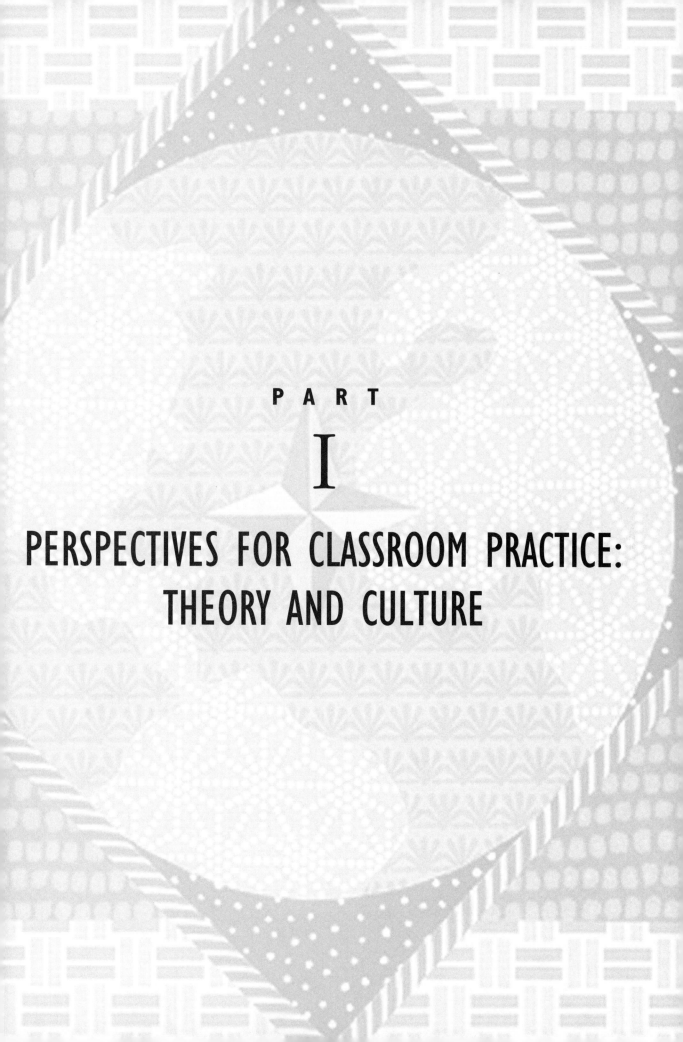

PART

I

PERSPECTIVES FOR CLASSROOM PRACTICE: THEORY AND CULTURE

CHAPTER 1

THEORETICAL CONSIDERATIONS

FIRST, DEMOGRAPHICS . . . AND THE NUMBERS KEEP RISING

All over the United States, growth of minority populations in public and private schools is rising, and the rate of that growth is increasing year by year. In the 11 school years from 1993–1994 to 2003–2004, the number of English language learners (ELLs) in public schools, kindergarten through 12th grade, rose 65.03% to just over 5 million. Total public school enrollment during those same years increased only 9.19% (National Clearinghouse of English Language Acquisition, 2005). Table 1.1 shows the annual enrollment growth of ELLs in relation to total K–12 enrollment growth. By all projections, the number of ELLs attending U.S. public schools will continue rising.

Every state in the nation is experiencing the effects of this growth. School districts, even the smallest ones, face the challenge of developing programs and services to help these students learn English, as well as math, science, social studies, and language arts. Schools and teachers are held accountable to demonstrate yearly progress of *all* students, including the ELLs. The challenge affects teachers of every grade level and subject area. The challenge is hard, and stakes are high—each year they seem to get harder and higher.

Why Content Teachers Can Help

Learning content is difficult for ELLs for reasons discussed later in this chapter and in Chapter 2. Teachers who are aware of these challenges and use techniques to make their content material more learnable can make a real difference in the academic lives of the ELLs in their classrooms. As ELLs learn more content, they begin to experience success as learners. They develop self-confidence in their academic ability that, in turn, increases their motivation to learn. Success breeds more success.

Teachers in content classrooms can help their ELLs develop an "I-can-do-it" attitude toward learning. Thinking you can goes a long way toward academic success.

How Content Teachers Can Help

Content teachers can help by using instructional strategies that increase comprehensibility of their content for the ELLs in their classrooms. Teachers can choose assignment and assessment strategies that evaluate ELLs' mastery of content knowledge without confusing it with their knowledge of the English language. These are the strategies presented in this text. However, to choose and use the strategies that work best for you, your content, and your students, you will first need a set of basic theoretical understandings.

Table 1.1 The Growing Numbers of English Language Learners (ELLs), 1993–1994 to 2003–2004

Year	Total K–12 Enrollment	K–12 Growth (%)	ELL Enrollment	ELL Growth Since 1993 (%)
1993–1994	45,443,389	—	3,037,922	—
1994–1995	47,745,835	5.07	3,184,696	4.83
1995–1996	47,582,665	4.71	3,228,799	6.28
1996–1997	46,714,980	2.80	3,452,073	13.63
1997–1998	46,023,969	1.28	3,470,268	14.23
1998–1999	46,153,266	1.56	3,540,673	16.55
1999–2000	47,356,089	4.21	4,416,580	45.38
2000–2001	47,665,483	4.89	4,584,946	50.92
2001–2002	48,296,777	6.28	4,747,763	56.39
2002–2003	49,478,583	8.88	5,044,361	66.00
2003–2004	49,619,090	9.19	5,013,539	65.03

National Clearinghouse of English Language Acquisition (NCELA) and Language Instruction Educational Programs. 2005 Poster. *The Growing Numbers of Limited English Proficient Students, 1993–1994 to 2003–2004.*

Why Theory First

Good teachers make good choices, and good choices are grounded in theory. To help their ELLs, content teachers must become familiar with select second-language acquisition principles and theory.

The strategies presented in this text facilitate instruction and assessment; they increase the comprehensibility of content through activities and assignments. Understanding the theories that inform these strategies empowers you to make the best choices and combinations. The question now becomes, what are the critical theories and principles an informed teacher should know?

THEORETICAL FOUNDATIONS

The theories, hypotheses, and principles of the following six theorists inform the strategies presented in this text:

- Cummins's differentiation between social and academic language
- Krashen's separate concepts of the affective filter and comprehensible input
- Vygotsky's zone of proximal development
- Swain's ideas about meaningful interaction
- Brown's principles of language teaching and language learning
- Bloom's taxonomy classifying levels of cognitive challenge

The sections that follow examine each of these important contributions. A final section shows how together they form a cohesive support system for teaching content to ELLs.

Cummins: Differentiation of Social and Academic Language

Jim Cummins (1984) contributed the concept that the language of the classroom requires more cognitively demanding language skills than the language of the outside world. He used the terms *cognitive academic language proficiency,* or *CALP,* to describe the language of the classroom and *basic interpersonal communication skills,* or *BICS,* to describe the social language of everyday life. Researchers, in recent years, have taken issue with the specificity of these concepts as separate entities, refuting them as simplistic and reductionist. Although some of these arguments may indeed be valid, Cummins's general concept about the differing demands of language usage inside and outside the classroom is still an important one for content teachers. For the purposes of this book, then, the differentiation between social and academic language will continue to form a foundation for understanding why the process and product of content instruction are challenging for ELLs. The concept of academic language underlies virtually every strategy in this text and deserves to be examined in detail.

Understanding Social Language

Language is a social construct: The purpose of language is communication. In a process closely resembling first-language acquisition, children learning English communicate to make friends with other children and to participate in the youth culture of sports, games, music, TV, video games, movies, fads, and fashion. They develop the social language skills of everyday activities through a process of natural acquisition by becoming immersed in the English-language-rich environments surrounding these activities. They learn to retell events, describe activities, express personal opinions, and maintain conversation. Children learning English develop these social language skills with an apparent ease that often awes adult learners. Because these children are immersed in an English speaking environment, it takes only 6 months to 2 years for them to develop this type of language competence (Cummins, 1981).

Understanding Academic Language

Schools have traditionally judged the proficiency level of ELLs by assessing their oral language communication skills, an often highly misleading indicator. Students can function at high levels in face-to-face social interaction and yet lack critical language skills for learning academic content.

The language of the classroom requires students to use language that is conceptually demanding and cognitively complex. Unlike the social language used to retell events, talk about experiences, describe activities, and give personal opinions, academic assignments require students to use different forms of language to accomplish the following:

- compare
- contrast
- list
- define
- order
- classify
- describe
- predict
- explain
- discuss
- analyze
- infer
- justify
- integrate
- evaluate
- deduce
- argue
- persuade
- defend

The challenge inherent in these uses of academic language for ELLs is made even more difficult by the need to apply them in all modalities of communication: speaking, listening, reading, and writing. The examples in Figure 1.1 contrasting social and academic language usage illustrate the distinct differences in the choice of words, the way the words are used, and the type of thought processing they require. The complex skills that comprise academic language are situation specific, cognitively demanding, and context reduced.

Academic language is *situation specific* because it is used exclusively in a classroom environment. It must be learned: Students do not acquire it naturally through immersion in activities of everyday life. With such limited exposure, it takes from 5 to 7 years to reach full development (Cummins, 1981). More recent research has shown that this type of

Social Language	Academic Language
Tell me about the girls in your gymnastics class.	Compare and contrast the main characters in the book.
Why do you want to do that?	Explain what you believe to be the most effective choice.
Is there an easier way to do this?	Can you propose and support an alternative technique to facilitate this procedure?
What do you think is going to happen?	Formulate a hypothesis that predicts the most probable outcome. Explain your reasoning.
Who's your favorite teacher?	Which of the characters do you find the most interesting? Justify and explain your choice.

Figure 1.1 Comparing Social and Academic Language

language competence can take up to 10 years to develop in language learners, depending on the amount of formal schooling students have received in their first language (Thomas & Collier, 1995).

Academic language is *cognitively challenging,* dealing largely with abstract concepts. It is beyond the realm of the "here-and-now"—those concrete personal experiences and activities that make social language easier to understand.

Academic language is *context reduced.* Oral and written academic tasks frequently lack the environmental clues to meaning that facilitate comprehension of social language.

Making Academic Language More Comprehensible

Cummins's next step addressed the issue of *how* to make the cognitive challenge of classroom oral and written academic language more comprehensible for ELLs. The key was to *embed* academic language in context. Providing contextual support in the form of *environmental clues* makes academically demanding content material easier for ELLs to understand. Cummins's concept is not dissimilar to the adage "A picture is worth a thousand words."

Figure 1.2 shows the graphic framework Cummins created to show what makes language easier or more difficult for these students. Difficulty is based on the relationship between two factors: the degree of the cognitive demand of the task and the amount of available contextual support.

Cognitive challenge of oral or written tasks is represented in the framework as undemanding (easy) in the two quadrants across the top of Cummins's chart or demanding

I Cognitively Undemanding + Context Embedded	II Cognitively Undemanding + Context Reduced
III Cognitively Demanding + Context Embedded	IV Cognitively Demanding + Context Reduced

Figure 1.2 Cummins's Framework for Evaluating Language Demand in Content Activities (Modified Format)

Cummins, J. (1984). *Bilingualism and Special Education: Issues in Assessment and Pedagogy.* San Francisco, CA: College-Hill Press. Used with permission.

(difficult) in the two lower quadrants. *Cognitively undemanding* tasks are either largely social or simply academically easy; *cognitively demanding* tasks are academically difficult, requiring higher levels of thought processing and language skills.

Contextual support, the second factor in Cummins's framework, assists comprehension by providing clues to the meanings of words. The more that spoken and written words are supported, or embedded, in context, the easier they are to understand. Contextual support for oral tasks comes from supplementing spoken language with facial expressions, gestures, body language, demonstrations, and visual cues from the physical environment. Contextual support for written tasks comes from supplementing text with pictures, graphs, charts, tables, and other textbook aids. Tasks—both oral and written—with a high level of contextual supports are *context embedded*. Tasks from which students must derive meaning solely from the spoken or written words themselves are *context reduced*.

The two quadrants on the left side of Cummins's chart represent tasks that are highly embedded and contextually supported. Tasks in the two quadrants on the right side are those that are context reduced. Combining the two elements of cognitive challenge and contextual support, the quadrants move in difficulty from I to IV. ELLs will generally find Quadrant I tasks easy because they are low in cognitive demand and high in contextual support. Quadrant IV tasks are at the other end of the spectrum; these tasks will be difficult for ELLs because they are academically demanding and lack contextual support.

Examples of tasks in each of the four quadrants, as shown in Figure 1.3, help to clarify Cummins's chart. Face-to-face conversation is classified as a Quadrant I task because the cognitive demand is low (most conversation is purely social) and the contextual support is high (observing the speaker's lips, facial expressions, and body language). The task moves to Quadrant II when the same conversation takes place over the telephone. The task is still social and, thus, cognitively undemanding, but here the listener loses the speaker's contextual support and must rely completely on auditory input for comprehension.

The tasks illustrating Quadrants III and IV are similar. On the lower half of the chart, the tasks are cognitively challenging. ELLs (and other students) will find mathematical word problems that offer the contextual support of manipulatives, graphics, and/or pictures easier to solve than problems without these environmental clues. Again, the level of difficulty changes in accordance with the degree to which words are embedded in context.

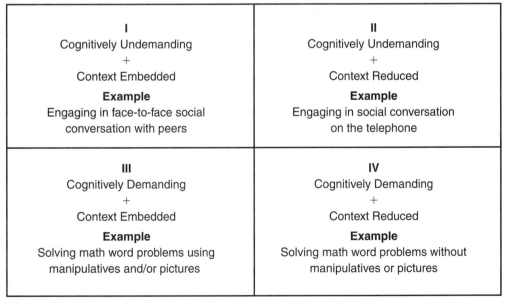

I Cognitively Undemanding + Context Embedded **Example** Engaging in face-to-face social conversation with peers	**II** Cognitively Undemanding + Context Reduced **Example** Engaging in social conversation on the telephone
III Cognitively Demanding + Context Embedded **Example** Solving math word problems using manipulatives and/or pictures	**IV** Cognitively Demanding + Context Reduced **Example** Solving math word problems without manipulatives or pictures

Figure 1.3 Cummins's Framework with Examples of Tasks for Each Quadrant

Cummins, J. (1984). *Bilingualism and Special Education: Issues in Assessment and Pedagogy.* San Francisco, CA: College-Hill Press. Used with permission.

Not every task can be neatly placed in a quadrant. Variables within a task itself or within a student's prior knowledge or experience can affect its placement on the chart. Solving simple computational problems in math, for example, would normally be considered a Quadrant III task. However, it would move to Quadrant IV if a student's native language used a different system of notation for writing numerals.

An even more complex example involves students' participation in physical education classes. It would seem, at first, to be a simple Quadrant I task, and indeed it would be if it involved *demonstrating* how to play a game or sport. However, it would become a Quadrant II task if the rules of play were explained orally with no accompanying demonstration. It would move into the cognitively demanding quadrants if it involved discussions and/or readings about complex rules and regulations of play or about the history of a sport. Placing these tasks in either Quadrant III or Quadrant IV would depend upon the amount of available contextual support.

Using Cummins's Principles

Strategies to embed academic tasks in context—to move them from Quadrant IV to Quadrant III—are commonly called *scaffolded instruction* or simply *scaffolding*. The term derives from the construction trades, where temporary external structures, scaffolds, provide support for workers as they construct a building. These scaffolds allow access to parts of the construction that would otherwise be impossible to reach. So, too, it is with scaffolded instruction.

In academics, scaffolds provide ELLs with the support they need to learn content while they are developing their English language skills. In ways figuratively similar to construction, scaffolding strategies allow language learners better access to content material. The scaffolds are progressively dismantled and discarded as they are no longer needed for support.

Scaffolding strategies facilitate comprehension for ELLs by moving academic tasks from Cummins's Quadrant IV to Quadrant III. For example, consider the Quadrant IV task of reading about materials that conduct electricity. Science teachers can shift this to Quadrant III by using the direct inquiry process. In class, students test materials such as plastics, woods, metals, and glass in a closed-circuit battery experiment to discover which materials are good conductors of electricity and which are not. Manipulating real-life objects turns abstract concepts into concrete academic tasks. It is a scaffolding strategy that allows students to formulate their own conclusions; real learning is taking place.

This example also illustrates the goal of maintaining a high level of cognitive challenge for ELLs. Direct inquiry learning of this type does not water down the curriculum. Embedding content in context maintains high levels of cognitive demand at the same time that it facilitates comprehension of important academic concepts.

Most learning in content classrooms falls into Quadrant IV because it is usually cognitively demanding and frequently context reduced. ELLs (as well as native English speakers whose academic skills are below grade level) typically find Quadrant IV tasks overwhelming and frustrating. Teachers can use the dual perspectives of cognitive challenge and contextual support to evaluate the difficulty of class instruction, activities, assignments, and assessments for their ELLs. It is a valuable tool to help teachers select, plan, and use appropriate strategies to scaffold content learning, moving it from Quadrant IV to Quadrant III.

Krashen: The Affective Filter

As part of his five-hypothesis Monitor Model of Second Language Acquisition, Stephen Krashen (1982) proposed the existence of an emotional filter that influences how much actual learning takes place in relation to input. The strength of the filter itself is determined by affective factors of learner anxiety, self-confidence, and motivation.

The affective filter may be conceived of as an emotional wall that blocks input from reaching the brain. Students who experience high learner anxiety, low self-confidence, and low motivation are said to have high affective filters that prevent them from successfully processing input. At the other extreme are learners with low affective filters. These learners, with little anxiety, good self-confidence, and high motivation, will learn much more from the same amount of input.

Using the Affective Filter Concept

Content teachers who use the strategies in this text give their ELLs the opportunity to experience academic success. With every small success comes an increase in students' self-confidence. The greater the gain in self-confidence, the more motivated the students become to continue learning. Increased self-confidence and motivation lower the affective filter and allow more academic input to be processed. The rewards of being a "good learner" are self-perpetuating.

Krashen: The Comprehensible Input Hypothesis

Krashen's second hypothesis that impacts content teaching deals with the concept of comprehensible input. He represented his idea in the formula $i + 1$, in which i is input—meaningful input based on real communication that is immediately comprehensible to the language learner—and $+ 1$ is the next level where language is advanced just enough so that the learner is challenged by it but able to learn it. This is the "teachable/learnable area"—the area between a student's actual and potential language development.

Extending the formula by logical implication, it is apparent that $i + 2$ would present too much challenge to be learnable and $i + 0$ would present no challenge toward more advanced levels of language development at all. To successfully advance language learning, then, comprehensible language input ideally should be $i + 1$.

Krashen's concept of language development can be compared to tennis players who, wanting to improve their skills, arrange games with players whose skill level is slightly more advanced than their own. The challenge motivates them, and the effort is rewarding. Playing with those whose skills are on par with their own offers little or no new input that might lead to improvement; playing with those at a much higher level of skill development leads only to feelings of frustration and defeat. As with language learning, tennis skills improve only in an environment of $i + 1$.

Using i + 1

Teachers can facilitate comprehension for the ELLs in their classrooms by incorporating strategies that expand the area between students' actual and potential levels of language ability. Scaffolding strategies that embed language in context use the $i + 1$ concept to allow students to advance to the next level of achievement.

Vygotsky: Zone of Proximal Development

Lev Vygotsky (1978) contributed the concept of the Zone of Proximal Development (ZPD), which he defines as "the distance between (a student's) actual developmental level as determined by independent problem solving, and the level of potential development as determined through problem solving under adult guidance or in collaboration with more capable peers" (p. 87). Figure 1.4 shows the three zones of possible development: the first in which a learner can solve problems independently; the middle in which the learner can solve them with assistance; and the third in which the learner will be unable to solve them at all because they are too advanced. Within the middle zone, according to Vygotsky's theory, learning occurs only when teachers offer opportunities for students to

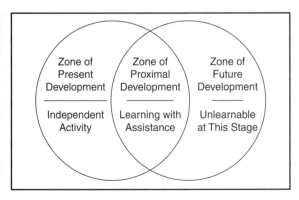

Figure 1.4 Understanding Vygotsky's Zone of Proximal Development

actively interact with their environments. Strategies that promote interaction in the classroom access students' zones of proximal development and allow students to extend their current levels of skills, knowledge, and experience.

Although Vygotsky's ZPD and Krashen's *i + 1* appear similar in content, the two differ in focus. Krashen applied his ideas narrowly to second-language acquisition and skill development and focused on the need to make language input comprehensible. Vygotsky applied his ideas more broadly to learning in general and focused on the importance of meaningful interaction with more advanced others. Both concepts are useful for content teachers with ELLs in their classrooms.

Using the Zone of Proximal Development

Applying the ZPD to the content classroom addresses *process* issues rather than *product* issues. Students learn most effectively by becoming active participants in their own learning. Students will progress to their fullest potential when teachers scaffold instruction with activity and assignment strategies that encourage working with teachers and peers, individually and in groups, in an atmosphere of guidance and collaboration.

Swain: Meaningful Output

Merrill Swain's 1985 concept of meaningful output supports Vygotsky's ZPD and enriches Krashen's comprehensible input. Swain views meaningful *output* as central to the process of language acquisition because it provides learners with opportunities to work with developing language in contextualized, meaningful situations. Swain believes that "it is not input *per se* that is important to second language acquisition but input that occurs in interaction where meaning is negotiated" (1985, p. 246).

The concept of *negotiated meaning* comes from the way people communicate with each other. To clarify meaning in conversation, speakers often participate in a certain amount of give and take—a kind of back-and-forth exchange that leads to more complete understanding. This happens among native speakers who want to better understand the details of the topic being discussed. However, among native and nonnative speakers, the give and take serve as a trial-and-error series of exchanges in which *language* becomes successively modified until both parties understand the communication.

Nonnative speakers receive input from their conversational partners. If the words are not understood, language learners request more comprehensible input by asking for repetitions or clarifications, causing the native-speaking listener to paraphrase or offer environmental clues—gestures, facial expressions, drawings, for example—to make meaning clearer. This is how meaning is negotiated through interaction.

Using Meaningful Output

Swain's concept of meaningful output has direct bearing on learning in content classrooms. The concept highlights the importance of small group interaction in long-term retention of both language and conceptual knowledge.

Content teachers can promote learning by choosing strategies that encourage students to negotiate meaning through paired or small group discussion. ELLs, in meaningful academic conversation with their peers, receive input and feedback that allow them to compare their language use (vocabulary, pronunciation, structures) and their conceptual understandings with those of their native-speaking peers. Manipulating language in meaningful classroom interaction clarifies input and makes it more comprehensible for ELLs.

Brown: Principles of Language Teaching and Learning

Of the 12 language teaching and learning principles upon which H. Douglas Brown (1994) based his entire methodology, 6 have direct bearing on teaching content to ELLs.

In some you will recognize the tribute he pays to the theorists discussed in the preceding sections.

Principle 2, *meaningful learning,* is the conceptual opposite of rote learning. Unlike the isolated, memorized facts and figures of rote learning, meaningful learning promotes long-term retention of knowledge.

Brown says that learning can be made meaningful for ELLs by appealing to their interests, by associating new topics and concepts to their existing knowledge and experience, by making abstract learning more concrete, and by choosing activities and assignments that go beyond drill and memorization (Brown, 1994, p. 18).

Principle 4, the *intrinsic motivation principle,* says that while virtually all human beings work, act, or behave in anticipation of a reward, "the most powerful rewards are those that are intrinsically motivated within the learner" (Brown, 1994, p. 20). When one's own needs, wants, and/or desires are the source of behavior, the behavior itself becomes self-rewarding.

Although it is true that students may be motivated to work for the tangible rewards of praise and grades, it is also true that motivation grows exponentially when students are shown the relationship between classroom learning and real-world use. More long-term learning takes place when students are motivated to learn because they perceive classroom activities and assignments to be "fun, interesting, useful, or challenging" (Brown, 1994, p. 20).

Principle 5, *strategic investment,* says that successful learning largely depends on the learner developing a set of strategies for understanding and producing the language involved in content learning. The greater the variety of strategies a learner can develop for processing information, the greater the possibility of academic success. Because students vary in their abilities to use individual strategies, the more opportunities teachers create to unlock the "secrets" of learning and to offer a variety of techniques for learning, the more teachers can promote student success.

Principle 7, *self-confidence* or the *"I Can Do It" principle,* states that "the eventual success that learners attain in a task is at least partially a factor of their belief that they indeed are fully capable of accomplishing the task" (Brown, 1994, p. 23). Brown believes that student self-assessment is a critical factor in learning.

Brown suggests building learner self-confidence in the classroom by using verbal and nonverbal approval and encouragement and by assigning tasks in sequence from easier to more difficult. Experiencing early successes motivates students to deal with successively more challenging tasks.

Principle 8, *risk taking,* states that students who feel self-confident as learners will be more comfortable attempting to use language for meaningful purposes: to ask questions and participate in small and large group work, for example. These are the students who are more willing to take calculated risks and to make educated guesses in the classroom. Willingness to use language about which the student is not completely certain promotes long-term retention and intrinsic motivation (Brown, 1994, p. 24).

Teachers can encourage risk-taking behavior by ensuring that the "atmosphere in the classroom . . . encourages students to try out language (and) to venture a response" (Brown, 1994, p. 24). Teachers need to "provide reasonable challenges in (their) techniques—make them neither too easy nor too hard" (p. 24) and to reward students' attempts with a response that encourages future attempts. ELLs who feel assured that language errors are a normal part of language learning will ultimately be more successful learners.

Principle 9, the *language–culture connection,* presents the concept that learning a new language involves learning a new culture: all those customs, beliefs, and values that deal with ways of thinking, feeling, and acting. Content teachers can develop an awareness that culture determines expectations of "proper" classroom behavior. Misinterpretations will be avoided by recognizing that the way ELLs act in class may be rooted in strong cultural components. Indeed, culture can even lead ELLs to confusion about particular concepts or topics. Brown suggests, that teachers "make explicit to your students what you may take for granted in your own culture" (1994, p. 25).

Meaningful Learning	Make learning meaningful and interesting to promote long-term retention of knowledge.
Intrinsic Motivation	Motivate student learning by making it interesting, useful, challenging, and fun.
Strategic Investment	Teach learners *how* to learn by actively teaching a variety of learning strategies.
Self-Confidence or the "I-Can-Do-It" Principle	Build learner confidence by creating a series of small successes that motivate learners to take on the challenge of more difficult tasks.
Risk Taking	Lower learner anxiety by creating a classroom environment in which language learners are encouraged to use language in meaningful ways and errors are accepted as part of the learning process.
Language–Culture Connection	Recognize that learning a new language involves learning a new culture and new ways of thinking, feeling, and acting.

Figure 1.5   Brown's Principles at a Glance

Using Brown's Principles

Brown's principles, shown in summary form in Figure 1.5, form a humanistic foundation for teaching language and, by extension, for teaching content. If these six principles intrigue you, you might enjoy taking a more thorough look at this highly readable text. Brown's writing includes a rarity in textbooks—humor!—making it educationally informative and pleasurable reading at the same time.

Bloom: Taxonomy

Benjamin Bloom (Bloom & Krathwohl, 1977) examined teacher question patterns and devised a system to categorize them according to the degree of cognitive challenge they elicited. He identified six levels of question types in his taxonomy and termed them *knowledge, comprehension, application, analysis, synthesis,* and *evaluation.* Questions at the knowledge and comprehension levels are simple and concrete and require only rote learning. At the higher levels of cognitive challenge, questions designated as application, analysis, synthesis, and evaluation are more abstract and increasingly complex. These are the questions that encourage critical thinking.

Starting at the lowest level of cognitive challenge, *knowledge* questions demand only isolated, memorized facts as answers. Questions in this category often start with *who, what, when,* and *where* and test recall and recognition of information.

Comprehension questions ask for short explanations or definitions of basic meaning in the students' own words. An example of a comprehension question might be, *What do we mean when we use the term _____?*

Application questions require students to apply known information to new situations, as in using rules and principles to produce a result. A question like *How is _____ an example of _____?* falls in this category.

Moving up the ladder of cognitive challenge, *analysis* questions focus on individual elements. Questions of this type ask students to consider the relationship of the separate parts to each other and to the whole. *What individual parts does _____ consist of?* is an analysis question.

Synthesis questions require putting elements together in a novel way. Questions like *What might happen if you combined _____ and _____?* and *How could you streamline the process of _____?* are typical of those in this category.

Evaluation questions, the most cognitively challenging level, ask students to make, justify, and defend judgments based on the information under consideration. In this category are questions such as *What criteria could you use to assess _____?* and *What do you believe would be the most effective solution?* Table 1.2 summarizes types of thought processing, associated verbs, and additional questions for each of the six levels of cognitive demand.

Table 1.2 Bloom's Taxonomy

Level	What Students Are Asked to Do	Useful Verbs	Sample Questions
Knowledge	• memorize • recognize • recall • remember • identify	tell state locate relate list find name choose define label select match	Who, what, when where, how? What happened after _____ ? How many _____ ? Which is true or false? Which one shows _____ ?
Comprehension	• interpret • paraphrase • organize facts • classify • condense • compare • contrast • summarize	explain restate outline compare describe distinguish convert estimate rewrite arrange	What was the main idea? Can you state this in your own words? What do you think is meant by _____ ? Does X mean the same as Y? What are the differences between _____ ? Which statements support _____ ? What information does the graph (table) give?
Application	• solve problems • use information to produce a result • extend what is learned to an unknown • make predictions • apply facts, rules, principles	apply interpret solve use demonstrate dramatize change compute calculate construct modify predict	How is X an example of _____ ? Why is _____ significant? How is X related to _____ ? How might you group these _____ ? What factors would change if _____ ? What would happen if _____ ?
Analysis	• identify component parts of a whole • examine relationship of parts to whole • understand underlying structures	analyze separate probe categorize connect arrange	What are the elements of _____ ? How would you classify _____ according to _____ ? How does _____ affect the whole? What are some different ways to categorize _____ ?

(continued)

Table 1.2 Bloom's Taxonomy (*continued*)

Level	What Students Are Asked to Do	Useful Verbs	Sample Questions
	• find patterns • draw conclusions • distinguish between fact and inference • recognize hidden meaning	divide dissect deconstruct group compare infer	Why did _____ changes occur? What were the motives behind _____? What assumptions are part of _____? What is the implication of _____?
Synthesis	• combine ideas or elements to form a new whole • generalize from given facts • relate knowledge from separate areas • predict, draw conclusions	combine integrate create design devise invent develop compose modify rearrange reorganize generate propose formulate hypothesize	What if _____? What would you predict from _____? How would you design a _____ to _____? What might happen if you combined _____? What solutions might you offer for _____? What are some unusual ways to use _____? What are some alternative ways to _____?
Evaluation	• make value decisions about issues and ideas • compare and discriminate information • verify value of evidence • recognize subjectivity • develop opinions, judgments, and decisions • make and justify choices	assess appraise evaluate decide rank rate recommend support defend convince judge discriminate prioritize deduce conclude criticize critique	What is your position on _____? Why? Is there a better solution for _____? How would you have handled _____? What evidence supports your position on _____? Do you believe _____ was a positive or negative influence? Why? What criteria are you using to evaluate _____?

Using Bloom's Taxonomy

It is discouraging to note that the great majority of teachers' oral and written questions fall into the two lowest levels of Bloom's taxonomy. Developing an awareness of question types focuses teacher attention on the levels of cognitive demand in teacher-directed discussions, classroom activities and assignments, and teacher-made quizzes and tests. An important objective of the strategies in this text is to maintain a high level of critical thinking for ELLs (actually, for *all* students) while simultaneously facilitating comprehension for them.

APPLYING THE THEORIES AND PRINCIPLES

The theories and principles presented in this chapter each contribute to the understanding of teaching content to ELLs. However, to be of real value, they must be combined in a way that addresses the central question:

> How can content teachers use these theories and principles to promote more effective learning for the ELLs in their classrooms?

The answer lies in distilling the essential elements of these separate theories and principles into a practical application that will guide all aspects of instruction and assessment of ELLs in content classrooms. The following Guidelines for Practice are the outcome of this process.

THEORY TO APPLICATION: GUIDELINES FOR PRACTICE

- Use scaffolding strategies with ELLs to facilitate comprehension of the specialized academic language of content classrooms.
- Use scaffolding strategies to challenge ELLs to advance beyond their present state of independent activity, into the areas of potential learning in which content is learnable with the assistance of teachers and peers.
- Use scaffolding strategies that embed the oral and written language of content material in a context-rich environment to facilitate learning for ELLs.
- Use scaffolding strategies that maintain a high level of cognitive challenge, but lower the language demand by embedding it in context.
- Maintain a high level of cognitive challenge by selecting content material for ELLs based on depth, not breadth.
- Make content material meaningful, interesting, and relevant to maintain a high level of cognitive challenge and to expand students' areas of potential learning.
- Actively teach learning strategies to give students a "menu" of ways to process and learn new information.
- Be aware that cultural differences may affect ELLs' models of classroom behavior and interpretation of specific content material.
- Activate and develop background knowledge to make new content meaningful and to form a foundation upon which new learning can be built.
- Provide opportunities for ELLs to negotiate conceptual understandings and to explore language usage through classroom interaction.
- Lower learner anxiety in the classroom to create students who are more willing to participate in class, to become risk takers in the learning process, and ultimately to become more successful learners.
- Provide opportunities for students to experience success in the classroom: Success in learning promotes more success by increasing learner motivation, interest, and self-confidence.
- Use scaffolding strategies to assess content knowledge separate from English language knowledge so students can *show what they know*.

Together, these theory-based guidelines form the cornerstone of effective instruction and assessment of ELLs in content classrooms. Individual guidelines have been selected and placed at the beginning of each strategy chapter. Certain guidelines are more broadly applicable, as, for example, the one about providing opportunities for success; this and others like it will appear in most, if not all, chapters. Others appear only when they specifically relate to the types of strategies that are presented in that chapter.

In combination, these guidelines serve as a solid foundation upon which each chapter's strategies are based. Let these guidelines inform your choices of strategies to maximize your ELLs' academic achievements.

Scaffolding strategies offer rewards not only for students but also for teachers. As your students begin to experience academic success, they will be rewarded with renewed interest and motivation to learn. Their feelings of self-confidence as learners will grow. They will begin to view school as a place of positive rewards.

Scaffolding strategies give you, the content teacher, a range and variety of options to help you make better instructional decisions. You will see that using these techniques, ideas, and activities in your classroom makes a real difference in the academic lives of your ELLs. Like your students, you too will derive greater satisfaction from your teaching. You will enjoy the renewed confidence that comes with being an even more accomplished professional.

QUESTIONS FOR DISCUSSION

1. Research statistics in your state and/or district for the number of ELLs enrolled in K–12 schools over the last 5 years. Compare that to the total enrollment in the same time period. Create a chart using actual figures and percentages of increases, similar to the chart shown in Table 1.1.

2. Using Cummins's quadrants, how would you classify each of the following tasks? The final three tasks can be placed in more than one quadrant; for those, justify and explain your placement.

   a. Listening to a tape-recorded presentation about caring for pets
   b. Listening to a presentation about pet animals that includes pictures and video
   c. Listening to a lecture on an unfamiliar topic
   d. Participating in a conversation with friends about politics or economics
   e. Reading a list of required school supplies
   f. Understanding written text through pictures and graphics
   g. Understanding written text through small group discussion
   h. Ordering dinner from a picture menu in a fast food restaurant
   i. Ordering dinner from a menu in a formal restaurant
   j. Reading Shakespeare's *Romeo and Juliet* in its original format
   k. Reading the illustrated (comic book) version of Shakespeare's *Romeo and Juliet*
   l. Writing research reports on assigned topics in social studies
   m. Solving math problems
   n. Doing a science experiment
   o. Learning about health and hygiene issues

3. Observe a class and keep a written log of the questions the teacher asks. Classify them according to Bloom's taxonomy. What percentage of the total are questions classified as knowledge and comprehension? Make up some additional higher level questions that the teacher could have used in this lesson.

4. If you are currently teaching, which of these theories, principles, and/or guidelines have you been practicing in your classroom? If you are not teaching, which of the theories

were implemented in classes in which you were a learner? Support your answers with specific examples.

5. If you have ever studied a foreign language, how successful were you in learning it? Can you explain your success or lack of it based on these theories, principles, and guidelines?

REFERENCES AND RESOURCES

Bloom, B. (Ed.). (1956). *Taxonomy of educational objectives, handbook I: Cognitive domain.* White Plains, NY: Addison Wesley.

Bloom, B., & Krathwohl, D. (1977). *Taxonomy of educational objectives; Handbook 1—Cognitive domain.* San Diego, CA: College-Hill.

Brown, H. D. (1994). *Teaching by principles: An interactive approach to language pedagogy.* Englewood Cliffs, NJ: Prentice Hall Regents.

Cummins, J. (1981). The role of primary language development in promoting educational success for language minority students. In California Department of Education (Ed.), *Schooling and language minority students: A theoretical framework* (pp. 3–49). Los Angeles: Evaluation, Dissemination and Assessment Center, California State University.

Cummins, J. (1984). *Bilingualism and special education: Issues in assessment pedagogy.* San Francisco: College-Hill Press.

Krashen, S. (1982). *Principles and practice in second language acquisition.* Oxford: Pergamon Press.

Krashen, S. (1985). *The input hypothesis: Issues and implications.* London: Longman.

National Clearinghouse of English Language Acquisition (NCELA), U.S. Department of Education (2005). *The growing numbers of limited English proficient students, 1992/93–2003/04.* Retrieved March 20, 2006 from http://www.ncela.gwu.edu/policy/states/reports/state-data/2003LEP/GrowingLEP_
0304_Dec05.pdf

Richard-Amato, P. A., & Snow, M. A. (Eds.) (2005). *Academic success for English language learners: Strategies for K–12 mainstream teachers.* White Plains, NY: Pearson Education.

Swain, M. (1985). Communicative competence: Some roles of comprehensible input and comprehensible output in its development. In S. Gass & C. Madden (Eds.), *Input in second language acquisition* (pp. 235–53). Rowley, MA: Newbury House.

Thomas, W. P., & Collier, V. P. (1995). Language minority student achievement and program effectiveness. *California Association for Bilingual Education Newletter, 17(5),* 19, 24.

Vygotsky, L. (1978). *Mind in society: Development of higher psychological processes.* Cambridge, MA: Harvard University Press.

CULTURE AND CONTENT INSTRUCTION

CULTURE AND THE PROCESS OF CONTENT INSTRUCTION

Teachers occasionally find themselves puzzled by certain classroom behaviors and reactions of their ELLs. What they are seeing may well be the effects of a deeply ingrained culture transplanted to new environments.

Culture may be defined as "the sum of attitudes, customs, and beliefs that distinguishes one group of people from another. Culture is transmitted, through language, material objects, ritual, institutions, and art, from one generation to the next" (Hirsch, 2002, p. 431). Culture is shared by individuals within the group and made up of many parts: values, beliefs, standards of beauty, ideas about celebrations, patterns of thinking, norms of behavior, and styles of communication. Among other things, culture determines how its group members interact with others. Culture goes beyond the sum of its parts: It is the eyes through which individuals view and interpret the world.

ELLs in U.S. schools are learning not only a new language but also a new culture, that of American schools. In this process, cross-cultural misunderstandings between teacher and ELL student may occur.

Because culture shapes its group members' ideas of politeness and etiquette, students from other cultures often react in class in ways that vary beyond the range of American cultural norms. The common parental admonishment to "behave in class," for example, may have some surprising results. To behave well in some cultures may mean to sit silently, even when asked a direct question.

Families who relocate to the United States carry their culture with them and respond with behaviors that are considered appropriate and polite within their own groups. When they enter U.S. schools, their children may exhibit patterns of behavior that are culturally different from their teachers' expectations. Their teachers, not realizing the cultural context of these responses, often mistakenly perceive these behaviors on a personal or individual level as rudeness, disinterest, or lack of knowledge. Awareness of culture as a potential source of student behavior will help teachers depersonalize the behavior, moving it from the personal to the cultural level. The next sections examine areas of frequently misunderstood school behaviors.

Class Work Patterns

The typical classroom uses whole class, small group, and individual work formats. In American schools, effective instruction consists of balancing the three types. In cultures that place more value on group cooperation, however, misunderstandings of intent can occur when individual work is required, as in a testing situation. Some cultures, in contrast, view the teacher as the academic authority and, as such, the only appropriate source of learning. Students from this type of educational background may view group work as nonproductive and may be reluctant to participate in it.

Instructional Patterns

Critical thinking, problem solving, and discovery learning are considered the gold standards of American instructional approaches. School programs in other countries, on the other hand, often put greater emphasis on techniques of rote memorization and recitation for learning. ELLs from these cultures may experience difficulty in understanding and participating in the instructional processes in which they find themselves immersed. The actual incident described in Figure 2.1 is an example of this type of misunderstanding.

Questioning Patterns

American classrooms reward students who ask questions, seek clarification, and challenge statements and ideas. Many cultures, however, do not encourage expressing personal opinions or questioning the teacher in class.

Students from some cultures may not be willing to participate in discussions that involve expressing opposing opinions or beliefs. For students whose culture teaches them that it is rude and disrespectful to disagree with an authority figure, offering an opinion

---

Yasmin's English skills were actually quite good, but she rarely participated in class. About halfway through the first semester, Ms. Dennis, her teacher, had a conference with her to talk about her lack of participation. Yasmin had a ready answer because it was a problem that she, too, was worried about.

Yasmin explained that each night she read and memorized all the information in the textbook. But the next day in class, the teacher asked "other" questions—not questions about the facts in the book.

It was a "lightbulb moment" for Ms. Dennis. Yasmin was 100% correct in her assessment of the situation. Ms. Dennis viewed the information in the textbook as a knowledge base and used class time to build upon that knowledge. Her questions guided students to extend their conceptual understandings by engaging them in critical thinking and problem solving tasks based on the textbook readings. Yasmin's prior academic experience had not prepared her for this approach to instruction.

Figure 2.1   A True Tale of Cross-Cultural Misunderstanding

that differs from that of the teacher is simply not an option. Even disagreeing with peers may seem impolite to students with this background.

Asking questions and seeking clarification may also be viewed in unexpected ways. Some students may feel it will cause the teacher embarrassment since not understanding reflects poorly on the teacher's knowledge and ability to teach. Other students may have been taught that questioning an adult is rude and disrespectful. Teachers who invite this type of interaction may be seen as lacking control and authority in their classrooms.

Teachers often lead discussions by asking questions and calling on students who raise their hands. Cultural beliefs, however, may prevent some students from volunteering answers. Students from cultures that deeply value humility may not raise their hands because displaying knowledge is considered a form of showing off.

In many cultures, adults are viewed as the figures of authority, and children are taught not to speak until they are spoken to. These students are following their cultural values by not volunteering information, not questioning for clarification, and not seeking additional information. On the other hand, calling on a student who doesn't volunteer may also produce an unintended effect. Students from cultures in which being correct is prized will feel they have brought shame on themselves, their families, even their communities, by giving a wrong answer.

Response Time Patterns

Americans, in general, value conversation and are uncomfortable with silence. Every culture has its own rules of conversation—rules for when to speak, how and when to interrupt, and how many people can speak at the same time. Those who follow the rules are thought to be polite. Interestingly, the rules vary not only across cultures but also regionally across the United States.

Americans often become anxious with conversational silences lasting longer than several seconds. Some cultures, however, are comfortable with much longer periods of silence. Children from these cultures learn that it is a sign of courtesy, respect, and wisdom to take time before responding. Other cultures, in contrast, value responses that are loud and quick. Those who jump right in to answer are seen as smart, interested, involved, and even strong.

These variations in culturally appropriate response patterns may cause teachers to misinterpret student behaviors during class discussions. Teachers may characterize students who don't immediately reply to questions as slow or lacking knowledge and those who jump right in as rude, domineering, or overanxious. Teachers who can depersonalize these behaviors by repositioning them in a cultural context will be able to see these students in a more positive light and to help them adjust to more appropriate behaviors for the American classroom.

Attention Patterns

Listeners in social and academic situations indicate that they are paying attention to the speaker through eye contact and head nods. Most teachers like to see every student looking directly at them while they teach. Although teachers may view lack of eye contact as a sign of disrespect or disinterest, other cultures view these behaviors differently.

Downcast eyes in some cultures denote respect for the speaker, particularly when the speaker is a figure of authority. Direct eye contact with an adult, especially a teacher, is considered overt boldness or defiant behavior.

Although teachers feel well understood and enthusiastically appreciated when students nod their heads during periods of instruction, in many cultures head nods do not indicate understanding or signify agreement. Head nods simply show that the speaker is being heard. In contrast, other cultures place great value on emotional control and discourage any show of enthusiasm or confirmation through changes in facial features.

Feedback Patterns

Americans are generally effusive in their use of praise. Teachers are generous in doling out intrinsic and extrinsic rewards as reinforcement for notable achievement and good behavior. They use praise to encourage students to continue their efforts to learn. Positive reinforcement theory recommends finding even small successes to praise.

In contrast, certain cultures believe that praise should be rewarded only for true excellence and outstanding performance. Praise given too generously is seen as insincere. Teachers who praise too much may even be viewed as inadequate: If students are so praiseworthy, perhaps the teacher just doesn't know all that much more than the students. Alternatively, effusive praise offered in front of the whole class may bring feelings of discomfort to students whose culture values humility.

Misunderstandings also can occur in the area of error correction. Some cultures strive for academic perfection to a greater degree than U.S. school culture does. To those students, a teacher's lack of constant correction may be viewed, like too much praise, as a sign of inadequacy.

Written feedback also may cause misunderstanding. Not all countries use the common notations of ✓ for right and ✗ for wrong. It is possible that such marks, too, may be subject to misinterpretation.

Patterns of Address

It is traditional in American schools to address teachers by using Mr. or Ms. and the last name. Teachers are often irritated to hear themselves called simply "Teacher" by their ELLs. You may be surprised to know that ELLs are according you great respect with this form of address. To them, it is the equivalent of the U.S. practice of addressing the physician as "Doctor" and the university instructor as "Professor." The next time a student calls you "Teacher," smile and enjoy the respect and admiration being offered you and your profession.

A Shift in Perception

Awareness of areas of potential cross-cultural misunderstanding allows teachers to develop cultural competency and to see their ELLs students in a clearer light. Reactively, thinking *culture* as the source of a student's behavior will help to refocus the way you perceive what is happening in your classroom. Proactively, the following are some of the things you can do to ease cultural adjustment issues for ELLs:

- Vary class work formats and explain the purpose of each type.
- Model and discuss commonly practiced classroom behaviors, such as asking and answering questions, offering an opinion or point of view, and taking turns.
- Praise something specific in a student's response rather than repeating the generic "Very good."
- Allow extended wait time to students whose culture values it.
- Explain the meaning of your written correction symbols.
- Learn about the cultures represented in your classroom by talking to adults familiar with those cultures or by doing Internet research on Web sites sponsored by unbiased sources.
- Talk about American cultural mores and behaviors to raise awareness for all students in your classes.

In addition to these specific proactive suggestions, it is also valuable to involve ELLs' parents whenever possible. They, too, are making a cultural adjustment. You can overcome language barriers in a number of different ways. Did you know that there are free Internet translation sites? These are listed in the *References and Resources* section at the end of this chapter. Another strategy is to identify bilingual contacts and liaisons who may be willing to serve as volunteers. Foreign language instructors at high schools or local colleges may also be able to help. These last two approaches work particularly well when coordinated as a whole-school effort.

One other suggestion to ease cultural adjustment for ELLs is to find opportunities to promote friendships between them and their native speaking peers. Students of every age and nationality share a need to belong and to contribute. Those who manage to form a friendship with even one schoolmate are more likely to make successful adjustments to academic life. Teachers can encourage this by assigning new students a buddy, a work partner, even a lunch partner. It's amazing what a big difference this one small step can make.

Cultural Behaviors Change Slowly

A change in culturally ingrained behavior may take some time. Students who become familiar with the variations in cultural expectations will probably not be able to put those behaviors into immediate effect. Understanding that American students who volunteer answers, for example, are not showing off will not make ELLs want to behave in that manner themselves, as the instructor in Figure 2.2 found out. In matters like these, emotional responses lag far behind rational understanding. The roots of culture are both strong and deep.

CULTURE AND THE PRODUCT OF CONTENT LEARNING

The effect of culture can extend beyond the patterns of ELLs' classroom behaviors; culture may also influence comprehension of content. Although issues such as the notation of dates and time shown in Figure 2.3 cross all content areas, teachers of math, science, social studies, and language arts all have to consider some content-specific cultural issues when teaching their subjects to ELLs.

Mr. Elkind thought he had a great idea for his advanced class of young adult ESL students. Learning about American humor, he reasoned, would provide an enjoyable forum for his students' language development through class discussion and, at the same time, expose them to deeper understanding of their new culture. He had a great sense of humor himself and couldn't wait to get right into the fun of it.

But Mr. Elkind was wrong, and the unit fell completely flat. What he didn't know at the time was that rational understanding of the culture behind the joke doesn't make it funny to someone whose culture doesn't share the same beliefs. He found that jokes about dogs having more creature comforts than the husband held no humor for those who believed that dogs are dirty and should *never* be allowed inside a home. Similarly, jokes about husbands' and wives' relationships with their mothers-in-law were not funny to those whose cultures elevate mothers-in-law to a position of great respect, esteem, even power.

In this particular situation, Mr. Elkind learned as much about culture as did his students. His students gathered new information about American cultural icons and beliefs, and Mr. Elkind learned that acquisition of new cultural knowledge doesn't automatically result in an immediate change in attitude. The unit on humor didn't turn out to be as enjoyable as he expected, but it was undeniably a great learning experience for everyone involved.

Figure 2.2   It's Just Not Funny

Figure 2.3 Differences in Writing Dates and Times

	U.S. Notation	Foreign Notation
DATES		
	month/day/year	day/month/year
	7/22/04	22/7/04
TIME		
	12-hour clock + a.m. or p.m.	24-hour clock with period
	hour:minute	hour.minute
	8:40 a.m.	08.40
	1:30 p.m.	13.30
	8:40 p.m.	20.40

Special Considerations for Teachers of Math

Starting at the most basic level, students from foreign countries may form the numerals differently from American notation. Figure 2.4 shows the numerals as a typical European-schooled student would write them. Additionally, some areas teach writing the 0 with a line through it, so it looks like this: Ø.

Numbers are highly ingrained in students' native languages. Counting in English is particularly difficult, even for those with well-developed English language skills. The fact that fully bilingual speakers can test which language is their dominant one by mentally observing the language they count in illustrates how deeply rooted numbers and counting really are. Reading large numbers correctly and understanding large numbers aurally are skills that improve slowly with a great deal of practice.

Mathematical usage of decimal points and commas in written notation is another area of potential confusion. Many foreign countries use a system that is the opposite of U.S. notation: Periods replace commas to mark off hundreds in large numbers, and commas are used in place of periods to mark off decimal places, as shown in Figure 2.5.

Additionally, in some countries, the meaning of *billion* varies from the U.S. concept of billion as one thousand million. In those places, 1 billion is equal to 1 million million.

Most of the world's countries use the metric system to measure weight, volume, and distance. Students schooled outside the United States will be accustomed to calculating measurements in meters, liters, kilograms, and kilometers. They will need practice to learn and become comfortable with the U.S. system of feet, quarts, pounds, and miles. And, since "knowing metric" is a real plus in the world economy, ELLs and native-speaking students could engage in reciprocal teaching to everyone's advantage.

Figure 2.4 European Notation of Numerals

	U.S. Notation	Foreign Notation
Grouping Hundreds	7,234,567	7.234.567
Marking Decimal Places	98.6	98,6
Showing Prices	$12.89	€12,89 (euro)
		£12,89 (pounds sterling)

Figure 2.5 Opposite Usage of Commas and Periods in Numeric Notation

Another area of possible cultural difference is in the focus on process so prevalent in American schools. Some cultures focus more on computational skills. For students coming from such cultures, the final answer is more valued than the process of finding the answer. The teacher's request to "Show your work" may not feel right to ELLs as their grades would have been lowered for doing so in their native countries.

Even the type of paper that students use for computation may seem strange to ELLs. In some countries, students are required to use graph paper for all math work to ensure that numerals are evenly spaced within the grid lines. When presented with blank paper, these students may experience difficulties that arise from the lack of structure.

Teachers of math also must be aware that culturally unfamiliar vocabulary in math word problems may prevent students from demonstrating their knowledge of the required mathematical functions. Word problems built around certain situations—such as a circus, a county fair, or American-style football—may not be solvable by ELLs not because they lack the computational ability to solve the problems but because they are stymied by the unfamiliar vocabulary involved in these events. It is not difficult, in problems like these, to substitute a known situation for the unfamiliar one.

Schools in foreign countries may also teach different algorithms for computation. Figure 2.6 through Figure 2.8 illustrate several alternative techniques for computation. If students in your classes are accustomed to using these approaches, it is best to let them continue such practices. Ask students to demonstrate their particular techniques to the whole class. You and your students will be fascinated by how they arrive at an answer, and your ELLs may, in the process, earn some extra esteem and respect.

Special Considerations for Teachers of Science

Teachers of science should be aware that for students from other parts of the world, science might not be as "pure" as Americans tend to think. Cultural backgrounds and religious teachings are strong determinants of beliefs. Students from other countries may hold conflicting views of commonly accepted scientific beliefs. Additionally, strong cultural taboos may affect the study of science. Activities such as dissecting animals and handling human bones, for example, may be forbidden.

Like math teachers, teachers of science are unquestionably aware of the difference between U.S. measurement systems and those used in most other countries. Students from countries using the metric system will be unfamiliar with our measurements of ounces, pounds, tons, cups, pints, quarts, gallons, inches, feet, yards, and miles. In terms of heat measurements, the centigrade scale is more widely used than the Fahrenheit scale. It will take some practice for students to feel comfortable using U.S. measurement systems.

Figure 2.6 Alternative Division Algorithms

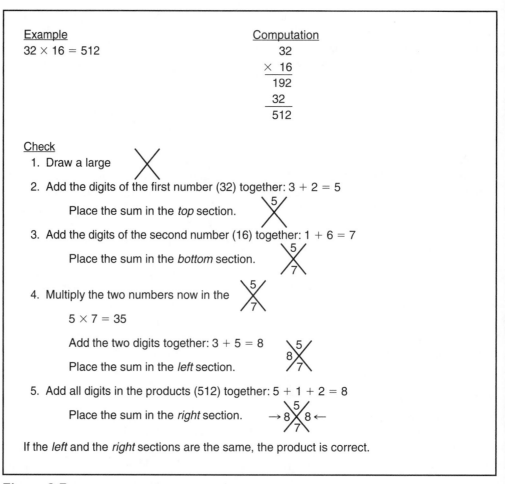

Figure 2.7 An Alternative Technique for Checking Multiplication Problems

Special Considerations for Teachers of Social Studies

Social studies is a nationalistic subject: Students everywhere learn about the people, places, and events that comprise the tapestry of world history from a nation-centered standpoint. The view is global, but the focus is local. Wars, conquests, alliances, power shifts, and leaders are subject to local interpretation. Inhabitants of neighboring countries, as well as those considerably more distant, may see the same historical events in a very different light. The particular understanding of history that ELLs are familiar with may differ from the one that U.S.-schooled students have learned. What, for example, might the World War II term *the Allies* mean to someone from Italy or Germany?

Another issue for teachers of social studies is that history in many parts of the world is rewritten as new rulers come into power. Current national, regional, ethnic, and religious perspectives color the way the past is seen. In his novel *1984,* George Orwell wrote, "Who controls the past controls the future: who controls the present controls the past." It is important that teachers recognize these potential disparities.

Special Considerations for Teachers of Language Arts, Reading, and Literature

As a teacher of language skills and literature, you know a great deal about the English language. Because you learned English as your first language or early in your childhood, you actually know even more about the language than you realize.

You know not only a great deal about grammar and vocabulary; you also know how to choose the right words and phrases to deal appropriately with a wide variety of

Example   Computation
89 × 47 = 4183   89
                                           47
                                          623
                                          356
                                         4183

Note: Only a single digit can be placed in the four sections of the ✕.

When the sum of any set of digits is more than a single digit, as in this example, add the second sum of digits together *again* to produce a single digit.

Check

1. Add the digits of the first number (89) together: 8 + 9 = 17

   Add the digits (17) together again: 1 + 7 = 8

   Place the sum in the *top* section.

2. Add the digits of the second number (47) together: 4 + 7 = 11

   Add the digits (11) together again: 1 + 1 = 2

   Place the sum in the *bottom* section.

3. Multiply the two numbers now in the

   8 × 2 = 16

   Add the two digits together: 1 + 6 = 7

   Place the sum in the *left* section.

4. Add all digits in the products (4183) together: 4 + 1 + 8 + 3 = 16

   Add the digits (16) together again: 1 + 6 = 7

   Place the sum in the *right* section.

If the *left* and the *right* sections are the same, the product is correct.
It *always* works!

Figure 2.8   It Always Works!

circumstances and people. You know the idioms, the proverbs, and the common cultural references of the language.

You understand intended meaning based on intonation. The messages of single words—*really, oh,* and *interesting,* for example—change entirely depending on how they are voiced. Few native speakers would confuse the meaning of *"Really?"* with *"Really!"*

You intuitively know how to order a series of adjectives that modify a noun. You would never say, for example, "the brick red big house." You recognize that certain words go together because of common usage. You say *heavy smoker* but *weighty matter*—and never *weighty smoker* or *heavy matter* (unless, of course, you're talking science).

You understand the subtle differences in meaning behind very close synonyms. Your choice of describing an acquaintance's appearance as *slim, thin,* or *skinny* or someone's behavior as *childlike* instead of *childish* has everything to do with your feelings of approval or disapproval.

You recognize that certain words are group nouns that cannot be counted individually. You say *three suitcases* but never *three luggages.* You know that prepositions can change the meaning of a phrase. You would never confuse a sign that said *On Sale* with one that said *For Sale.*

Idiomatic Speech

Let the cat out of the bag
Bite the bullet
Keeping up with the Joneses
Tongue in cheek
Pop the question
Take the cake
Four-letter words

Beat around the bush
See eye to eye
Brain trust
By the book
Read between the lines
Pay lip service
Eleventh hour

Proverbs and Adages

Nothing succeeds like success.
The wish is the father of the deed.
Any port in a storm.
A word to the wise is sufficient.
Curiosity killed the cat.
Too many cooks spoil the broth.
Forewarned is forearmed.
Necessity is the mother of invention.
When it rains, it pours.
A stitch in time saves nine.
Make haste slowly.
Out of the frying pan, into the fire.
Once bitten, twice shy.

Iconic References to American People, Events, and Places

Washington and the cherry tree
The Blue and the Gray
The father of our country
Uncle Sam
First Amendment rights
Paul Revere's ride
Underground railroad
Big stick diplomacy
Ellis Island
Prohibition and the Roaring Twenties
Watergate

Iconic References to Literature in English

She seems always to have an albatross around her neck. (Coleridge)
His ambition is matched only by Captain Ahab's. (Melville)
They were smiling like Cheshire cats. (Carroll)
Those two are like Tweedledum and Tweedledee. (Carroll)
You found it! Well aren't you a regular Sherlock Holmes! (Doyle)
My boss is a real Simon Legree. (Stowe)
I'm just starting out in my profession. I've got miles to go before I sleep. (Frost)
She should be wearing the scarlet letter. (Hawthorne)

Iconic References to Nursery Rhymes and Children's Stories

Be like the tortoise, not like the hare.
It was like trying to fix Humpty Dumpty.
His personality was a match for the Grinch.
They're killing the goose that lays the golden eggs.
She reacted to the spider like Little Miss Muffet.
He thinks he's Peter Pan.
It's a case of the boy who cried "Wolf."
Look at her now—a real ugly duckling.

Figure 2.9 Culturally Familiar References

Amazing, isn't it? You, as a fluent speaker of English, possess an enormous amount of language knowledge. When you learn English as a first language or early in childhood, you acquire all this knowledge without giving much thought to its subtleties and nuances. It would not be unusual that now, as a teacher, you intuitively use all the rules of the English language correctly but cannot explain exactly what those rules are.

The good news is that a number of teacher resources are available to you. If a student asks you about ordering adjectives, as in the examples of "the brick red big house," or the *luggage/suitcases* issue, you can find answers in a rules-based grammar book written specifically for ELLs. If the question refers to the connotation of words, as in the example of *childish* and *childlike*, you can refer to a special ELL-designed thesaurus that defines and explains shades of meaning and usage. If you wonder why your Russian students never use articles (the, a, an) when they speak or write English, you can turn to books that explain specific language interferences. (The interference here is caused by the Russian language having no articles.) These reference materials are listed in the *References and Resources* section at the end of this chapter.

An additional area of potential difficulty for ELLs in language arts/literature classes involves the use of common cultural references that virtually all native speakers know. These include idiomatic speech, proverbs and adages, and iconic references to American people, events, and places; to English language literature; even to nursery rhymes and children's stories. Examples of each of these are shown in Figure 2.9.

References of these types are troublesome for ELLs in several ways. Teachers may be unaware of the need to explain them because they appear so commonly in print and speech. And, even if explained, there may still be confusion if the symbolism or usage is not the same. Tuesday, the 13th, for example, is the unlucky day in Greece and Spain; and the owl, for some Native Americans, is a portent of death rather than a symbol of wisdom.

Not only ELLs, but also many young native English speakers, are unfamiliar with some proverbs or iconic references. Teaching these expressions to both native and nonnative English-speaking students can be as enjoyable as it is educational. A cultural-literacy dictionary in your classroom and instruction in how to use it serves as an excellent resource for ELLs to gain understanding of important cultural referents.

A final area of potential difficulty for ELLs in language arts and literature classes lies in the use of dialectic speech in novels that students may read in class. Conversations between characters in novels, such as Mark Twain's *The Adventures of Huckleberry Finn* and Zora Neale Hurston's *Their Eyes Were Watching God,* will tax ELLs' reading skills to the limit. A useful strategy for scaffolding such novels is to offer *Cliff Notes* or an ELL-simplified version as a supplement to the actual novel. Indeed, this may also be a good solution for native-speaking students whose reading skills are considerably below grade level.

As a final note to this chapter, it is worth repeating that human beings are products of their culture. Culture and cultural beliefs are deeply ingrained; the behaviors they control are not easily changed or discarded. Teachers of all subjects must develop an awareness of cultural determinants of behavior and a sensitivity to possible cultural conflicts to learning in American classrooms.

QUESTIONS FOR DISCUSSION

1. What qualities, characteristics, and behaviors are valued by the American culture?
2. What personal behaviors and beliefs do you feel have been shaped by the culture of your own family, religion, and/or ethnicity?
3. Have you ever visited a foreign country where you felt "out of place" because expectations of behavior were different from those you were accustomed to? Please explain.
4. Sometimes a move to a new area of the United States involves a cultural adjustment, even though it doesn't involve learning a new language. Have you ever had any experiences of this type?

5. Do you know people who immigrated to the United States from a foreign country? If so, interview them or their first-generation American children to find out about the cultural difficulties they experienced as they adjusted to life in their new country.

6. Use the Internet or personal resources to research proverbs, adages, animal symbolism, and cultural icons of a country or ethnicity of your own or your instructor's choice. Compare them with U.S. cultural references.

7. For 1 hour, listen either to a pair or group of people in conversation or to people talking on television. Create a list of the adages, idioms, and cultural references that you hear. Are there any that are unfamiliar to you?

REFERENCES AND RESOURCES

Diaz-Rico, L. T., & Weed, K. Z. (2005). *The cross cultural, language, and academic development handbook: A complete K–12 reference guide* (3rd ed.). Boston: Allyn and Bacon.

Firsten, R., with Killian, P. (2002). *The ELT grammar book: A teacher-friendly reference guide.* Burlingame, CA: Alta Book Center Publishers.

Helmer, S., & Eddy, C. (2003). *Look at me when I talk to you: ESL learners in non-ESL classrooms.* Portsmouth, NH: Heineman.

Hirsch, E. D., Jr. (2002). *The new dictionary of cultural literacy: What every American needs to know.* New York: Houghton Mifflin.

Igoa, C. (1995). *The inner world of the immigrant child.* New York: St. Martin's Press.

Longman Language Activator (Thesaurus, 2nd ed.). (2002). White Plains, NY: Pearson Education.

Scarcella, R. (1992). Providing culturally sensitive feedback. In P. A. Richard-Amato, & M. A. Snow (Eds.), *The multicultural classroom* (pp. 126–141). Reading, MA: Addison-Wesley.

Stewart, E. C., & Bennett, M. (1991). *American cultural patterns: A cross-cultural perspective.* Boston: Intercultural Press.

Swan, M., & Smith, B. (Eds.) (2001). *Learner English: A teacher's guide to interference and other problems.* Cambridge, England: Cambridge University Press.

Watkins-Goffman, L. (2001). *Lives in two languages: An exploration of identity and culture.* Ann Arbor: The University of Michigan Press.

The TechConnection

Free Internet Translation Sites

www.babelfish.altavista.com
www.itools.com

Culture-Specific Information

www.culturalorientation.net/pubs.html
www.culturegrams.com
www.interculturalpress.com

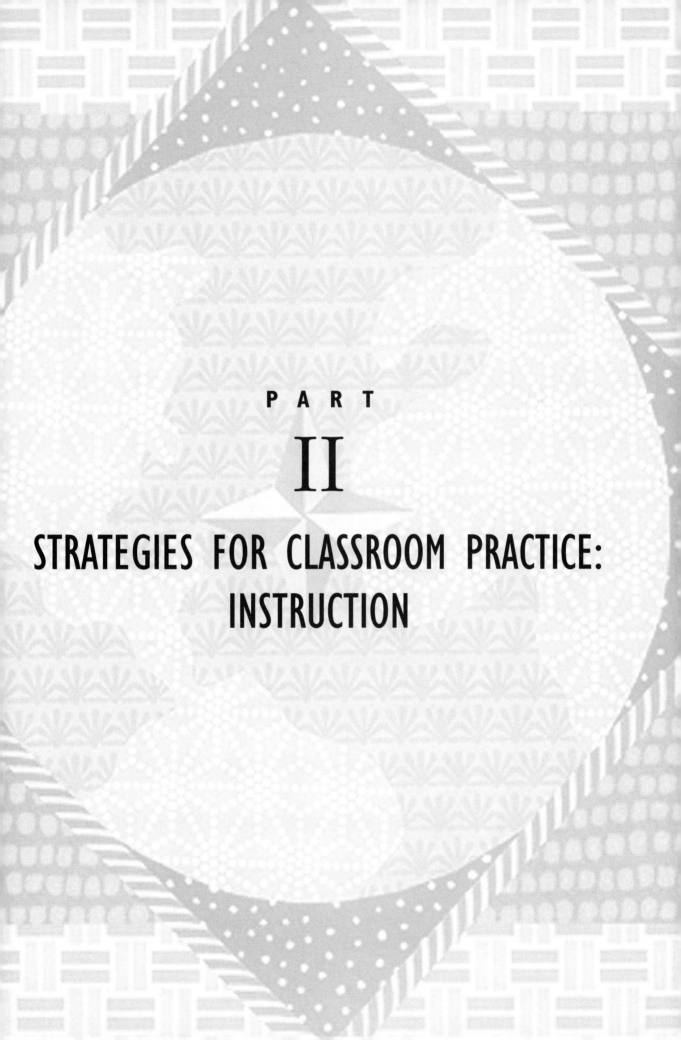

PART

II

STRATEGIES FOR CLASSROOM PRACTICE:
INSTRUCTION

CHAPTER 3

MEETING STATE OBJECTIVES AND STANDARDS: MAKING GOOD CHOICES

THEORY TO APPLICATION: GUIDELINES FOR PRACTICE

- Maintain a high level of cognitive challenge by selecting content material for ELLs based on depth, not breadth.
- Make content material meaningful, interesting, and relevant to maintain a high level of cognitive challenge and to expand students' areas of potential learning.
- Provide opportunities for students to experience success in the classroom: Success in learning promotes more success by increasing learner motivation, interest, and self-confidence.

State academic standards serve as rigorous goals for teaching and learning. They specify what students should know and be able to do in designated core areas of instruction as a result of their K–12 schooling. Standards align classroom instruction and establish a content base for statewide assessment.

State standards are not drawn arbitrarily. They are derived from a detailed web of topics, concepts, and skills essential for each grade level that professional organizations in each of the major content areas have created. States have used this information to develop their own sets of state standards and grade-level curricula. Classroom content teachers know these standards well—better, perhaps, than those that relate to the ELLs in their classrooms.

STANDARDS FOR ENGLISH LANGUAGE LEARNERS

In 1997, the organization Teachers of English to Speakers of Other Languages (TESOL) created a set of English as a Second Language (ESL) standards designed to complement the content area standards created by other professional associations. In 2006, TESOL extended and refocused those standards in a new document, *PreK–12 English Language Proficiency (ELP) Standards*, which reflects a number of trends relating to standards, content-based instruction, ELLs, and the provisions of the No Child Left Behind (NCLB) Act of 2001. The new standards set high expectations for achievement in the realms of English language and general academics.

Standard 1: ELLs communicate for social, intercultural, and instructional purposes within the school setting.

Standard 2: ELLs communicate information, ideas, and concepts necessary for academic success in the area of English language arts.

Standard 3: ELLs communicate information, ideas, and concepts necessary for academic success in the area of mathematics.

Standard 4: ELLs communicate information, ideas, and concepts necessary for academic success in the area of science.

Standard 5: ELLs communicate information, ideas, and concepts necessary for academic success in the area of social studies.

Figure 3.1   TESOL's 2006 PreK–12 English Language Proficiency Standards

The five ELP standards (see Figure 3.1) acknowledge the central role of language in the achievement of content. They form the bridge between language learning and national standards in the core curriculum areas of English language arts, mathematics, science, and social studies.

The standards are organized in a matrix that delineates expectations by grade level cluster, language proficiency level, and language domain (see Figure 3.2) for specific topics in the core academic content areas. By aligning academic content standards with language domain and proficiency levels, TESOL has produced a framework that can serve teachers, schools, and districts in establishing realistic expectations and meaningful instruction for their ELL student populations. The clear standards and model performance indicators define concrete goals for student achievement at each level of language proficiency. They serve to ensure that all students reach their full potential for academic success.

THE DILEMMA OF STANDARDS

Academic standards, whether discipline specific or ELP, specify what students should know and be able to do at each grade level and in each of the core content areas. They establish common yardsticks of instruction and curriculum. The dilemma they present to classroom teachers is one of curricular depth versus breadth: Should students spend a longer time on fewer topics or a shorter time on more topics?

Teachers have long felt torn between conflicting beliefs. On one hand, covering fewer curricular objectives and topics in greater depth allows opportunities to approach subject material in creative ways that can increase students' interest and motivation. On the other hand, teachers also believe that they have a responsibility to expose their students to all objectives and topics in the curriculum to prepare them, at least minimally, for future learning.

The issue of depth versus breadth has become even more serious for teachers in light of high-stakes testing. Because state accountability tests are directly linked to the standards,

Grade Level Clusters	Language Domains	Language Proficiency Levels
PreK–K: The Early Years	Listening	Level 1: Starting Up
Grades 1–3: Primary Grades	Speaking	Level 2: Beginning
Grades 4–5: Middle Elementary	Reading	Level 3: Developing
Grades 6–8: Middle School	Writing	Level 4: Expanding
Grades 9–12: High School		Level 5: Bridging Over

Figure 3.2   Differentiated Areas of TESOL's 2006 PreK–12 English Language Proficiency Standards

teachers feel themselves under intense pressure to cover these standards in the course of a school year. If this is a challenge with the *native* English-speaking students in their classes, can teachers possibly meet those standards with their ELLs? And if not, then what?

SELECTING STANDARDS, TOPICS, AND OBJECTIVES

The Objective: Analyze Standards, Topics, and Objectives to Make Sound Choices.

The Rationale

The preceding questions must be addressed realistically. ELLs, simply because they are in the process of learning English, may not be able to master the complete curriculum, but they will be able to learn a great deal of it. While the 2006 ELP Standards serve as a valuable guide, it is ultimately teachers' responsibility to select the standards, concepts, topics, and skills they believe are most essential for their ELLs. Those chosen should be core concepts that are individually interesting and cognitively challenging.

 ## STRATEGY 1   SELECT CORE CONCEPTS

IN CONCEPT

Core concepts are those that most benefit students' future learning. Take a close look at the standards, objectives, unit topics, and subtopics in your curriculum. It will be obvious that all have not been created equal. Some standards encompass high-level thinking skills and broad concepts; others are more narrowly based on separate, discrete skills and information. Topics, as well, can be viewed in a similar manner. Certain topics in your curriculum contain *core* concepts, those that recur and are conceptually extended in each successive year of schooling. Concepts such as those shown in Figure 3.3 form the foundation of knowledge upon which the understanding of more advanced and complex information, ideas, and relationships will depend and, as such, should be given higher priority.

IN PRACTICE

You can best help the ELLs in your classroom today by selecting and concentrating *first* on the core topics, skills, and standards that they will be expected to know and do in the academic years that follow. Start by examining the content standards and benchmarks—the topics, concepts, and skills—for your grade or grade grouping, and then compare them to those at the next higher level.

The Sunshine (Florida) State Science Standards, for example, are delineated by strands and by grade level groupings. Figure 3.4 shows the standards and benchmarks of

Math	Science	Social Studies
equality	adaptation	culture
operations	energy	liberty
equivalence	force	change
symmetry	matter	exploration
number systems	properties	rights/responsibilities

Figure 3.3 Some Core Topics in Math, Science, and Social Studies

Grades 6–8 Earth and Space

Standard 1: The student understands the interaction and organization of the Solar System and the universe and how this affects life on Earth.

1. understands the vast size of our Solar System and the relationship of the planets and their satellites.
2. knows that available data from various satellite probes show the similarities and differences among planets and their moons in the Solar System.
3. understands that our sun is one of many stars in our galaxy.
4. knows that stars appear to be made of similar chemical elements, although they differ in age, size, temperature, and distance.

Standard 2: The student recognizes the vastness of the universe and the Earth's place in it.

1. knows that thousands of other galaxies appear to have the same elements, forces, and forms of energy found in our Solar System.

Grades 9–12 Earth and Space

Standard 1: The student understands the interaction and organization of the Solar System and the universe and how this affects life on Earth.

1. understands the relationships between events on Earth and the movements of the Earth, its moon, the other planets, and the sun.
2. knows how the characteristics of other planets and satellites are similar to and different from those of the Earth.
3. knows the various reasons that Earth is the only planet in our solar system that appears to be capable of supporting life as we know it.

Standard 2: The student recognizes the vastness of the universe and the Earth's place in it.

1. knows that the stages in the development of three categories of stars are based on mass: stars that have the approximate mass of our sun, stars that are two-to-three stellar masses and develop into neutron stars, and stars that are five-to-six stellar masses and develop into black holes.
2. identifies the arrangement of bodies found within and outside our galaxy.
3. knows astronomical distance and time.
4. understands stellar equilibrium.
5. knows various scientific theories on how the universe was formed.
6. knows the various ways in which scientists collect and generate data about our universe (e.g., X-ray telescopes, computer simulations of gravitational systems, nuclear reactions, space probes, and supercollider simulations).
7. knows that mathematical models and computer simulations are used in studying evidence from many sources to form a scientific account of the universe.

Figure 3.4 Sunshine State Science Standards: Earth and Space Strands for Grades 6–8 and Grades 9–12

Florida Department of Education. (2005). *Sunshine State Standards for Science, Grades 6–8.* Retrieved April 26, 2006, from *http://www.firn. edu/doe/curric/prek12/pdf/science6.pdf.*

Florida Department of Education. (2005). *Sunshine State Standards for Science, Grades 9–12.* Retrieved April 26, 2006, from *http://www.firn. edu/doe/curric/prek12/pdf/science9.pdf.*

the Earth and Space strand for Grades 6–8 and 9–12. A middle school science teacher, after examining the corresponding high school standards, will recognize that the single benchmark in Standard 2 for Grades 6–8 is more critical than it might seem at first glance. It forms the core of understanding for the seven benchmarks at the next level. Its importance as a key to understanding future benchmarks makes it a core topic.

Keep in mind that ELLs are learning a new language at the same time they are trying to learn content. Focusing on core concepts for your ELLs does not lower your expectations—it simply repositions them at a more realistic level.

 ## STRATEGY 2   SELECT INTERESTING TOPICS

IN CONCEPT

Inherent interest in a topic is a natural motivator to learning. Students learn better—more quickly and in greater depth—when they are motivated. Developing a great deal of knowledge about a single topic, rather than a little bit of knowledge about a lot of topics, also promotes long-term retention of learning.

In general, students are interested in topics that relate to previous personal experiences, to prior learning, and/or to real-world connections. Linking standards, topics, and skills to the individual interests of students makes learning meaningful to them, and meaningful content is understood more easily and retained longer.

IN PRACTICE

There is no doubt that you will have to make some content choices for the ELLs in your classrooms. You can facilitate their learning by offering them a degree of choice in selecting topics that appeal to them.

The four benchmarks in Grades 6–8 Standard 1 (see Figure 3.4) cover a range of interesting topics: the planets, their moons, satellite probes, the sun, the stars. ELLs may discover a particular fascination with one of these topics. Encourage them to select that topic for in-depth study. Their motivation and personal interest may lead them toward expanding their knowledge of science and, in the process, building their English language skills as well.

 ## STRATEGY 3   SELECT CHALLENGING TOPICS

IN CONCEPT

Any topic selected for study by teacher or student must maintain a high level of academic challenge. ELLs will not benefit in the long or short run from a watered-down curriculum or from lowered expectations. Thoughtful selection of content involves combining cognitively demanding topics and concepts with activities that require the use of higher level thinking skills.

IN PRACTICE

To achieve this, allow your ELLs to focus on content *depth* rather than *breadth*. Turn your ELLs into class specialists by having them concentrate their attention on a narrow section of content instead of trying to cover all the information that the other students will be

Figure 3.5
Topics for Class
Specialists in Earth
Science

Unit	Expert Focus
Freshwater resources	Water pollution
Ocean motions	Currents
Weather factors	Precipitation
Energy resources	Fossil fuels

Figure 3.6
Topics for Class
Specialists in Life
Science

Unit	Expert Focus
Human anatomy	Skeletal system
Human physiology systems	Circulatory system
The sense organs	The sense of sight
Mammals	Mammal habitats

learning. Figures 3.5 and 3.6 offer samples of subtopics for your ELL specialists to study. Table 3.1 includes suggested assignments.

Offering ELLs a choice of areas to develop as their field of expertise will feel empowering and motivating to them. ELLs can be working on their expert topics at their own pace independently, in pairs, or in small groups, producing an example such as the graphic shown in Figure 3.7, while you continue your lessons with the class.

Table 3.1 Topics for Class Specialists in American History

Unit	Expert Focus	Assignment Type
The Constitution	Amendments	Timeline
	The 7 Articles	Graphic representation
	Separation of powers	Graphic representation
	U.S. government vs. system of government in ELLs' native countries	Venn diagram
The Civil War	Life in the North vs. life in the South	Venn diagram
	One battle: Antietam	Map, outcome graphic
	One general: Lee or Grant	Timeline
	The two generals compared	Venn diagram
Growth of the West	Railroads	Timeline, map
	Mining	Map, products
	Effects on Native American tribes	Graphic representation
The Progressive Era	The rise of unions	Timeline
	Reforms for women	Timeline
The Great Depression	Causes of the Depression	Graphic representation
	New Deal program summary	Graphic representation

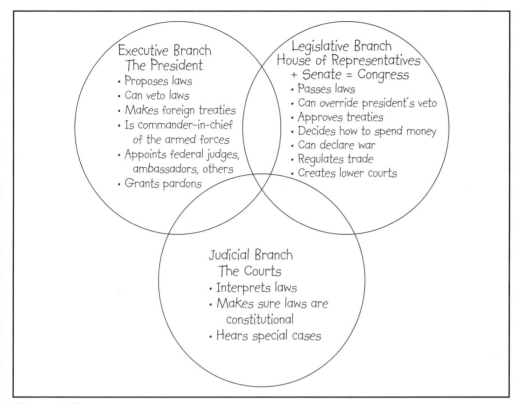

Figure 3.7 A Specialist's Report: The Three Branches of Government

When ELLs complete their individual assignments, they present their areas of expertise to others in a group information exchange. This pattern of assignment allows all aspects of a topic to be covered—the five senses, for example—but with each student assuming a reasonable language/academic challenge. Through this type of cooperative or shared activity, ELLs learn a great deal about content, concept, and language. It also creates the opportunity to show your ELLs in a positive light when you "call on the experts" to share knowledge as their topics arise during class discussion.

Inviting ELL students to become specialists in a narrow field of study is a pedagogically sound approach to learning. Long-term retention of knowledge is dramatically increased when learning is focused on the principle of *learn more about less*. Students who merely learn facts for the test often retain the information only until the test is over. Memorized lists are quickly forgotten, while information that has been thoroughly researched is often long remembered.

Combining depth of study with choice based on interest will give your ELLs a solid chance to learn challenging material. You will have offered them the best possible means of becoming actively and effectively involved in their own learning.

STRATEGY 4　SELECT PRACTICAL TOPICS

IN CONCEPT

Standards, objectives, topics, and concepts may vary in terms of practicality. A practical approach involves selecting topics that are easier to make comprehensible to ELLs because they are more concrete and demonstrable in content and process. These will be linguistically easier for ELLs to understand because they lend themselves to graphic representation and perhaps even direct inquiry learning.

IN PRACTICE

If you are deliberating among several topics that appear to offer equal challenge and long-term importance such as those in the Grades 6–8 benchmarks of Standard 1 (Figure 3.4), use practicality as a criterion of selection. The first benchmark about the solar system and the relationship of the planets and their satellites contains content that is practical because it can be broken into small, concrete chunks of information and then slowly built into the whole through demonstration, discovery learning, and multimedia graphics. Practical content offers you more ready access to the variety of strategies that scaffold instruction.

IN SUMMARY: SELECTING STANDARDS, TOPICS, AND OBJECTIVES

State standards are, at their best, a means to raise expectations for *all* students by improving the quality of learning in classrooms. At their worst, when too closely tied to high-stakes tests, state standards narrow curricula into little more than test preparation. Realistically, in the broad middle range, state standards maintain content integrity and use assessment to inform instruction. For better or worse, however, state standards are something all teachers have to work with for all their students.

It would be wonderful if all students could meet all the standards and learn everything in your curriculum. In an ideal world they could, but in the real world in which you teach, some of your students will do it all and some will not. Many ELLs, because they are learning the language while they are learning the content, will be in the group that will not. The medium of instruction is, for them, as challenging as the instruction itself.

The reality is that you must make curricular choices. Your most sincere attempts to cover the entire range and breadth of requirements with your ELLs—to meet all the standards—may well result in little real learning and a great deal of confusion and frustration. You can help ELLs so much more by maintaining high expectations that focus on topics, concepts, and standards that are important, foundational, cognitively challenging, interesting, and practical. You will be giving them the gift of academic success.

QUESTIONS FOR DISCUSSION

1. How do the strategies for selecting content reflect the *Guidelines for Practice* presented at the beginning of this chapter?
2. Research the state standards for the grade(s) and content area(s) you are now teaching or will soon teach. Then research the state standards for ELLs. To what degree are the two sets of standards related to each other? If they are less than fully interrelated, propose a plan or outline for improvement.
3. What is the relationship between your state's standards and its accountability system? What advantages and disadvantages do you see in this arrangement? If you are not yet teaching, interview a teacher in your field about this and report the results.
4. Investigate the accommodations made for ELLs in your state accountability systems. Do they reflect the guidelines for practice at the beginning of the chapter? In what ways do you believe they should be modified?

REFERENCES AND RESOURCES

Echevarria, J., & Graves, A. (2005). Curriculum adaptations. In P. Richard-Amato & M. A. Snow (Eds.), *Academic success for English language learners: Strategies for K–12 mainstream teachers* (pp. 224–247). White Plains, NY: Pearson Education.

Echevarria, J., Short, D., & Powers, K. (2003). *School reform and standards-based education: How do teachers help English language learners?* (Technical report). Santa Cruz, CA: Center for Research on Education, Diversity, and Excellence.

Falk, B. (2005). Possibilities and problems of a standards-based approach: The good, the bad, and the ugly. In P. Richard-Amato & M. Snow (Eds.), *Academic success for English language learners: Strategies for K–12 mainstream teachers* (pp. 342–362). White Plains, NY: Pearson Education.

Freeman, Y. S., Freeman, D. E., & Mercuri, S. (2002). *Closing the achievement gap: How to reach limited-formal schooling and long-term English learners.* Portsmouth, NH: Heineman.

Lachat, M. (2004). *Standards-based instruction and assessment for English language learners.* Thousand Oaks, CA: Corwin Press.

Teachers of English to Speakers of Other Languages (TESOL), Inc. (2006). *PreK–12 English language proficiency standards.* Alexandria, VA: TESOL, Inc.

The TechConnection

www.inspiration.com
    Find activities and learning tools matched to individual state standards.

Professional Organizations

The following professional organization Web sites contain a wealth of information on standards and topics that students should know at each grade level. Those relating to ELLs are listed first, followed by the national organizations for the major content areas.

California Association for Bilingual Education (CABE), *www.bilingualeducation.org*

National Association for Bilingual Education (NABE), *www.nabe.org*

TESOL, Inc. (Teachers of English to Speakers of Other Languages), *www.tesol.org*

National Council of Teachers of English, *www.ncte.org*

National Council of Teachers of Mathematics, *www.nctm.org*

National Science Teachers Association, *www.nsta.org*

National Council for the Social Studies, *www.socialstudies.org*

Information and Research Centers

These Web sites make available extensive information relating to the education of ELLs, including answers to questions, research findings, databases of education literature, and links to additional Internet resources.

Education Resources Information Center (ERIC), *www.eric.ed.gov*

Center for Applied Linguistics (CAL), *www.cal.org*

National Clearinghouse for English Language Acquisition (NCELA) and Language Instruction Educational Programs, *www.ncela.gwu.edu*

Center for Research on Education, Diversity, and Excellence (CREDE), *www.crede.org*

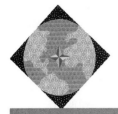

CHAPTER 4

LEARNING STRATEGIES FOR ENGLISH LANGUAGE LEARNERS

THEORY TO APPLICATION: GUIDELINES FOR PRACTICE

- Actively teach learning strategies to give students a "menu" of ways to process and learn new information.
- Use scaffolding strategies to challenge ELLs to advance beyond their present state of independent activity, into their areas of potential learning in which content is learnable with the assistance of teachers and peers.
- Provide opportunities for students to experience success in the classroom: Success in learning promotes more success by increasing learner motivation, interest, and self-confidence.

THE IMPORTANCE OF LEARNING STRATEGIES

Learning strategies are the keys to academic success for all students. Effective learners in all subject areas are those who have discovered and developed techniques of learning that work best for them. They have available to them a repertoire of learning strategies and know which to select to meet their immediate learning needs. They have acquired the tools for successful academic learning.

All students need to use learning strategies, but not all students develop them intuitively. It is surprising that many students believe that those who achieve high grades do so because they are "smart," not because they work hard and study effectively.

All students benefit from direct instruction in choosing and using learning strategies. ELLs, even more so, need this guidance to overcome the challenge of learning a new language while trying to use that language as the means to learn content.

Learning Strategies Defined

Learning strategies are techniques that facilitate the process of understanding, retaining, and applying knowledge. They are the "specific actions taken by the learner to make learning easier, faster, more enjoyable, more self-directed, and more transferable to new situations" (Oxford, 1990, p. 8). These "tricks of the learning trade" come in many varieties, but not all strategies work equally well for all learners, nor do they work equally well in all learning situations. Exposure to different types allows students to develop their own personal menu of strategies—a repertoire of techniques that work well for them.

Students choose appropriate strategies in combination with their personal learning styles to fit the type of knowledge they need to learn. For ELLs in content classrooms, these tricks of the learning trade take on extra importance and value.

Learning Strategies and Teaching Strategies: Same or Different?

Learning strategies and teaching strategies are often thought of interchangeably, but they are definitely *not* the same. Learning strategies are used *by the student* to understand, retain, and apply new knowledge. They are not readily visible or immediately identifiable.

Teaching strategies are used *by the teacher* to facilitate understanding for students and to make content more accessible to students. These are the techniques, approaches, activities, and assignments that teachers use to help students process new information and apply prior learning. Teaching strategies are immediately visible and identifiable: Indeed, they are what administrators evaluate when they do classroom observations. The subset of teaching strategies used for ELLs is part of *scaffolded instruction*. Teaching strategies are concerned with how teachers *send* the message; learning strategies deal with how the message is *received*, and that is the focus of this chapter.

Learning Strategies and Learning Styles: Same or Different?

Again, learning strategies and learning styles are *not* the same thing. Learning styles involve preferences of particular work patterns *within* an individual. Learning styles are personal, enduring, and often unconscious choices of ways to learn, such as individual or group work, auditory or visual input, a quiet environment or background noise, and single-task or multitask focus. Learning strategies, in contrast, are learned, changeable from task to task, and often consciously chosen.

Although learning styles are individual, teachers should be aware that education systems around the world value and reward different learning styles. As discussed in Chapter 2, ELLs may prefer styles of learning that have been shaped by their cultures.

THE TYPES OF LEARNING STRATEGIES

Having now sorted out any confusions about what learning strategies are and are not, it is time to focus on ways of classifying them. Much has been written about how students learn and the strategies they use in the process. The classification of strategy types used in this text is built largely upon the research and writings of O'Malley & Chamot (1990) and Oxford (1990).

Learning strategies for ELLs fall into four broad types—metacognitive, cognitive, social, and compensation—with a subtype within the cognitive category, memory strategies. It is important to understand how each of these strategy types helps students learn.

Metacognitive Strategies

Metacognitive strategies are those that involve *thinking* about learning. These can be divided into two subtypes of techniques: those that deal with *organizing* and *planning* for learning, and those that deal with *self-monitoring* and *self-evaluating* learning.

Examples of Metacognitive Strategies Dealing with Organizing and Planning for Learning
- Using a homework notebook to write down all assignments.
- Keeping a calendar/organizer to write down long-term assignments.
- Dividing long-term assignments into shorter segments and tasks.
- Setting deadlines for completion of each segment or task.

- Determining the most appropriate and efficient strategies to learn specific content.
- Planning *how* to study for a test

Examples of Metacognitive Strategies Dealing with Self-Monitoring and Self-Evaluation of Learning

- Recognizing your own knowledge gaps or weaknesses
- Discovering strategies that work best for you (and those that don't)
- Training yourself to monitor your own progress in learning—to awaken the little voice in your head that asks, "How am I doing?" and "Am I understanding this?"
- Checking your progress frequently by responding to that little voice
- Recognizing the need to find a new strategy if the one you're using isn't working

Cognitive Strategies

Cognitive strategies are those that involve any type of *practice* activity. These are techniques that promote deeper understanding, better retention, and/or increased ability to apply new knowledge. The techniques that fall into this category are familiar to successful learners and are used on a regular basis.

Examples of Cognitive Strategies

- Making specific connections between new and old learning
- Making specific connections between English and the student's native language
- Highlighting important information while reading
- Dividing a large body of information into smaller units
- Note taking (even in student's native language)
- Condensing notes to study for a test
- Making and using flash cards to test yourself
- Making visual associations to aid in retention
- Creating graphic organizers, maps, charts, diagrams, timelines, and flowcharts to organize information
- Making categories and classifications

Cognitive strategies form the core of learning techniques. They fall into the general category that students call *studying*. Cognitive strategies that are creative, interesting, even gamelike in nature, put a positive spin on studying, making it more motivating and productive to all students.

Memory Strategies

Memory strategies consist of any technique that aids *rote recitation* of learned material. Memory strategies are devised simply to recall elements without any attempt to understand the material more completely. They are a subtype of cognitive strategies because their purpose is to trigger the recall of specific groups of items, concepts, or ideas that have been learned through other cognitive techniques.

A simple example of a memory strategy is the *Alphabet Song* learned by young children often long before they have any concept of letters. It is strictly a rote memory device—a *mnemonic*—and indeed, a very effective one. Later, as children learn to recognize and write their letters, they use the *Alphabet Song* to remind themselves of alphabetic order.

Mnemonics in academia are created, often by individual students, to help remember rules, key words, lists, and categories. Memory strategies such as poems, songs, acronyms, sentences (the first letter of each word in the sentence is the same as an item in an ordered list), and word patterns are very effective in triggering the recall of much larger bodies of information that have been learned through other cognitive approaches. ELLs can even use their native languages to create their own memory devices.

Figure 4.1 Two Mnemonics to Remember the Number of Days in the Months

You May Know This Poem:

Thirty days hath September
April, June, and November
All the rest have thirty-one
Excepting February alone
It has twenty-eight days time
And each leap year twenty-nine

But Do You Know The Knuckle Technique?

Hold your hand forward, palm down, and make a fist.

Starting with the knuckle above the index finger, count off the months, naming a month as you touch *each knuckle and the spaces* between.

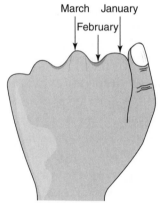

March   January
February

When you get to July at the pinky knuckle, touch that knuckle again for August and reverse direction.

Have you noticed that all the months that fall into the spaces have fewer than thirty-one days?

Examples of Familiar Mnemonics

- The "I before E" poem to recall spelling rules
- The poem and the "knuckle technique" for remembering which months of the year have less than 30 days (see Figure 4.1)
- The made-up word to remember the color spectrum in which the letters recall the colors in their correct order (see Figure 4.2)
- The silly sentence to remember the notes on a treble staff (see Figure 4.2)
- The "tricks" of the multiplication table (see Figure 4.3)

Figure 4.2 More Mnemonics

For the Color Spectrum

"Roy-G-Biv" = **r**ed, **o**range, **y**ellow, **g**reen, **b**lue, **i**ndigo, **v**iolet

For the Notes on a Treble Staff

E, G, B, D, F = **E**very **g**ood **b**oy **d**oes **f**ine.
                Every **g**ood **b**oy **d**eserves **f**udge.

Figure 4.3 Multiplication Mnemonics

The 9 Times Trick

Hold both hands in front of you with your fingers spread out.
For 9 × 3, bend your third finger on your left hand down.
   (9 × 4 would be the fourth finger, and so on.)
You have 2 fingers in front of the bent finger and 7 after the bent
   finger. And there's the answer: 27.
This technique works for the 9 times tables up to 10.

The 4 Times Trick

For this one, you only need to know how to double a number.
Simply, double a number and then double it again!

The 11 Times Trick

To multiply 11 by any two-digit numbers:
Example 1
Multiply 11 by 18. Jot down 1 and 8 with a space between:
   1   8
Add the 1 and the 8 and put that number in the middle: 198.
   11 × 18 = 198
Example 2
When the digits of the multiplier add up to 10 or more, do it this way:
Multiply 11 by 39. Jot down 3 and 9 with a space between:
   3   9
Add the 3 and the 9 to get 12.
Put the 2 in the middle between the 3 and the 9, then add the 1
   to the 3:
   4
   3 2 9   11 × 39 = 429

As students recognize the efficiency of mnemonics as a recall tool and feel comfortable using them, you can assign the creation of a mnemonic as a creative homework assignment, as described in Figure 4.4.

Social Strategies

Social strategies are of two types. In the first type, language learners attempt to learn English by interacting with the environment. They expand their vocabularies by listening as English is being spoken and by attending to written English as it appears around them.

The second type of social strategy is more closely related to the classroom. Here language learners work with one or more other students to learn information or to complete a task. Group work and cooperative learning are social learning strategies. Because social strategies are, as the name states, social, they often feel less like practice and occasionally even like fun.

Figure 4.4 Assign a Mnemonic for Homework: It's Challenging, Fun, and Effective

Ask students to create a mnemonic designed to recall the elements in a set of information. The mnemonic can be an acronym that sounds good or a silly sentence that works.
   Students will have to process the content under study to complete this assignment, but they'll hardly know they're doing it!

Figure 4.5 Questions and Requests: A Social Strategy for English Language Learners

> Please say that again.
> Would you write that word on the board, please?
> Could you speak more slowly, please?
> Can you give more examples, please?
> Would you please explain what _____ means?
> Can you say the directions again, please?

Examples of Social Strategies

- Working in class in pairs or small groups to clarify content, solve problems, and complete projects
- Playing teacher-made or professionally designed games to sharpen skills
- Doing homework with a friend
- Studying with a partner for a test
- Watching select television programs
- Observing peers to learn more about culture and language
- Asking questions and making requests (see Figure 4.5)

Compensation Strategies

Compensation strategies are techniques used to make up for something that is either unknown or not immediately accessible from memory. Proficient speakers of English regularly use this type of strategy in conversations when they use words or phrases such as *whatchamacallit,* the *thingamajiggy,* or just plain *that thing—you know what I mean* to replace the language they are searching for but cannot find at the moment.

Examples of Compensation Strategies

- Stalling for time while we think of an appropriate response
- Making an educated guess that extends and generalizes what we know to what we don't know
- Using a circumlocution, a substitute phrase that "talks around" the word we don't know or "writes around" the word we can't spell

Figure 4.6 Examples of Compensation Strategies

Stalling for Time

- Repeating the question or statement
- Using fillers like *Well. . .* or *Hmmm. . . .*
- Using expressions such as *"That's a tough question"* or *"That's a complicated issue"*
- Coughing or clearing your throat
- Any combination of the above

Making Educated Guesses

- Using *airplane driver* as an extension of known expressions, such as *truck driver* and *taxi driver,* when the word *pilot* is not known

Using Circumlocutions

- Using the descriptive phrase *the man who drives the airplane* instead of the unknown word *pilot*
- Using the phrase *the machine that cooks the bread dark* in place of the unknown word *toaster*

Figure 4.6 gives examples of specific usages of each of these compensation strategies. Explaining the concept of compensation strategies to your ELLs and encouraging them to use them may go a long way toward making ELLs feel more willing to participate in class.

WORKING WITH LEARNING STRATEGIES

The Objective: Combine Strategies and Strategy Types.

The Rationale

While all students need to use a variety of strategy types, ELLs, in particular, will benefit from using strategies in combination. Using two or more cognitive strategies in tandem or sequentially, or grouping one or several cognitive strategies with social strategies, offers ELLs more opportunities to hear the language structures and vocabulary that support the conceptual ideas.

STRATEGY 5   USE TWO OR MORE COGNITIVE STRATEGIES TOGETHER

IN CONCEPT

Trying to learn by repeating one cognitive strategic technique over and over is often not the most productive approach to learning. Using several techniques in combination strengthens the effectiveness of each and reinforces student learning.

IN PRACTICE

Show students how powerful learning strategies can be when they are combined sequentially. A guided whole-class activity that takes students through a series of cognitive learning strategies to learn information and concepts presented in a reading passage can demonstrate the value of combining strategies. Using a photocopied reading passage, guide students as they read and highlight important information and concepts for them. As the next step, have students write up a set of notes based on the highlighted sections. Then have them condense their notes and make flash cards to study in preparation for a quiz. The grades on the quiz should speak well for this combined strategic approach.

You also may want to underscore the effectiveness of combining strategies by doing a guided whole-class activity, either prior to or following this activity, in which your students use only one cognitive strategy to learn the elements of a similar reading passage. Comparing the two approaches to learning should bring about a lively class discussion.

STRATEGY 6   USE SOCIAL AND COGNITIVE STRATEGIES TOGETHER

IN CONCEPT

ELLs increase their opportunities for academic success when they work in collaboration with their native English-speaking peers, using interaction to negotiate meaning of both language and content. Working in pairs and small groups serves to widen the language learner's zone of proximal development (Vygotsky's theory, discussed in Chapter 1).

Figure 4.7   Is This Math Class or English Class?

> Wei looks at the assigned word problems in his math book and knows that there is no way he can possibly figure out any of the answers. It's not that Wei's math skills are weak—in fact, he knows he's really pretty good at computation. He also knows that, once again, it's all those words in the problem that will bar his way to success. Wei is an English language learner.

IN PRACTICE

Students have, for many decades, spontaneously created their own strategy combinations. You may remember making flash cards to help you learn large sets of information. Then you used them to check yourself to see how much you really knew. Finally, you and a friend or classmate quizzed each other. You were combining a cognitive technique with a social one, which is an excellent way to learn.

To see the benefit of combining strategy types, look at the scenario described in Figure 4.7. Math word problems are almost always a challenge for ELLs. ELLs need a plan to help them separate the actual math knowledge required to solve the problem from the English language knowledge that is impeding them. The multistep approach called *streamlining*, a structured combination of cognitive and social learning strategies shown in Figure 4.8, offers this kind of support.

WORKING WITH LEARNING STRATEGIES

The Objective: Actively Teach Learning Strategies.

The Rationale

You may already be aware that strategy training should not be subtle. It needs to be taught explicitly and overtly. For students to recognize the usefulness of learning

Figure 4.8   Streamlining: A Multistep Approach for Math Word Problems

> **Step 1: Make language substitutions.**
>
> In pairs or small groups, students look for words or phrases that can be eliminated or replaced with more simple language. They use a bilingual dictionary or a student dictionary as needed.
>
> **Step 2: Determine the information presented.**
>
> Students, still in pairs or groups, reread the now-simplified wording of the problem. They search out and write down all information given in the problem.
>
> **Step 3: Determine the information needed for solution.**
>
> Students now look for words that offer clues to the information needed in the solution. They first eliminate extraneous words and information, and then write out the words and phrases that tell how to process the information in the problem.
>
> **Step 4: Determine the process needed for solution.**
>
> Using the words or phrases from Step 3, students figure out the process needed to find the solution.
>
> **Step 5: Solve the problem.**
>
> Students perform the necessary computations and compare results.

strategies in general, specific strategies must be directly tied to learning specific content as they are taught.

STRATEGY 7   USE THE FIVE-STEP APPROACH TO TEACH LEARNING STRATEGIES

IN CONCEPT

Strategy teaching is a five-step process. First, introduce the strategy to your students and *label* it as a new learning strategy. Next, *identify* it with a name and explain how it is used. Then, *demonstrate* how to use it by applying it directly to specific content. Next, give students the time and opportunity to *practice* using it with that content. Finally, *discuss* with your students how effective they found this strategy to be for them and ask them for which other types of tasks this new strategy might be good. These steps are summarized in Figure 4.9.

IN PRACTICE

The clearest way to understand the five-step approach is to examine in detail an actual example of a strategy lesson. The teacher in this example has observed when he teaches that few of the students are able to distinguish the important concepts and ideas from the less important details. The lesson he planned will give students a strategy for listening for key pieces of information during class lessons and discussions.

For Step 1—*Introduce it and label it as a new strategy*—he opens the lesson with a question: "Do you have trouble knowing what's *really* important when I teach? Today we're going to learn a new strategy that will help you with this."

Moving immediately to Step 2—*Identify it by name and explain its use*—he says, "We're going to call this strategy *Listening for Key Words* *. (The asterisk symbolizes words that the teacher writes on the board as she or he speaks them.) Here's how it works."

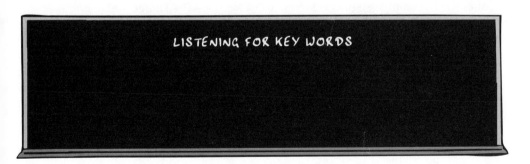

"When I teach, I often use phrases like 'This is really important *,' and 'Here's the important part *,' and 'This is a key point *.' Have you ever heard me say any of those? Or have you heard me *repeat words or phrases* * or say something several times? I do that because I want you to know it's really important."

Figure 4.9 Strategy Teaching in Five Steps

---

1. *Introduce* it and label it as a new strategy.
2. *Identify* it by name and explain its use.
3. *Demonstrate* how to use it.
4. Give students time and opportunity for *practice*.
5. *Discuss* effectiveness and application to other tasks.

> LISTENING FOR KEY WORDS
>
> *"This is really important."*
>
> *"Here's the important part."*
>
> *"This is a key point."*
>
> REPEAT words or phrases.

"So look at what I've written on the board. Let's call these *listening cues* *. They're like flags that wave at you to tell you to listen and remember."

> LISTENING FOR KEY WORDS
>
> *"This is the important part."*
>
> *"Here's the important part."*   LISTENING CUES
>
> *"This is a key point."*
>
> REPEAT words or phrases.

The teacher continues to Step 3—*Demonstrate how to use it*—by saying, "OK, let's try it. For the next five minutes, while I teach, I want you to raise your hand every time you hear me say one of these phrases (Teacher points to and repeats phrases on board). Then we'll talk about how they tell you that something important is coming up next."

After the five-minute segment, he moves to step 4—*Give students time and opportunity for practice*—explaining to the students that they are to listen carefully for these phrases for the rest of the instructional period. Any time they hear one, they are to write down the information that comes immediately after the phrase.

In Step 5—*Discuss its effectiveness and application to other tasks*—the students share the information they have written down. The strategy session concludes with a discussion about whether they found the strategy helpful as a means of recognizing important facts and concepts during oral instruction, as well as where else they think this strategy might be useful.

The students have learned a specific strategy for recognizing important pieces of information. To reinforce this learning, this teacher will remind students to use this strategy at the opening of subsequent lessons and class discussions.

STRATEGY 8 USE THINK-ALOUDS AND MODELING

IN CONCEPT

Think-alouds and modeling demonstrate the step-by-step process involved in completing many types of activities. In think-alouds, you, the teacher, explain how your brain is working at each step on the way to the solution of a problem. Modeling does the same

Your student correctly infers information from the text.

ASK: *Where did you find the information that helped you with that answer?*

Your student solves a complex problem.

ASK: *How did you arrive at that answer?*

Your student presents an informed opinion on a topic.

ASK: *What information led you to this opinion?*

Your student gets a good grade on a test.

ASK: *How exactly did you study for this test?*

Figure 4.10   Think-Aloud Applications for Strategy Training

but with actual samples and examples of steps along the way. The two techniques are nonexclusive; indeed, they work most effectively when used together.

IN PRACTICE

Technique I

When students are faced with a complicated learning task, you might say something like "If I had to learn this, I would probably . . . ," giving a detailed, step-by-step description of the *process* you would use. You are, in effect, modeling the how-to of learning.

Technique II

Students themselves can be a good source for think-aloud strategy training. Guided questions such as those in Figure 4.10 about how they knew or learned specific information will allow ELLs (and others, of course) to see how their peers approach a task and to learn directly from them.

If one of the students describes a way of learning that is new to the class, you can label that strategy with the name of the student who contributed it. Imagine how empowering it is to have a strategy named for you!

STRATEGY 9   BRAINSTORM LEARNING STRATEGIES

IN CONCEPT

While some students may easily organize their plans for learning, for others it is a daunting task. Brainstorming ideas for learning in a class discussion can be a productive strategy.

IN PRACTICE

When students are facing a difficult learning task—memorizing the table of periodic elements in chemistry, for example—you can conduct an open-ended discussion about which learning strategies they think they could use to accomplish this feat. Discuss with them any specific strategies they've used in the past that they think might help them to learn the type of content they're facing now. It is of equal value to include in the discussion approaches to learning that probably will *not* be particularly helpful.

STRATEGY 10 IDENTIFY STUDENTS' PERSONAL PREFERRED STRATEGIES

IN CONCEPT

Because not all learning strategies work for all students in all situations, it is important that students understand that strategy usage is personal and individual.

IN PRACTICE

Teachers can help students identify their own current learning strategies through survey questions and discussion. To keep learning strategies at the forefront of students' thinking, use a bulletin board or wall space to make a display naming the strategies and showing how they are used. As each new strategy is taught, add it to the wall poster or bulletin board. Students can keep their own learning strategy logs or journals. In either case, students will have a ready reference—a menu or guide—from which to draw.

STRATEGY 11 INTEGRATE LEARNING STRATEGY TRAINING INTO DAILY INSTRUCTION

IN CONCEPT

The more seamlessly you integrate learning strategy training into your instruction, the more students will incorporate learning strategies into their thinking about learning. Making conscious decisions about which learning strategies to use for which tasks will become a deeply ingrained pattern for learning.

IN PRACTICE

Technique I

Give students frequent tips—strategies to help them manage their time, take notes, classify and categorize information, and study for tests. Before students begin a class or homework assignment, ask them which learning strategies they think might be most appropriate, effective, and efficient to achieve a successful outcome. Make sure the students remember to refer to the wall display as a resource.

Technique II

Students of every age love to hear about the lives of their teachers. They will listen in rapt attention when you talk about your own personal learning experiences. Tell them about the successful and not-so-successful strategies you used to learn things. Talk about how you learn now. Take advantage of every possible opportunity to bring learning strategies into class lessons and discussion.

IN SUMMARY: WORKING WITH LEARNING STRATEGIES

Teachers who recognize the value of learning strategies and the potential of each strategy type, alone and in combination, understand the importance of making strategy training an ongoing part of their classroom instruction. Their students will develop a repertoire of effective learning strategies and know how to make task-appropriate choices. Actively teaching learning strategies offers students the best chance to meet with academic success.

QUESTIONS FOR DISCUSSION

1. How do the strategies for teaching learning strategies reflect the *Guidelines for Practice* presented at the beginning of this chapter?

2. Label each of the following examples of learning strategies by type—metacognitive, cognitive, memory, social, or compensation:

   a. Helping friends with homework

   b. Making flash cards and using them to study

   c. Substituting a synonym for a word you can't pronounce or spell

   d. Breaking an assignment into its component parts, ordering the parts, and setting timelines for completion

   e. Taking notes from highlighted text sections

   f. Reading the questions at the end of the passage before actually reading the text

   g. Using "the next day" instead of "tomorrow" in writing

   h. Testing your understanding by making up your own quizzes

   i. Actively reading and interpreting street signs and billboards

   j. Asking another student or a sibling to quiz you

   k. Guessing at new words

   l. Keeping a vocabulary journal

3. Classify by learning strategy type each step in streamlining, shown in Figure 4.8.

4. Think about the learning strategies you used as a learner. Which ones were successful for you? How did you learn them? Did you have any learning strategies that you discarded because you realized they weren't working well for you?

5. Analyze the learning strategies that you now use most frequently. Do you use different strategies for different types of tasks?

6. Prepare a think-aloud demonstration (Strategy 8) to present in class. Your colleagues will offer verbal feedback or a written critique.

REFERENCES AND RESOURCES

Chamot, A. U., Barnhardt, S., El-Dinary, P. B., & Robbins, J. (1999). *The learning strategies handbook*. White Plains, NY: Pearson Education.

O'Malley, J. M., & Chamot, A. U. (1990). *Learning strategies in second language acquisition.* New York: Cambridge University Press.

Oxford, R. (1990). *Language learning strategies: What every teacher should know.* New York: Newbury House.

Reid, J. (Ed.). (1998). *Understanding learning styles in the second language classroom.* Upper Saddle River, NJ: Prentice Hall Regents.

CHAPTER 5

A SOLID START: BUILDING AND ACTIVATING BACKGROUND KNOWLEDGE

THEORY TO APPLICATION: GUIDELINES FOR PRACTICE

- Activate and develop background knowledge to make new content meaningful and to form a foundation upon which new learning can be built.
- Make content material meaningful, interesting, and relevant to maintain a high level of cognitive challenge and to expand students' areas of potential learning.
- Lower learner anxiety in the classroom to create students who are more willing to participate in class, to become risk takers in the learning process, and ultimately to become more successful learners.
- Provide opportunities for students to experience success in the classroom: Success in learning promotes more success by increasing learner motivation, interest, and self-confidence.

BACKGROUND KNOWLEDGE AND LEARNING

What makes something easier or harder to learn? Most answers to this question would include two factors among possible others: motivation and preexisting knowledge.

Motivation

People learn what they want or need to learn. They learn because it is important to some aspect of their lives, perhaps even to their very survival. How fast they learn depends on how valuable, interesting, or necessary they perceive the new learning is to them. The greater the felt need or desire to learn, the easier and faster the learning will be. Motivation is a powerful influence on the learning process.

Preexisting Knowledge

The other factor influencing the learning process is the amount that is already known about the topic (Leinhardt, 1992). People learn most readily by adding new data to preexisting information. It is a far greater challenge to learn something entirely new.

Learning something completely new is like gathering individual grains of sand. Imagine each new fact as a single grain of moist sand. At the start, it is hard to form a whole from the tiny disparate grains because each grain can stick to so few others. Eventually enough sand accumulates to form a small mass. Then, new grains have an easier time finding a spot to fit in.

So too it is with facts: Like sand, each new fact about an unknown topic is unrelated to any other and must be processed individually. Eventually, enough facts accumulate to form a small mass of knowledge. As the mass of facts grows, new facts begin to relate more easily to what has already been learned, and this is where background knowledge enters the picture. Background knowledge *is* the mass that makes new facts meaningful. The larger the mass of background knowledge and the more it can be actively recalled, the easier it will be for new knowledge to find a place to fit in.

All Students Need Background Knowledge

The student's own background knowledge forms the building blocks upon which new learning is built. Why, then, is this a special issue for ELLs?

A school curriculum is planned around a set of basic assumptions about common academic background and life experience of students at each grade level. Students entering U.S. schools from other countries, however, have generally had differing sets of personal, cultural, and academic experiences. Teachers with ELLs in their classrooms must first determine that these students actually *have* prior learning or experience that is relevant to their success in learning new content. The second step is then to *build* background knowledge where it is lacking before presenting the new material.

WORKING WITH BACKGROUND KNOWLEDGE

The Objective: Use Varied Techniques to Activate and Build Background Knowledge.

The Rationale

All students, not only language learners, learn more effectively and efficiently when teachers make explicit connections between past and present learning and take time to build up weak foundational backgrounds. Indeed, a strong indicator of how well a student will learn new content is the amount of relevant background knowledge or experience he or she already has. That is why activating students' prior knowledge is an essential teaching strategy.

Activating background knowledge not only makes learning easier; it also makes learning meaningful, awakens interest in the topic, and increases motivation. Students who can see the relevance of a topic to their own lives will be interested in learning about it. Teachers who understand the importance of background knowledge and motivation can facilitate learning for their students. Finding the right connection pulls students directly into the material.

Strategies to build background knowledge aim to connect what students already know with what they will be learning and to develop a strong foundation of background for new learning. The strategies presented in this section simultaneously activate prior knowledge for students who have it and build new knowledge for those who need it.

STRATEGY 12 BEGIN WITH BRAINSTORMING

IN CONCEPT

Brainstorming is the strategy of asking students to think about and tell what they already know (or think they know) about a new topic before it is actually introduced. It activates

Figure 5.1 Carousel Brainstorming

Tape sheets of chart paper on the walls at various locations around your classroom. At the top of each sheet, write a word or phrase pertaining to the new topic to be studied. For large groups and to save time, have several sets of the same words or phrases.

Following your signals, students walk around the room in small groups writing their associations to the word at the top of the paper. Allow no more than two minutes before signaling time to move to the next location.

existing background knowledge in those students who have it, fills gaps for those students who lack it, and engages student interest for all.

For ELLs, brainstorming may be a first exposure to new vocabulary as they hear the pronunciation of a word and see it written at the same time. Teachers benefit, too, by being able to immediately assess whether or not students have enough background knowledge to move ahead.

IN PRACTICE

Technique I

To begin brainstorming, write a topic word on the board or on an overhead transparency. Accompany it with the open-ended question *"What do you think of when I say the word _____?"*

As students respond, write their words and phrases around the topic word to form a graphic display. Accept all answers, right or wrong. When you feel ready to move on with the lesson, tell students that you will return later to reexamine these ideas by saying something like *"Let's save these answers. We'll come back to them later to see what we found out about them."*

Technique II

A variation of this strategy is called *carousel brainstorming* (see Figure 5.1). This technique offers the additional benefits of getting students up and physically moving, involving all students simultaneously. It is exciting to watch students' faces as they think of new ideas triggered by reading what other students have written. At the end of the activity, groups can read out items from each sheet of chart paper as you create a single brainstorming graphic based on all the information written.

Technique III

Use the brainstorming graphic at the end of the lesson as the lesson summary and review. Ask, as you point to each item, *"Did we talk about this?"* Students can review what they learned in the lesson. They can add new words and phrases and correct misconceptions. You can make connections to subtopics to be covered in later lessons.

Technique IV

Write the initial brainstorming graphic on an overhead transparency or chart paper and save it to start the next day's lesson. Students can add newly learned information as they review previous learning.

 STRATEGY 13   USE THINK–WRITE–PAIR–SHARE

IN CONCEPT

Think–Write–Pair–Share is a technique that encourages participation at the same time that it activates students' prior knowledge. It is a way of getting students actively and immediately involved in learning new concepts and topics.

IN PRACTICE

Start with the same open-ended question as in the brainstorming activity, but this time, instead of asking the class for an immediate oral response, give students a short time—no more than two minutes—to *think* about and *write* down any relevant words or phrases they can come up with. For the next minute or two, *pair* each student with a partner to discuss and expand each individual's list. Finally, invite students to *share* their ideas with the rest of the class. A great way to do this is to ask students to tell you an idea they either *had* or *heard*.

STRATEGY 14 USE K–W–L CHARTS

IN CONCEPT

A graphic organizer that complements the think-write-pair-share activity is the K–W–L chart (see Figure 5.2). This is a strategy that is best completed in a small group environment. Talking about the topic helps students generate the ideas and vocabulary needed to complete the columns.

IN PRACTICE

Technique I

Students are asked to write what they already **k**now (or think they know) about a topic in the **K** column. Then, with a partner or in a small group, they discuss what they **w**ant to know to complete the **W** column. The **L** column gets completed at the end of the lesson with students, again in pairs or small groups, listing what they **l**earned. K–W–L charts, used to open a lesson on a new topic, may help bolster confidence and motivation as students begin to realize that they already know something about the forthcoming material.

As topical information builds, making daily entries in each column provides an ongoing means of activating students' prior knowledge and stimulating critical thinking. The completed K–W–L chart at the end of a unit serves as an excellent source of summary information from which to study for tests.

What do I **k**now?	What do I **w**ant to know?	What have I **l**earned?

Figure 5.2 K–W–L Chart

What do I know?	What do I want to know?	What have I learned?	How did I learn it?

Figure 5.3   K–W–L–H Chart

Technique II

You may want to include two additional columns on your K–W–L charts. The first (see Figure 5.3) adds an **H** column for students to write **h**ow they learned the information in the **L** section. Including an **H** column is an effective way of focusing awareness on learning strategies.

The second variation is to add a **Q** column, "What **q**uestions do I still have?" (see Figure 5.4). The **Q** section may seem, at first, repetitive of the **W** section, but it is not. The **W** column, "**W**hat do I want to know?" is anticipatory—it is designed to get students thinking about the topic. The **Q** column, on the other hand, deals with questions students may have about information they just learned and added to the **L** column. These questions can cover anything students are not completely sure about: concepts, vocabulary, even how to go about learning the material. Student-generated items in the **L** and **Q** sections are a good way to open the next day's lesson: They activate background knowledge and serve as an immediate connection between past and present learning.

What do I know?	What do I want to know?	What have I learned?	What questions do I still have?

Figure 5.4   K – W – L – Q Chart

STRATEGY 15 PERSONALIZE THE LESSON

IN CONCEPT

Students enjoy sharing their own and hearing about others' life experiences. They also are universally fascinated with stories about their teachers' experiences. Personalizing a lesson is an attention-getting way to begin a new topic.

Students, especially those who have lived in other countries and cultures, may have had personal experiences that relate to some aspect of the content being introduced. Asking students to talk about these experiences is an excellent way to activate and build background knowledge for all students. It increases motivation by stimulating student interest in and curiosity about the topic and demonstrating its relatedness to the real world.

IN PRACTICE

ELLs may be able to contribute interesting and uncommon items of topical knowledge and life experience. An introduction to a unit on the Civil War, for example, often includes a discussion of how differences among individuals and groups can lead to conflict. Students who have lived outside the United States may lack background knowledge about the U.S. Civil War, but they may have firsthand knowledge of conflicts based on political, ethnic, or religious differences in their native countries. On a more personal level, some students, including the native English speakers, may want to share stories about family feuds.

For another example, ELLs may know little about the American Revolution, but they may have lived in an area that had its own revolution from a colonial power in the much more recent past. Students may have heard family stories about life in times of war or conflict. They even may be willing to share with the class their own firsthand experiences of difficult times.

In science, some students may have firsthand knowledge of terrain or weather uncommon to your area. Can any of your students talk about living in or near rainforests, mountains, deserts, oceans or rivers, or experiencing a tornado, hurricane, or earthquake? Some may have lived in or near areas with visible air or water pollution. Sharing this type of knowledge awakens immediate personal interest and allows you to draw comparisons and make generalizations.

In math, ELLs often come from educational systems that introduce concepts and processes earlier in the curriculum than is common in the United States. Those students can show others the particular algorithms or explain real-life applications. They can serve as peer tutors for their classmates in an unusual role reversal that will raise their peers' respect and bolster their own self-confidence.

STRATEGY 16 SPARK INTEREST

IN CONCEPT

Interest in a topic is a natural motivator to learning. Activities that create an element of excitement or curiosity will raise students' interest levels at the same time that they activate background knowledge.

IN PRACTICE

Technique I

Try something graphic and visual to catch your students' interest in a new topic. Obvious choices are photos, videos, or short films relating to the topic.

Rank these forms of transportation in order from slowest to fastest. Write number 1 next to the one you think is the slowest, up to number 10 next to the one you think is the fastest. When you finish numbering, write down a speed for each one.

_____ Motorcycle
_____ Train
_____ Skateboard
_____ Race car
_____ Tractor
_____ Bicycle
_____ Inline skates
_____ Rowboat
_____ Jet plane
_____ Ship

Figure 5.5   What Do You Know About Speed?

Magazines and newspapers, not necessarily current, are other good sources of material appropriate for building motivation and interest. Or start with an exciting science demonstration to capture student interest and imagination. Try to recapture that "Wow!" sensation for your students, like the first time you witnessed the effect of dry ice in water. Interest acts as a motivator that facilitates learning for students.

Technique II

Another means of jump-starting student interest is to engage students in a short activity that might be named *Start Your Brain Engines!* or *Think About It!* There are many variations of this type of activity, several of which are shown in Figure 5.5 through 5.8.

Regardless of its form, this activity serves as an ungraded pretest, designed to get students thinking of the new topic in advance. It is inherently motivating: Students like to see how close they came to the right answers. Those who did better than they expected may be more motivated to learn when they discover that they already know more than they think about a topic.

Anticipation activities, first introduced by Readence, Bean, and Baldwin (1981), can be done individually, but they will be completed more productively in pairs or small groups. Class discussion when students' answers are checked and compared serves as an introduction that forms a natural bridge to new learning.

Directions: Number these events in the order you think they occurred. Write the number 1 next to the first (or earliest) through number 7 for the last. Can you "smart-guess" how long ago each of these happened?

Number   **How long ago?**

_____ Humans acquire language.   _____
_____ Humans learn to grow crops.   _____
_____ Humans invent the wheel.   _____
_____ Humans make the first tools.   _____
_____ Humans invent writing.   _____
_____ Humans make tools from metals.   _____
_____ Humans discover fire.   _____

Figure 5.6   Wake Up Your Thinking About Prehistoric Times

Look at the pictures below. Read what is in each cup. Working with your partner, decide which cup is the lightest. Mark it number 1. Which cup is the heaviest? Mark it number 6. Mark the other four cups in order of their weight.

#_____   1 cup of water

#_____   1 cup of glass marbles

#_____   1 cup of cotton balls

#_____   1 cup of sand

#_____   1 cup of cooked rice

#_____   1 cup of flour

From *Earth and Physical Science: Content and Learning Strategies* by Mary Ann Christison and Sharron Bassano © 1992 by Pearson Education, Inc., publishing as Addison-Wesley (p. 67.) Used by permission.

Figure 5.7 What Do You Know about Matter, Mass, and Molecules?

Is what you "know" really true? For each of the following statements, decide whether or not it is true. If it is true, write FACT, and if it not true, write FICTION.

_____ Sound travels in waves.
_____ Sound is caused by vibrations.
_____ Sound travels through the air.
_____ Sound travels through water.
_____ Sound travels through steel.
_____ Sound always travels at the same speed.
_____ Sound travels faster than light.
_____ Sound is measured in amperes.
_____ Technically, there is no real difference between music and noise.
_____ When people have excellent hearing, they can hear every sound that is made.
_____ Sound can be unhealthy for people.

Figure 5.8 Fact or Fiction?

STRATEGY 17 LINK LESSONS

IN CONCEPT

Every lesson benefits from linking students' past learning and experiences to new concepts about to be presented. Making explicit connections among concepts serves as a form of

Before we learn more about meteorology, check yourself to see what you remember about clouds. Next to each statement, put a T for TRUE or an F for FALSE. If you think the statement is false, rewrite it to make it true.

_____ Clouds are masses of water droplets and ice crystals.
_____ Clouds change shape because of wind and sunlight.
_____ Clouds are grouped into classes according to their size.
_____ Certain clouds are formed entirely of ice crystals.
_____ High, thin clouds cause thunderstorms.
_____ Clouds cause tornadoes and hurricanes.
_____ Clouds at night lower ground temperature.

Figure 5.9   How Much Do You Remember About CLOUDS?

reinforcement and review. Explicit linking also helps students understand the interrelatedness of information as it exists in the real world. The more frequently you revisit conceptually important pieces of information, the more opportunity students have for learning. By regularly stimulating background knowledge, you facilitate students' continuing conceptual development and increase the potential for new learning and enhanced retention.

IN PRACTICE

Technique I

Simple questions form effective links to prior knowledge. Start your daily instruction by activating previous learning with questions like these:

What did we talk about yesterday when we were discussing the _____?

Who remembers the reasons for _____?

What did we learn about _____?

Who remembers some examples of _____?

What were some new words we used yesterday when we discussed _____?

Technique II

Another type of linking attempts to reactivate previously taught concepts that may serve as background knowledge for new learning. Review questions at the ends of chapters make excellent material to create this type of linking activity, an example of which is shown in Figure 5.9 You can also reintroduce topics using questionnaires similar to those illustrated in Figures 5.5 through 5.8.

STRATEGY 18   PREVIEW THE LESSON

IN CONCEPT

Previews create a framework for understanding a challenging reading on a new topic at the same time that they supply critical pieces of background information. Previewing information makes a new undertaking appear more learnable and facilitates students' comprehension.

IN PRACTICE

When you recognize that a reading passage may present difficulties for students, give them a written introduction that outlines important information they will need for comprehension.

Include such items as definitions of new vocabulary and explanations of complex concepts. Add supporting visuals (graphics, maps, tables, charts, photos) as an extra aid to understanding. Think of previewing as the *Cliff Notes* of background knowledge.

For example, previewing is an excellent strategy to use at the start of a long and detailed work of fiction. Students might receive a preview with a list of the major characters, including some details about their personalities and their relationships to others in the book, brief notes about historical events and cultural understandings that are important to the plot, and maps showing routes of journeys or places of significance to the story line. Previews are useful initially in providing requisite background knowledge, and then continue to guide students as they read.

STRATEGY 19 MAKE NEW LEARNING FEEL LEARNABLE

IN CONCEPT

Many ELLs feel intimidated by the amount of learning they are expected to undertake and complete. A new topic can feel overwhelming in its breadth and scope. Strategies that make new learning feel learnable help students build confidence in themselves as learners. They are an important tool to success. The previewing strategy previously described builds students' self-confidence in their abilities to learn at the same time that it builds background knowledge.

IN PRACTICE

Technique I

For some students, the thought of a new topic is daunting. The vast amount of information to be learned feels much like starting a 1,000-piece jigsaw puzzle—just too many little, indistinct pieces. When introducing a new topic to students, use *Spiraling* to actively tie new information to concepts that have been learned in the past; this has the dual purpose of building self-confidence as it builds background knowledge.

Spiraling strategies reactivate known concepts that are related to a new topic. Showing students that they already have some pieces of the puzzle in place gives them a more positive attitude with which to approach the new topic.

Technique II

When you announce that students will be learning a completely new topic, start by acknowledging that it *is* complex. Then explain that *all* new topics appear complex before you learn them. Help them recall other topics they learned that seemed so difficult at the beginning but were, after all, quite learnable. Assure them that this new topic is no different. A positive mind-set motivates learning.

STRATEGY 20 COMBINE STRATEGIES TO INCREASE EFFECTIVENESS

IN CONCEPT

All the individual strategies in this section are effective in building and activating background knowledge for your students. However, pairing individual strategies often produces

Try	With
Think–Write–Pair–Share (Strategy 13)	→Carousel brainstorming (Strategy 12)
Brainstorming (Strategy 12)	→ Previews (Strategy 18)
Interest awakeners (Strategy 16)	→K–W–L charts (Strategy 14)
Think–Write–Pair–Share	→ Numbered heads (Strategy 43, chapter 7)
Numbered heads	→ Brainstorming

Figure 5.10 Mix and Match Strategies

even better results. The more background knowledge students develop, the more easily they will process, retain, and apply new information.

IN PRACTICE

Using the Think–Write–Pair–Share strategy (Strategy 13) in combination with carousel brainstorming (Strategy 12), for example, offers an extra opportunity to hear ideas related to the new topic. Interest awakeners (Strategy 16) also lend themselves well to pairing with other background knowledge strategies. Figure 5.10 lists these and other suggested pairings for mixing and matching strategies. Combinations are limited only by your own creativity and imagination.

IN SUMMARY: WORKING WITH BACKGROUND KNOWLEDGE

It is worth repeating: How well a student learns new content is directly related to the amount of relevant background knowledge and/or experience he or she already has. The minutes—even hours—you spend in class activating and building background knowledge will pay you and your students back many times over by facilitating their learning and maximizing their possibilities for academic success.

QUESTIONS FOR DISCUSSION

1. How do the strategies dealing with activating and building background knowledge reflect the *Guidelines for Practice* presented at the beginning of this chapter?

2. Think back to something you learned from scratch. How did you feel as you were starting? Did you feel like you were looking up from the bottom of a tall mountain and feeling very small? Can you think of anything that would have made you feel better about starting on the new topic? At what point did you realize that you were finally "getting it?" Did your ability to learn and/or your feeling about learning change after that? If so, how?

3. *If you are currently teaching:* Select a lesson you taught that began with a particularly effective introduction to build and activate background knowledge. Describe the strategies you used and why you believe they were effective.

   If you are not currently teaching: Work with a partner or a small group to plan interesting ways to build and activate background knowledge as an introduction to the following topics:

   Violent weather: Thunderstorms, tornadoes, earthquakes, and hurricanes

   The rise of labor unions

   Human anatomy: Skin, muscles, and bones of the human body

REFERENCES AND RESOURCES

Chamot, A. U., & O'Malley, J. M. (1994). *The CALLA handbook: Implementing the cognitive academic language learning approach.* (pp. 84–86, 199–200, 263–264, 283–284, 293–294). Reading, MA: Addison-Wesley.

Echevarria, J., & Graves, A. (2005). Curriculum adaptations. In P. A. Richard-Amato & M. A. Snow (Eds.), *Academic success for English language learners: Strategies for K–12 mainstream teachers* (pp. 224–247). White Plains, NY: Pearson Education.

Leinhardt, G. (1992). What research on learning tells us about teaching. *Educational Leadership, 49* (7), 20–25.

Readence, J. E., Bean, T. W., & Baldwin, R. S. (1981). *Content area reading: An integrated approach* (2nd ed.). Dubuque, IA: Kendall/Hunt.

The TechConnection

http://www.state.ia.us/educate/ecese/tqt/tc/prodev/reading_activating.html

Summaries of research studies about activating background knowledge with compilations of grade-leveled strategies and links to more information.

CHAPTER 6

PRESENTING NEW MATERIAL: TEACHING THE LESSON

THEORY TO APPLICATION: GUIDELINES FOR PRACTICE

- Use scaffolding strategies with ELLs to facilitate comprehension of the specialized academic language of content classrooms.
- Use scaffolding strategies to challenge ELLs to advance beyond their present state of independent activity, into the areas of potential learning in which content is learnable with the assistance of teachers and peers.
- Use scaffolding strategies that embed the oral and written language of content material in a context-rich environment to facilitate learning for ELLs.
- Use scaffolding strategies that maintain a high level of cognitive challenge, but lower the language demand by embedding it in context.
- Lower learner anxiety in the classroom to create students who are more willing to participate in class, to become risk takers in the learning process, and ultimately to become more successful learners.
- Provide opportunities for students to experience success in the classroom: Success in learning promotes more success by increasing learner motivation, interest, and self-confidence.

You've introduced the new topic to your students and sparked their interest. You've activated your students' prior knowledge and built a foundational background for those who needed it. You've motivated your students by demonstrating the usefulness to real-life applications. Your students now seem ready to learn the material that you've planned to teach. The strategies in this chapter will help you present information in ways that will make it easier for the ELLs in your class to understand it.

ORAL ACADEMIC LANGUAGE

Have you ever had the experience of trying to talk to someone in a foreign language? You may have had an opportunity to visit a country whose people speak a language you studied in school. Perhaps you tried to learn a few useful phrases in preparation for a trip.

You managed to ask *Où est la gare?* or *¿Dónde está la playa?* You felt delighted to be understood. Then you got the answer—and poof! the bubble of satisfaction burst. You didn't have the faintest idea where the train station or the beach really was. The words seemed to be coming at you so fast that you couldn't make sense of them at all.

Why do speakers of foreign languages seem to be speaking so fast? It's actually not because of the rate of speech but rather the rate of listening: nonnative speakers are *slow listeners*. They need extra time to bring meaning to what they're hearing, to actively process the incoming language. That is not easy to do, especially while trying to pay attention to the flow of new words that continue to be spoken.

Imagine now that these foreign words are not about something as simple as the price of a souvenir or the directions to the restroom. Imagine instead that they deal with complex academic concepts in math, science, and social studies. That is the challenge faced by ELLs in content classes.

The Difficulties of Oral Academic Language

The spoken language of academic instruction is difficult for language learners for several reasons. First, oral language is ephemeral in nature. Words, once spoken, are gone. You cannot rehear them for review.

Second, the nonnative listener takes more time to process the incoming words than the speaker takes to deliver them. Concentrating on the meaning of one spoken sentence interferes with the ability to listen to the next one. Listening is such a complex task that even native speakers have occasional difficulty processing spoken language in some circumstances, such as listening to TV news or radio traffic reports.

Third, English, the language students are trying to learn, is the *medium* through which academic content is delivered. For ELLs, the language itself adds an additional burden of complexity to understanding the content. Understanding academic concepts depends not just on *what* the teacher says but also on *how* the teacher says it. For ELLs, the *how* can help bring meaning to the *what*.

TEACHER TALK

The Objective: Pace Your Speech.

The Rationale

Oral instruction becomes more comprehensible for ELLs when the speaker focuses on *how* the words of instruction are delivered. Although most teachers speak clearly enough for native English-speaking students, ELLs benefit when those teachers use strategies to enhance the clarity and reduce the complexity of the language they use when presenting new information. Language-sensitive instruction facilitates the challenge of academic listening for ELLs.

STRATEGY 21   SLOW DOWN!

IN CONCEPT

The simplest and most helpful strategy to modify the way you speak is to slow down. The goal is to speak at a slightly slower pace—but not so slowly that it feels or sounds unnatural. A good way to slow down speech is to pause for an extra beat or two at natural breaks between phrases or sentences.

IN PRACTICE

Examine in Figure 6.1 the pausing the teacher uses in her delivery of this overview of the eighth-grade American history curriculum on the first day of school. The dots between phrases represent pause time, two dots for shorter pauses and four dots for longer ones. Each pause offers ELLs valuable extra time to process the language of the incoming content.

Figure 6.1   Pausing Slows Down Speech

What are we going to study this year? . . . . This year . . we'll be studying the significant . . historical . . events . . . . that led to the development . . of our nation's traditions . . . . We'll survey American history . . . . with a special emphasis . . on the nineteenth century . . . . First, . . we'll examine in detail . . the Declaration of Independence . . . . and the Constitution . . . . because they're fundamental . . to the history of the United States . . . . Then . . we'll study topics such as slavery, ... the Civil War, ... reconstruction, ... industrialization, ... and the United States as a world power.

 STRATEGY 22   ENHANCE THE INTONATION OF YOUR WORDS

IN CONCEPT

Enhanced pronunciation helps you to enunciate the words you speak. Highlight important words by raising or lowering your voice level and your pitch. Giving special intonation when speaking key content words is the equivalent to underlining, bolding, or italicizing words in writing. Clearly enunciated, well-paced speech with interesting patterns of tonal variation is much more enjoyable to listen to and easier to understand than speech that is rapid or monotonal or—even worse—both.

IN PRACTICE

Return now to the social studies course overview in Figure 6.1. Even with the pausing, it is a heavy dose of language for ELLs. Using rising and falling intonation to emphasize important content words signifies to ELLs which words to focus on at the same time that it slows the pacing of speech even further. Read aloud the overview in Figure 6.2, this time giving special emphasis to the boldfaced words. You should be able to hear the difference pauses and intonation can make for your ELLs.

To demonstrate how effective this strategy is, look at the list of words in Figure 6.3. These are the boldfaced words designated for enhanced intonation that appear in Figure 6.2. Reading through the list of just those words *alone* gives you a pretty good idea of the message the passage will convey. You can make your oral instruction easier to understand for your ELLs by speaking more clearly through pausing and intonation.

Figure 6.2   Enhanced Intonation Slows Speech Even More

What are we going to study this year? . . . . This year . . we'll be studying the significant . . **historical** . . **events** . . . . that led to the development . . of our **nation's traditions.** . . . . We'll survey **American history** . . . . with a special emphasis . . on the **nineteenth century** . . . . **First,** . . we'll examine in detail . . the **Declaration of Independence** . . . . and the **Constitution** . . . . because they're **fundamental** . . to the history of the United States. . . . . **Then** . . we'll study topics such as **slavery,** . . . . **the Civil War,** . . . . **reconstruction,** . . . . **industrialization,** . . . . and the United States as a **world power.**

Figure 6.3   Getting the Message from Only the Boldfaced Words

historical events
nation's traditions
American history
nineteenth century
First
Declaration of Independence
Constitution
fundamental
Then
slavery
the Civil War
reconstruction
industrialization
world power

TEACHER TALK

The Objective: Simplify Your Speech.

The Rationale

Native speakers use speech patterns that differ greatly from patterns used in writing. Simply put, we speak differently than we write, and it is all perfectly normal and correct. Speakers tend to use familiar or informal words in short, simple sentences. Often they use phrases instead of complete sentences. Speakers lose their place and backtrack, or they repeat themselves, or they correct themselves. They make false starts and use extraneous words as fillers or spacers. They regularly use contractions and merge words together. Teachers can facilitate comprehension of spoken academic language by making minor adaptations to their normal speech patterns.

STRATEGY 23   LIMIT USE OF CONTRACTIONS

IN CONCEPT

All fluent English speakers contract words when speaking. It is one of the normal differences between spoken and written English, as well as a salient difference between language learners and native speakers.

For ELLs, contractions are a source of misunderstanding. Words like *they're* and *it's* are easily confused with their other forms: *there/their* and *its*. Another issue is the two ways of contracting the phrase *it is not*. Do *it isn't* and *it's not* really mean the same thing? Many ELLs do not connect the spoken *should've,* which sounds like *should of,* with its written form, *should have.* And almost every listener has experienced the difficulty of hearing the difference between *can* and *can't.*

IN PRACTICE

You can help your ELLs by using the full form of these and other contracted words—such as *they are, it is, it is not,* and *cannot*—as often as you can. The uncontracted forms help ELLs not only by making the meaning more apparent but also by slowing down your rate of speech.

STRATEGY 24   USE FEWER PRONOUNS

IN CONCEPT

ELLs can bring meaning to spoken language more readily when they hear more nouns and fewer pronouns. Pronouns involve some extra language processing and can slow down comprehension.

IN PRACTICE

Although it may sound a bit strange or stilted to you, try to repeat names and other nouns more frequently than you might normally. Look at the nouns in the following sentence:

> The colonists who participated in the Boston Tea Party were willing to risk deprivation, even their lives, for the principle of *no taxation without representation*.

For ELLs, any pronoun that might follow in the next sentence will require a great deal of grammatical processing to determine its antecedent noun. Instead of *they,* repeat *the colonists;* instead of *it,* repeat *the Boston Tea Party* or *no taxation without representation.* Even native speakers occasionally become confused when pronouns like *it* or *they* are used too many times.

 ## STRATEGY 25   SIMPLIFY YOUR SENTENCE STRUCTURE

IN CONCEPT

Teachers often bring to class articles or books to supplement information in their lessons or in students' textbooks. They read aloud passages that were meant to be read silently and processed slowly. The long, complex sentences of written text make them difficult to process orally.

IN PRACTICE

Modify the text materials you read aloud during oral instruction by shortening the sentences and simplifying the structure. Consider the following textbook sentence:

> The Civil War, which took more American lives than any other war in our history, divided the people of the United States, so that in many families, brother fought against brother.

You could facilitate the listening comprehension of this passage for your ELLs by subdividing the sentences and paraphrasing the wording to this:

> The Civil War divided the people of the United States. It even divided families. In many families, brother fought against brother. More Americans died in the Civil War than in any other war in American history.

 ## STRATEGY 26   USE FAMILIAR WORDS AND BE CONSISTENT

IN CONCEPT

Varying your word choices with synonyms and colorful words may make speech sound more interesting, but for ELLs it adds another source of confusion. Oral academic language can be made more comprehensible for ELLs by using high-frequency words instead of less common ones and by repeating known words instead of using synonyms. Familiar and recognizable spoken words and phrases allow ELLs to focus more clearly on the concepts you are trying to convey. The more consistent your terminology and word patterns, the more readily your ELLs can process the content.

IN PRACTICE

Technique I

All students can benefit from exposure to a wide range of interesting vocabulary through the technique of association. Every time you use low-frequency words, pair them immediately with their more familiar synonym, as *autonomy* with *independence* and *emancipation* with *freedom*. Frequent pair repetition solidifies the association, and the unfamiliar word soon becomes readily recognized.

Technique II

Be consistent in the words you use to give oral directions for assignments and activities. Teachers are often unaware that they are using different words to give the same set of directions, as in the following:

> Circle the word that best describes _____.
>
> Draw a circle around the best word choice for _____.
>
> Find the word that best fits each question and then circle it.

Choosing one word pattern to communicate these directions and using it on a regular basis simplifies oral input for ELLs.

Technique III

The words you speak in class should also be consistent with the words and phrases used in the students' textbooks. A brief examination of the words used in the textbook to give directions or to discuss a topic can help you decide which words and phrases to use in presenting and discussing the material. When you believe that directions written in the text seem overly complicated, like those in Figure 6.4, explain them through paraphrase and discussion. For ELLs, maintaining consistency of the words they hear in class and the words they read in their textbooks is another strategy to facilitate comprehension.

Technique IV

"Translate" the current pedagogical jargon in your school district usage by pairing such terminology with more traditional forms of expression. Some widely used examples are shown in Figure 6.5. Use jargon if you must, but be sure that all your students know what the new words really mean.

Figure 6.4 Simplify Unclear Directions from the Textbook

> **If the textbook says:**
>
>   Evaluate the following expression for the given value of the variable.
>
>   A + 5 =   For A = 2; A = 6.
>
> **Paraphrase to:**
>
>   **(Good)**   Find A + 5 when A = 2.
>   Find A + 5 when A = 6.
>
>   **(Better)**   If A = 2, then A + 5 = ?
>   If A = 6, then A + 5 = ?

Today's Terminology	Traditional Terminology
an extended constructed response a brief constructed response selected response questions making text-to-text connections	an essay a paragraph multiple-choice questions comparing books

Figure 6.5 Current Terminology May Be Difficult to Understand

STRATEGY 27   BECOME AWARE OF IDIOMATIC LANGUAGE

IN CONCEPT

Idioms and figurative speech make speech colorful and interesting. Language learners feel they are learning the "real English" when they learn idioms, and perhaps they are. Native speakers use them liberally in speech. Unfortunately, idioms and figurative speech also confuse ELLs because the meaning of the individual words, even when each word is well known, does not reflect the actual meaning of the whole message.

IN PRACTICE

Teachers use figurative language to get their students' attention. A teacher, wanting to check students' understanding of new material, might begin a question session with an enthusiastic opener, such as "Okay. I'm going to pitch some practice questions. Let's see who can hit a home run here!" It definitely adds an element of fun, but the ELLs in this classroom are likely to respond by looking around the room for a baseball and bat.

It is not possible to avoid using idioms and figurative speech, nor would you want that. Such language personalizes and flavors speech and often injects interest and humor. Developing an awareness of the idioms and figurative speech you use as you speak allows you the opportunity to paraphrase or explain your language choices in a simple way.

TEACHER TALK

The Objective: Enhance Your Words.

The Rationale

Why do families no longer listen to the radio as evening entertainment? Why is MTV so popular? The answer is that television enhances spoken words and music in ways that engage people. Enhancing words of instruction in the classroom will engage your students, too.

Adding visual elements to speech embeds it in context and facilitates comprehension of the oral language of instruction. Using strategies that move oral instruction from Cummins's Quadrant IV to Quadrant III (Figure 1.3 in Chapter 1) makes it easier for ELLs to understand concepts and content.

STRATEGY 28   USE GESTURES

IN CONCEPT

Some people say they couldn't talk if their hands were tied behind their backs. Americans, and speakers of many other languages, use their hands to make gestures to help convey the meaning of their words. Hand gestures, along with facial expressions and body language, make speech easier to understand. Consider the difference in the ease of comprehension between watching a videotaped lecture and listening to the same lecture on audiotape. Gestures help embed the context of oral language.

IN PRACTICE

In classroom instruction, ELLs will become more involved if you make oral language as visual an experience as it can be. Make ample use of the gestures and facial expressions that come naturally. When you tell your students "There are three important things to remember," hold up three fingers for your students to see. Continue using one, two, and three fingers as you explain each piece of information. Point prominently to your first finger when you review by asking "What was the first thing we discussed?" Students form a visual picture that helps them retain the information.

Take advantage of any pictures or objects in the classroom that you can use to illustrate a particular word. Try pantomime to help explain a new or difficult term; it is a surefire way of getting the attention of all your students.

STRATEGY 29   USE VISUALS AND GRAPHICS

IN CONCEPT

Support your words with graphic representation. Seeing words and phrases in written form reinforces oral language and facilitates content comprehension.

IN PRACTICE

Technique I
Use the "chalk–talk" approach. Write key vocabulary words and phrases on the board or on an overhead transparency as you speak them. ELLs may not recognize spoken words, such as those in Figure 6.6, as the same ones that they know in their written forms. In some cases, the pronunciation is totally unlike the spelling. In other instances, it may be a word previously encountered only in print that, when spoken, differs from a student's silent pronunciation. It may also be a word that is indistinguishable orally because its spelling is close to too many others, as in the last column of words in Figure 6.6. Seeing a word in writing as you speak it facilitates comprehension for ELLs students.

Technique II
Extend the chalk–talk approach beyond just writing words and phrases to include graphic organizers as a regular part of your teaching. Graphic organizers (discussed at length in Chapter 10) contextually embed oral language. They help ELLs see relationships and understand vocabulary and concepts in a linguistically simplified way.

Figure 6.6 Pronunciation Puzzlers

sovereignty	epitome	tough
pneumatic	psychology	though
phlegm	posthumous	through
mnemonic	hegemony	thorough
choir	conscience	thought

Technique III

Incorporate pictures, photos, maps, graphs, tables, or anything else you may have on hand to help illustrate the meaning of your words. Draw a picture of an object—even stick figures and rough sketches are helpful. Refer to them as you talk. Remember the adage *One picture is worth a thousand words*. For language learners, this is a primary principle.

Technique IV

Supplement class lectures and discussions with filmstrips, slides, videotapes, DVDs, and CD-ROM programs. While these media types work well to create interest and decrease reliance on language, their soundtracks may present ELLs with some difficulties.

You can take any of several approaches to remedy the soundtrack difficulty. Consider finding some class time to allow ELLs a preview without sound. If this is not feasible, give students an outline or a list of key words and phrases to guide them as they watch.

Technique V

Encourage students to find and share content-appropriate Web sites on the Internet. You might maintain space on a bulletin board or chalkboard for students to write in new and interesting finds that support class content.

Technique VI

Bring in *realia* to explain and interest your students. Realia are authentic, real-world objects that illustrate a concept in ways that allow students to make meaningful connections to their own lives and to the world outside the classroom. Using bank deposit slips and check registers for a unit on banking or working with copies of actual floor plans to calculate square footage can motivate student learning. Suggest that students contribute their own realia—that may provide an interesting cultural experience for you and all your students.

 STRATEGY 30   DEMONSTRATE YOUR WORDS

IN CONCEPT

Demonstration and modeling are effective ways to facilitate comprehension of the words of oral instruction. Students can "see" how to find an answer or solve a problem.

IN PRACTICE

Take your students through a step-by-step process to explain how to reach the end result. For each step, do a *think-aloud* to demonstrate *why* you choose to do it a certain way and why you choose *not* to do it in other ways. Ask out loud the questions you would normally ask yourself silently as you show the steps you take. For example, in a lesson about classifying objects, after asking the question, you might say something like "Now how will I know whether it is A or B? I have to think about. . . ." It is important to *not* make it seem too simple: Students need to realize that thinking, adjusting, and readjusting are a natural part of the learning process. Figure 6.7 shows some appropriate classroom applications of this strategy.

Figure 6.7 Use Think-Aloud
Demonstration to Show Process

How to classify information
How to sequence information
How to summarize information
How to locate information to answer a question
How to highlight important information
How to select the main idea and supporting details

STRATEGY 31   BE DRAMATIC

IN CONCEPT

Dramatic lessons are memorable lessons. Make your lessons memorable by hamming them up.

IN PRACTICE

Dramatize, emote, role-play, pantomime. Have a good time! Come to class in a costume or an unusual outfit. Doing such things gives your students tacit permission to be dramatic, too. Groups of students may enjoy staging mini reenactments of events or acting out imaginary dialogs between historical or scientific figures. Students will remember the material and probably you, too.

CLASSROOM ROUTINE AND REVIEW

Routines create patterns of consistency, and review creates patterns of opportunity. Both lower levels of anxiety for the students in your classroom.

Routines lessen the need for wordy explanations that may confuse ELLs and, in doing so, raise their anxiety levels. Review offers students multiple opportunities for reinforcement of instructional information. Creating and using classroom routines can free up valuable extra minutes for review.

The Objective: Streamline Your Class Schedule.

The Rationale

Students often enter the classroom over a period of several minutes. Of course you're not going to start until everyone is in their seats and ready. How many minutes does it actually take until you are doing something instructional? (*Hint:* Students stall as long as possible.) Routines will remedy this situation.

STRATEGY 32   USE THE FIRST 5 MINUTES PRODUCTIVELY

IN CONCEPT

Students should know what to do immediately upon arrival and what is expected of them during the class period. Think about the ways you take attendance and correct homework. Techniques to streamline the process so it gets accomplished automatically and without your leadership will save valuable time at the beginning of each class period.

IN PRACTICE

Technique I

Designate a group captain (selected either on a regular rotation basis or as an academic reward) whose job is to take attendance and visually check completed homework assignments as soon as the students enter the room.

Technique II

The same group captain can next lead a discussion and comparison of the answers to the homework assignment. Among his or her responsibilities is to report to you any items that seemed problematic for the group or for which group members' answers differed. This gives you the option of spending valuable class time on only those items that need review, reinforcement, and possibly reteaching.

Students should have their homework clearly visible on their desks as you walk around the room to supervise and offer help during the homework discussion time. Group captains can also collect the papers for you if you want to see them every day.

Technique III

Teachers often wage an internal debate about whether and how often to collect homework. Collecting and correcting it on a daily basis adds another burden to teachers' already heavy workloads, but some teachers feel it may be the only way to ensure that all the students have actually completed the assignments.

An effective technique to resolve this situation is to do a homework check on random days of the week, anywhere from two to six days apart. The idea of this is to give the students just enough time to copy out the answers from the particular assignments you have listed on the board. If they've done their homework, it is an easy task to simply locate the items you request, rewrite them on a separate sheet, and submit them. If they have not done their assigned work, they will not be able to answer the questions and complete the required tasks in the allotted time. The details of this technique are illustrated in Figure 6.8.

---

1. Students fold a blank sheet of paper into four or six sections.
2. Students number each box one through four or one through six.
3. Teacher writes on the board four or six items to transfer to the appropriate box.

    Examples:
        Box 1. Tuesday, Question 5, page 138.
        Box 2. Wednesday, Question 2, page 151.

1. Tuesday, Q 5, P 138	2. Wednesday, Q 2, P 151
3. Thursday, Q 1, P 167	4. Friday, Q 3, P 189

4. Teacher allots only enough time to *copy* answers, not to respond or compute them.
5. Teacher collects and corrects the papers.

Figure 6.8 Homework Check

STRATEGY 33   DISPLAY THE CLASS PLAN

IN CONCEPT

Routines involving lesson objectives create a sense of security through structure for your ELLs.

IN PRACTICE

Write lesson objectives, topics, and activities for the day or for the week on the board or in another prominent place so that ELLs (and other students) can use them for reference. Seeing what they will be doing next in class decreases the reliance on oral language input for ELLs, resulting in lower levels of anxiety and greater ability to focus on classroom tasks.

STRATEGY 34   POST THE HOMEWORK

IN CONCEPT

Teachers often run out of time at the end of the lesson. The homework assignment, usually the last piece of information in the class, often gets delivered in a hurried rush of words as students are packing up their books and getting ready to leave. For ELLs, this can be a confusing and difficult situation.

IN PRACTICE

Write homework assignments ahead of time in the same place everyday. The place you choose can be on a small section of the board, on chart paper, or on an overhead transparency. If you don't want your students to see the assignment at the beginning of class because they may be tempted to work on it during class time, keep it covered until an appropriate point in the lesson. The main objective is to avoid rushing it out orally as the bell is ringing. Make sure students know that homework information will appear in the same place every day. Your students can never use the excuse that they didn't hear you.

CLASSROOM ROUTINES AND REVIEW

The Objective: Get into the Routine of Review.

The Rationale

If background knowledge forms the building blocks of learning, then review is the cement that holds the learning together. It reinforces learning and makes it more solid. Mini-reviews during the lesson and a final review at the end benefit all students. Those who know will shine, and those who don't know will get another opportunity for learning. You get the opportunity to hear and correct any misconceptions. It's a win–win situation for everyone. Frequent review during and at the end of every class period far exceeds in value the minutes devoted to it.

STRATEGY 35   REVIEW WHILE YOU TEACH

IN CONCEPT

All students benefit from a quick review of content as the lesson progresses. Multiple mini reviews keep student attention and concentration focused throughout class time. For ELLs, in particular, repetition and review offer extra opportunities for language input that can reinforce and enhance their conceptual understanding.

IN PRACTICE

Technique I

As you teach, ask frequent questions so students can repeat, review, paraphrase, and summarize content. Those who know the material get a chance to reinforce their learning, and those who don't get the opportunity to hear the information again.

As often as every 5 or 10 minutes, ask appropriate questions:

So, what did we just cover?

Who remembers the reasons for _____?

Who can explain the process we just saw?

Why did we say _____ was important?

A good challenge is to ask simple yes/no questions that contain misinformation, such as "General Grant led the Confederacy's army, right?" Misinformation questions promote critical listening and encourage students to think before answering. You may find that your students like the idea of correcting your misstatements.

Technique II

One middle-school teacher treated review questions as a gamelike challenge. At any point in the lesson, she would announce, "Quick check!" The students became instantly alert in anticipation of the question and the opportunity to score bonus points. They loved it—perhaps your students will, too.

STRATEGY 36   END EACH LESSON WITH REVIEW

IN CONCEPT

Teachers, with the objective of utilizing every minute of class time for learning, often find themselves with no time at the end of class to conduct a review. With all good intentions, those who do this discard a critically important teaching strategy.

All students benefit from spending the last 3 to 5 minutes of class time in review. Every lesson needs closure, even those that will be continued the next day.

IN PRACTICE

Technique I

Just before class ends, either return to the brainstorming graphic for review or ask the simple question "So, what did we talk about today?" If important information is omitted, make your question more specific, as in "What about _____? What did we say about that?"

Figure 6.9   Elbow Buddy Review

> "Turn to your elbow buddy and tell him or her. . . ."
>
>   2 causes of _____
>
>   3 substances that _____
>
>   the definition of _____
>
>   3 reasons for _____
>
>   2 places that _____

Technique II

In *Elbow Buddy Review* you ask your paired students to turn to their partners—their "elbow buddies"—and tell them a specific piece of information that you announce. Several ideas for this type of review are listed in Figure 6.9.

Technique III

Partner Review pairs students who are designated as Partner A or B. (Use a simple technique to designate As and Bs, such as the student whose first name comes first alphabetically is partner A.) Using the same types of prompts as in Figure 6.9, ask Partner A to tell Partner B the items for review, alternating partners with each request for additional review items. To ensure that the information being exchanged between partners is correct and complete, you can ask students to share with the class what they just discussed with their partners.

Technique IV

Another way to review that is fast, effective, and fun is 3–2–1. At the end of the lesson, students write three facts they learned, two new words, and one item of particular interest, as shown in Figure 6.10.

The review format in Figure 6.11 offers the interesting addition of a "0" line for other aspects of the topic that students hope to learn in future lessons. You can combine this strategy with *Elbow Buddy Review* or *Partner Review*, using this as a follow-up written form after the oral partnered review. If you use the *3–2–1* review by itself, you will get a more satisfactory result by doing it as a paired or small group activity, perhaps structuring it with a *Think–Write–Pair–Share* (Strategy 13, Chapter 5) approach.

Technique V

A different type of strategy involves using graphic organizers as review. Working again in pairs, students can use any of the graphic organizers discussed later in Chapter 10 to sum-

Figure 6.10   3–2–1 Review

> 3 facts I learned today are:
>
>   1. _____
>
>   2. _____
>
>   3. _____
>
> 2 words I want to remember are:
>
>   1. _____
>
>   2. _____
>
> 1 thing I found very interesting is:
>
>   1. _____

Figure 6.11   Variation on the 3–2–1
Review: Add a Zero

3 facts I learned today are:

　　1. _____

　　2. _____

　　3. _____

2 words I want to remember are:

　　1. _____

　　2. _____

1 thing I found very interesting is:

　　1. _____

0! I still don't know anything about _____ and I
would like to!

marize and review information. *K–W–L* charts (Chapter 5, Figures 5.2–5.4) and learning logs (Chapter 9, Figures 9.10 and 9.11) also can be used for review. At some point, perhaps as a homework assignment, students can transfer the review items to the L section of their *K–W–L* charts to their learning logs.

STRATEGY 37   MAKE ACTIVE USE OF REVIEW NOTES

IN CONCEPT

As important as review is to reinforcing knowledge, it can become an even more powerful technique when students become aware that their daily reviews can help them in other ways.

IN PRACTICE

Have students keep their daily written reviews in a separate section of their notebooks or even in a completely separate review notebook. The review notes can be used daily to activate prior knowledge as you begin the next day's lesson on the same topic. Students can be encouraged to use their review notes to study for tests. These same notes can be used to link new information with previously learned material providing even more reasons to make review a regular class routine.

IN SUMMARY: TEACHING THE LESSON

It is apparent that good classroom instruction begins with speaking in a manner that facilitates comprehension for your ELLs. The challenge, however, lies in changing highly ingrained speech habits and mannerisms that may interfere with clarity. The first step in the process, and perhaps the hardest, is becoming aware of what you actually do.

An interesting way to start thinking about the way you use oral language in your classroom is to record—on videotape or audiotape—a lesson you teach. As you replay it, listen closely to your use of language, and select one or two areas you would like to improve. Choose the strategies you think would help and begin to incorporate them into your patterns of oral instruction. When those feel comfortable, try working on others, one or two at a time. Each modification you add enhances the clarity of your oral instruction for your ELLs.

A second part of good instruction involves classroom routine and review. For ELLs, predictable classroom routines and frequent content review lower anxiety and support language development at the same time that they facilitate comprehension of content. For teachers, routines save time, effort, and energy. They are clearly good for everyone. Try getting into your own routines for arrival, homework, review, and dismissal. You're going to like what happens.

QUESTIONS FOR DISCUSSION

1. How do the strategies dealing with teacher talk and classroom routine and review reflect the *Guidelines for Practice* presented at the beginning of this chapter?

2. *If you are currently teaching a class,* audiotape or videotape a lesson in which you are actively teaching. Analyze the type of language you use and your pace of delivery. What advice would you give yourself to facilitate comprehension of your oral language for the ELLs in your classroom?

   If you are not currently teaching, get permission to audiotape or videotape a lesson in which the teacher is actively teaching. Analyze the recording as described above.

3. In pairs of one who is currently teaching and one who is not, compare and critique each other's analyses of the recorded lessons.

4. Prepare a text passage for reading aloud in class. After your reading, your colleagues will give you verbal feedback or a written critique.

5. Prepare a "Get-the-message-from-the-boldfaced-words" activity (Strategy 22). Read it to your peers in class. Did they get the message?

6. *If you are now teaching a class,* what routines do you think you could create to lower language input for your ELLs and, at the same time, make your class period more time efficient?

   If you are not currently teaching a class, arrange to observe a teacher and keep a written record, minute to minute, of classroom activities from the arrival of the first students through the final dismissal. In what ways do you think this teacher could benefit from creating routines?

REFERENCES AND RESOURCES

Fillmore, L. W., & Snow, C. E. (2005). What teachers need to know about language. In P. A. Richard-Amato & M. A. Snow (Eds.), *Academic success for English language learners: Strategies for K–12 mainstream teachers* (pp. 47–75). White Plains, NY: Pearson Education.

Richard-Amato, P. A., & Snow, M. A. (2005). Instructional strategies for K–12 mainstream teachers. In P. A. Richard-Amato and M. A. Snow (Eds.), *Academic success for English language learners: Strategies for K–12 mainstream teachers* (pp. 197–223). White Plains, NY: Pearson Education.

CHAPTER 7

DID THEY GET WHAT I TAUGHT? CHECKING COMPREHENSION

THEORY TO APPLICATION: GUIDELINES FOR PRACTICE

- Use scaffolding strategies with ELLs to facilitate comprehension of the specialized academic language of content classrooms.
- Use scaffolding strategies to challenge ELLs to advance beyond their present state of independent activity, into the areas of potential learning in which content is learnable with the assistance of teachers and peers.
- Use scaffolding strategies that maintain a high level of cognitive challenge, but lower the language demand by embedding it in context.
- Provide opportunities for ELLs to negotiate conceptual understandings and to explore language usage through classroom interaction.
- Lower learner anxiety in the classroom to create students who are more willing to participate in class, to become risk takers in the learning process, and ultimately to become more successful learners.
- Provide opportunities for students to experience success in the classroom: Success in learning promotes more success by increasing learner motivation, interest, and self-confidence.

CHECKING COMPREHENSION

You've taught the lesson. Now it's time to check comprehension: Do your students understand what you've taught?

With the goal of ensuring that their instruction has been understood, teachers almost always follow up the presentation section of a lesson with a question-and-answer session. The Q and A routine follows a traditional pattern: Teacher asks, teacher calls on student, student answers. If the response is incomplete, teacher calls on more students to add information. If the response is adequate, teacher moves on to the next question. It is always the same students who raise their hands to participate. Teachers' attempts to involve others in the class often result in uncomfortable silences.

The strategies in this chapter will help you expand student participation and increase the success of your question-and-answer sessions.

QUESTIONS, ANSWERS, AND PARTICIPATION IN THE CLASSROOM

The Objective: Formulate Questions in Ways that Encourage Participation.

The Rationale

Students hesitate to participate in class for a number of reasons, but the three most likely ones are they didn't understand the question; they don't know the answer; or they are fearful or shy about speaking in class. More students will willingly participate when you use strategies that involve selecting question types, offering assistance in answers, and lowering the affective filter.

 ## STRATEGY 38   DON'T FALL INTO THE "DOES EVERYONE UNDERSTAND?" TRAP

IN CONCEPT

Teachers sincerely want to make sure that students *really* understand the new material that has just been taught. Teachers willingly seek to clarify, repeat, explain, give more examples, and correct misunderstandings before moving ahead. So at several points in the lesson, teachers stop to check student comprehension with questions such as these:

Does everyone understand?

Does anyone have any questions?

Does anyone need me to repeat any part of this?

OK, so everyone gets it, yes?

The fact is that no matter how little the students have actually understood—no matter how completely confused they are—they just don't raise their hands in response to such questions. And why don't they? The answer lies in the way the questions are phrased. In effect, what the students hear is "Will the one really dumb person in this class who didn't get this please raise your hand and publicly identify yourself?" Why would anyone want to do a thing like that? Better just to sit there and *feel* dumb than to raise your hand and have everyone *know* how dumb you really are! The unintended effect of these questions is exactly the opposite of the teacher's objective.

IN PRACTICE

How, then, can you word a question that will actually achieve your desired goal? Try this:

"It's question time. Who's got a question for me?"

These words make it sound like questions are a normal and expected part of every lesson.

You can reinforce your accepting attitude toward questions even further when you respond to a student's question with something very positive:

"That's a great question!"

"Thank you for asking that!"

"Good question!"

Responses like these actually make students feel *rewarded* for asking for clarification instead of penalized by drawing negative attention to themselves. You, too, will be rewarded by your students' responses when you change "Does everyone understand?" to "Question time. Who's got a question for me?"

STRATEGY 39   SELECT QUESTION TYPES

IN CONCEPT

Teachers' questions vary in difficulty depending on their conceptual and/or linguistic complexity. Selecting the types of questions you direct to your ELLs promotes their participation.

IN PRACTICE

Even those in the early stages of second-language acquisition may be willing and able to respond with answers requiring only a minimum number of words, especially if they can refer to key words and phrases that you have written previously on the board. Pattern your questions to elicit nonverbal, yes/no, either/or, or one-word responses, as in the examples shown in Figure 7.1.

It is tempting to ask lower-order questions, such as those in Figure 7.1, to the ELLs in your class because they are linguistically simple to answer. The drawback of these questions, however, is that they do not involve much thought processing. Responses to these types of questions call for only simple recall of information.

To become critical thinkers, students must engage in processing higher order questions that ask them to explain, analyze, synthesize, and evaluate information (see *Bloom's Taxonomy* in Chapter 1). It is not the cognitive level of these questions that may present a challenge for ELLs but rather the higher levels of language ability required to answer them.

The strategy of directing follow-up questions to ELLs is a technique that balances both linguistic and cognitive demands. ELLs can engage in complex thought processing while answering the following types of questions with relatively simple English:

Do you agree with Ilya's answer?

Why?

Why not?

Can you add anything to Shihan's answer?

STRATEGY 40   MAKE STUDENTS ACTIVE LISTENERS

IN CONCEPT

What happens immediately after the teacher calls on someone to give an answer? In most classes, all the other students simply turn off their thinking and listening until the teacher asks the next question. Students can be helped to become active listeners throughout the lesson.

Point to.	Can you show us the location of Washington, DC, on the map?
Yes/no	Do Bedouins live on grassy plains?
Either/or	Is the Ukraine east or west of the major part of Russia?
Add more information	Who can give me another example of a deciduous tree?

Figure 7.1   Select Questions for English Language Learners

Figure 7.2 Follow-up Questions Encourage Active Listening

> "Brahim, can you tell me in your own words what Raoul just said?"
>
> "Rosalba, do you agree or disagree with what Raoul just said, and why?"
>
> "Irina, Raoul gave such a good answer. I think we all need to hear what he said again."

IN PRACTICE

Encourage active listening by following up a student response with a request for another student to paraphrase or evaluate what was just said. Frequent follow-up questions, such as those in Figure 7.2, make students aware of other students' thinking and problem-solving strategies. They also keep students tuned in and ready to respond.

The easiest follow-up question is simply "Do you agree with that answer?" Teachers routinely ask this question when the answer is wrong. The first time you try it when the answer is correct, you will witness a fascinating reaction. Students are accustomed to hearing "Do you agree with that answer?" exclusively as a means of correcting misinformation. The question renders students virtually speechless when you ask it as a follow-up to a *correct* question—after all, they've never encountered it used that way.

After you've used this questioning technique once or twice, remind students at the start of Q and A and discussion sessions that you will frequently ask them if they agree or disagree with other students' answers. Using this type of follow-up question as a regular part of your teaching will make your students active listeners. They are never "off the hook" because they know they may be called on to affirm or deny any student's answer.

STRATEGY 41   VARY WHOLE-CLASS RESPONSE TECHNIQUES

IN CONCEPT

When teachers want the whole class to answer a question, they most commonly use the choral response technique. The problem with this approach is that the teacher can never be sure who is answering correctly and who is not. The following three techniques allow ELLs to participate in a linguistically simple and nonthreatening manner. The entire class is actively involved and you, the teacher, get immediate feedback about the students' level of understanding.

IN PRACTICE

Technique 1

Students make the *Thumbs Up/Thumbs Down* sign in response to a series of short yes/no questions. Thumbs in the mid-position can mean "sometimes" or "depending on circumstances" or even "I'm not sure."

Students can also hold up one to five fingers to indicate their responses to choices you've written on the board. Think of this as a sort of oral multiple-choice technique. It works particularly well for classification activities. If you see more than one response, you have the immediate opportunity to discuss the item and to clarify misunderstandings.

In this technique, as well as the ones that follow, students should not answer instantly. It is important that you allow enough wait time (see Strategy 45 later in this chapter) for all students to think the question through. Students respond only after you give the signal to do so.

Technique II

Before beginning a question or review session, students make *response cards* with content-specific words or symbols written on index cards or small squares of paper. Information on each card could be numbers, mathematical signs denoting processes, categories, identifying names, descriptive phrases, the words *yes* and *no,* or the symbols + for presence or − for absence of a quality. Students hold up the appropriate card or card combinations in response to your series of questions.

Technique III

Students use markers or dry-erase boards to write brief responses to your questions. At your signal, they hold up the boards for you to see. Students can work individually or in pairs. They love this strategy because it feels like the TV show *Jeopardy.*

You can get the dry-erase boards from large hardware and home improvement stores. These stores willingly donate the scrap ends from customers' custom cuttings to teachers who request them. Stores will save them up to make class sets and will generally trim them to size.

STRATEGY 42   "PRE-PAIR" TO RESPOND

IN CONCEPT

Students dread looking foolish in front of peers and often avoid answering teachers' questions for this reason. You can lower students' anxiety by offering them the opportunity of testing out an answer with a partner before stating it in front of the whole class.

IN PRACTICE

The *Pre-Pair* strategy invites students to check with a partner before volunteering an answer. After you pose a question to the class, allow 10 to 20 seconds for one member of prearranged pairs to tell the other member his or her ideas. One partner can be A and the other B, and you can specifically designate after each question whose turn it is to talk and whose to listen. At the end of the designated time, students can raise their hands to share an idea they had or one they heard.

STRATEGY 43   TRY "NUMBERED HEADS"

IN CONCEPT

Numbered Heads is a structured strategy that promotes student participation by allowing small groups of students to discuss possible responses before one group member is selected to answer. It is a strategy that offers extra linguistic support for ELLs and reinforces conceptual understanding for all students. It promotes student participation by building self-confidence and also increases student–student interaction. It is a source of authentic language input for language learners. Best of all, perhaps, students like it because it feels like a game.

IN PRACTICE

Students sit in groups of four. Each student has a designated number, one through four, decided by the members of each group (see Figure 7.3). After each question, the teacher gives the groups a brief period, from 20 seconds to 2 minutes, depending on the complexity of the question, to discuss their answers. When time is up, the teachers calls out

Figure 7.3 Numbered Heads

a number—number three, for example. All the students designated number three raise their hands. The teacher chooses one number-three student to answer the question and continues calling on other number threes until enough information has been given. This procedure is repeated with each question.

A randomized process for choosing numbers works best here. Teachers can make a spinner with four quadrants, use numbered popsicle sticks or balls, or put numbered slips of paper in a box or paper bag. Psychologically, random drawings make students feel that no one number is being favored, neglected, or picked on. Even better, random drawings keep all students focused and on task for every question by removing the possibility that they won't be called on two or more times in a row.

STRATEGY 44   USE THINK–PAIR–SHARE

IN CONCEPT

Think–Pair–Share (a modification of Strategy 13, *Think–Write–Pair– Share*, in Chapter 5 to activate background knowledge) works equally well in question-and-answer sessions. Like *Numbered Heads*, the *Think–Pair–Share* strategy actively scaffolds learning by offering ELLs the opportunity to negotiate their conceptual understandings through interaction with peers. ELLs will experience less participation anxiety when they are able to test their content knowledge and language usage in the shelter of a small group setting.

IN PRACTICE

Prepare students by informing them that they will be using the *Think–Pair–Share* strategy prior to raising their hands to answer questions. During your Q and A sessions, allot 10 to 20 seconds for students to think about an appropriate response after you ask a question. Follow this "think time" with another 20 second segment during which students discuss the ideas they thought of with a partner or small group. Here again, students may find themselves more willing to participate because they can share either an idea that they had or one that they heard.

STRATEGY 45   ALLOW EXTRA WAIT TIME

IN CONCEPT

Wait time is the period of silence given to students to formulate an answer to a question. You probably first encountered the concept of wait time early in your teacher training classes. It would not be unusual if you have not given it much conscious thought since then.

Wait time is important because all students need time to sort out the meaning of the question and process the content required to answer it. Wait time is even more essential for ELLs because they have the additional layer of language processing to go through.

IN PRACTICE

Language learners benefit from wait times of 5 seconds for simple questions to as much as 10 to 20 seconds for more complicated questions. One way to ensure adequate time is to count slowly to yourself. The sound of silence may be uncomfortable to you at first, but extended wait times help lower the feelings of anxiety that often accompany being called on to produce an answer in a new language.

 ## STRATEGY 46   GIVE CREDIT FOR TRYING

IN CONCEPT

Teachers hear wrong answers every day. How you respond to them can make the difference between students who are willing to participate and those who are not. Acknowledging incorrect answers with a pleasant, positive response takes at least some of the risk out of classroom participation.

IN PRACTICE

Try saying one of the following with sincerity and a smile when students offer misinformation:

Good try.

Almost.

Thank you for trying.

Not quite, but you're thinking.

What an interesting (unusual) way to look at it.

Such responses lessen the stigma and anxiety of wrong answers and encourage continued attempts at participation. Wrong answers become an acceptable and normal part of learning.

 ## STRATEGY 47   OFFER FACE SAVERS

IN CONCEPT

Offering your students a face-saving way to not answer a question also lowers anxiety levels. It lowers students' affective filters and makes them more willing to take academic risks in the classroom.

IN PRACTICE

Technique I

Make it an accepted practice for students in your class to exercise a *Pass* option. Students who cannot answer a question simply say "Pass," after which you can add "Fine. We'll get back to you later." Be sure that you do.

You might consider using actual pass tokens that sit on students' desks until redeemed at some point during the class period. Students have to return them by answering a later question or by contributing to the review at the end of the class.

Technique II
A second face-saving strategy is to allow students to call on another student for assistance. To make this an effective learning technique, the student you initially called on should paraphrase or repeat the information given by the student who assisted in answering the question.

STRATEGY 48   WATCH FOR STUDENT READINESS

IN CONCEPT

Sometimes you can sense that certain students would like to try to answer but can't quite bring themselves to raise their hands. This is a good time to *invite* their participation.

Start by making friendly eye contact and smiling at each of the students who seem reluctant to participate. Look closely at those students' faces when you direct a general question to the whole class. Call on them when you detect readiness, but ensure that they have positive early participation experiences by giving them positive feedback and assisting their efforts.

IN PRACTICE

Technique I
Smile and nod while you encourage ELLs to use visual aids to support their words. Point to anything in the classroom that might help them with their responses, particularly the key words and phrases you wrote on the board during the period of instruction. There may also be charts, pictures, or places on maps displayed on bulletin boards around the room that can help them complete their responses.

Technique II
Smile and nod as you expand their few words into more complete thoughts. Use your words to augment theirs, as in Figure 7.4. Follow up a one-word student response with "Good—tell me more" or "True, but tell me why you think so." Affirming the correctness of the original answer gives students the confidence to continue.

Teacher Question	Student Response	Teacher Expansion
What is the name of the courts directly under the Supreme Court?	Circ . . . circa . . . circle courts.	Yes, the Circuit Court of Appeals. (Write the word *Circuit* on the board.)
Why do objects in motion continue to move in a vacuum?	No friction.	Exactly, a vacuum is a frictionless environment.
When would you use a bar graph and when a line graph?	Bar graph . . . to count . . . to put together . . . line for much change . . . long time.	Excellent! A bar graph shows data that can be counted and compared, and a line graph shows change over time.

Figure 7.4 Expanding Students' Responses

Technique III

Smile and nod when you prompt students by supplying the word or phrase they are searching for or stumbling over. Fill in the missing word or phrase and perhaps they will be able to continue with their responses.

STRATEGY 49   FOCUS ON CONTENT

IN CONCEPT

When ELLs attempt to answer questions, keep your attention on the message, not on the medium. Focus on the *content* in the response rather than on the language used to express it.

IN PRACTICE

ELLs will participate more readily if their language usage and pronunciation are not constantly and overtly corrected. Instead, model correct usage, as shown in Figure 7.4, by rephrasing student answers using complete sentences with correct grammar, vocabulary, and pronunciation.

Restructuring responses should be a subtle, not obvious, form of correction. Too much overt correction raises students' affective filters and decreases their willingness to participate.

QUESTIONS, ANSWERS, AND PARTICIPATION IN THE CLASSROOM

The Objective: Fine Tune Your Awareness of Student Participation.

The Rationale:

Successful learning takes place in classrooms that promote student participation. Teachers try to involve every one of their students in class discussions, but few really know if they actually succeed. The next strategy will fine-tune your awareness of student participation in your classroom.

STRATEGY 50   MONITOR YOUR INTERACTION PATTERNS

IN CONCEPT

Many teachers have a distinct *action zone* (Richards & Lockhart, 1996, p. 139), that is, a localized area of the classroom that they favor. This is the section of students toward whom they direct their instruction and discussion. Unconsciously, they look at and call on the students in this zone much more than the others.

IN PRACTICE

You can systematically determine if you have a particular action zone by videotaping a class you teach. (The suggestions in Figure 7.5 will ensure that you do not violate any privacy laws when you do the recording.) Making the videotape is easy if your school can provide an audiovisual team member to operate the camera as you teach. If that is

Schoolwide Permission

Many schools routinely send home forms requesting permission to videotape for educational purposes. Parents sign and return the forms at the beginning of the school year. If your school does this, you are covered.

Individual Permission

If your school doesn't do this, you must request parental permission with a letter similar to this one:

Dear Parents,

In my ongoing pursuit of excellence in teaching, I would like your permission to videotape *myself* as I teach a lesson in our classroom. The focus will be exclusively on me and my teaching, and only I will view the tape. I will be observing myself as a teacher to become aware of any ways that I might improve the quality of instruction. My goal is to become the very best teacher I can be for your children, who will be the beneficiaries of this experience.

Thank you very much.

(Your Signature)

I give permission to videotape for this purpose only.

Parent's Signature _____

Student Name _____ Date _____

Figure 7.5   Getting Permission to Videotape

not the situation, you can set the camera, focused on you, on a tripod in the rear of the room. Reviewing the videotape will help you determine whether you favor a particular section of the classroom. It will also allow you to observe your patterns of interaction. You may make some unexpected discoveries.

As you watch your videotape, look carefully at where you direct your attention and which students you actually call on. Use a class-seating chart to carefully note where you stand and who you look at as you teach. Note which students you call on and how many times. Your tallies may make you aware of an action zone and an interaction pattern you never knew you had.

Teachers have made many interesting discoveries from viewing themselves teaching. Some were surprised that they had called on several of their students so many times. Others saw that they had neglected to call on several very quiet students in the class, even though they were positive that they had actively involved every single student. Still others realized that they might improve student participation by working on smiling more and moving around the room.

Use the videotape to develop an awareness of other aspects of teaching discussed in this chapter. If you like what you see, give yourself a pat on the back. If, on the other hand, you feel you should find ways to increase student participation, you might try any of several techniques. A simple strategy that teachers use is to check off students' names on a class list or seating chart as you call on them. You can readily see participation patterns and frequency.

Another approach is to write students' names on popsicle sticks, place the sticks name side down in a cup, and randomly draw one after asking a question. (Use your teacher prerogative if you think the question may be too difficult for the name you draw by saying "Oops, I just called this name" or "Absent.") One teacher instituted a rule that all students who didn't participate during the lesson itself had to conduct the review at the end of the class. It was amazing how the participation in that class increased!

IN SUMMARY: CLASSROOM QUESTIONS, ANSWERS, AND PARTICIPATION

Teachers who strive to create a classroom environment that promotes and encourages participation invite students to become active learners. Active learners make better learners. Strategies that increase participation maximize potential for students to show what they know and to begin to experience feelings of academic success.

QUESTIONS FOR DISCUSSION

1. How do the strategies dealing with classroom questions, answers, and participation reflect the *Guidelines for Practice* presented at the beginning of this chapter?
2. Research additional question types used in classrooms, such as rhetorical, inquiry based, closed, open ended. Give examples of all question types. Discuss the effect of each type of question on student participation.
3. How does lowering the affective filter promote classroom participation? Give some specific examples.
4. Compare a class you took in which you enjoyed participating with one in which you did not. Evaluate what the instructors did or did not do to encourage/discourage participation.
5. Respond to the following scenario individually if you are currently teaching a class and with a partner if you are not.

    You have just been assigned a student teacher and you want to start him/her out right. Write a list of at least five practices that encourage classroom participation and five practices that are sure to discourage participation.

REFERENCES AND RESOURCES

Brown, H. D. (1994). *Teaching by principles: An interactive approach to language pedagogy* (pp. 157–169). Englewood Cliffs, NJ: Prentice Hall Regents.

Freeman, Y. S., & Freeman, D. E. (1998). *ESL/EFL teaching: Principles for success*. Portsmouth, NH: Heinemann.

Richards, J. C., & Lockhart, C. (1996). *Reflective teaching in second language classrooms*. Cambridge, England: Cambridge University Press.

CHAPTER 8

EXTENDING COMPREHENSION: TEXTBOOK VOCABULARY STRATEGIES

THEORY TO APPLICATION: GUIDELINES FOR PRACTICE

- Use scaffolding strategies to challenge ELLs to advance beyond their present state of independent activity, into the areas of potential learning in which content is learnable with the assistance of teachers and peers.
- Use scaffolding strategies that embed the oral and written language of content material in a context-rich environment to facilitate learning for ELLs.
- Use scaffolding strategies with ELLs to facilitate comprehension of the specialized academic language of content classrooms.
- Use scaffolding strategies that maintain a high level of cognitive challenge, but lower the language demand by embedding it in context.
- Actively teach learning strategies to give students a "menu" of ways to process and learn new information.

If ELLs could tell you what part of their content classes they found the most challenging, the majority would say their textbooks. The written language in student textbooks combines the difficulties of highly abstract and cognitively demanding concepts with content-specific words and advanced academic vocabulary, all written in language appropriate to the grade for which they are intended. Fortunately, textbooks can be made more comprehensible to ELLs—and to native English-speaking students who read below grade level—through the creative application of scaffolding strategies. This chapter focuses on vocabulary strategies that facilitate comprehension of the textbook, and the next will focus on reading strategies.

NEW VOCABULARY: WHICH WORDS TO TEACH?

Many ELLs believe that the key to understanding English lies in the vocabulary. It is difficult to argue against this point of view: Knowing what words mean is unquestionably critical to comprehension.

Textbooks and their accompanying teachers' editions do a creditable job of identifying and defining new vocabulary that appears in each chapter. These words are content specific or technical in nature, words students must learn if they are to understand the concepts that follow. If it were only these words that needed explanation, teachers and students would have an easy task.

Other than obvious technical or content-specific vocabulary in textbooks, four other categories of words may be unknown or misunderstood by ELLs. These are (1) synonyms, (2) idioms, (3) new usages of familiar words, and (4) just plain new words.

Synonyms

All writers use synonyms to add interest and variety to text. Indeed, it would be boring to read the same noun, adjective, or verb over and over in a piece of writing. While synonyms have the positive effect of adding flavor to writing, they also have the unintended negative effect of burdening ELLs with more unknown vocabulary. Consider the number of synonymous phrases we use to talk about the following simple arithmetic problem:

$$\begin{array}{r} 8 \\ -\ 5 \\ \hline \end{array}$$

Subtract 5 from 8.
5 from 8 equals ____.
Take 5 away from 8.
Take away 5 from 8.
How much less is 5 than 8?
How much is 8 less 5?
8 minus 5 equals ____.
What is the difference between 8 and 5?

At a more advanced level, think about the different words and phrases that are used to represent the concept of *freedom* in written texts. A search through several high school social studies textbooks produced this list:

liberty	liberation
independence	autonomy
sovereignty	emancipation
self-determination	self-government
self-sufficiency	self-reliance
home rule	

To make the situation even more confusing for ELLs, words and phrases used during class discussions may vary significantly from the wording used in the textbook. It's not hard to see why vocabulary is such a challenge.

Idioms

ELLs love to learn idioms because they feel, and perhaps rightly so, that if they understand idioms, they *really* know English. Idioms are more than the sum of their parts. These groups of words have meanings unrelated to knowledge of the actual words, and analyzing them on a word-by-word basis often produces some odd images. Visualize the literal meaning of the following widely used idiomatic expressions:

She really put her foot in her mouth.
It's raining cats and dogs.
I'm all ears.
He's got two left feet.

Idiomatic expressions are also used in academic writing. The phrases in Figure 8.1 are frequent idiomatic references in social studies textbooks. It is not difficult to imagine an ELL thinking "Why did they stand under a flag to fight?"

About the Civil War	About the American Flag
a house divided fighting under the Confederate flag on the home front loss of lives	the Stars and Stripes Old Glory the Red, White, and Blue

Figure 8.1 Idiomatic References in Social Studies

New Usages of Familiar Words

Think of the word *strike*. In what context might ELLs be familiar with this word? Did you think of baseball, perhaps bowling or fishing? Students will be familiar with these usages of the word *strike* from watching or participating in these activities or having parents who do.

Apart from sports, *strike,* as used in everyday conversation, has multiple meanings depending on the context in which it appears. Here are several:

Police thought the murderer would *strike* again.

He hoped a brilliant idea would *strike* him.

She tried unsuccessfully to *strike* up a conversation.

He tried again to *strike* the match.

She tried to *strike* a bargain.

   (Did she light any fires?)

The dog was *struck* by a car.

He was *struck* by the beauty of the sunset.

   (Was he hurt, too?)

We heard the clock *striking* midnight.

The similarity was *striking.*

   (And loud, too?)

In textbooks, however, the word *strike* appears in wholly different contexts. Think now of how it relates to these topics;

Industry: The workers went on *strike.*

Mining: The prospectors were hoping to *strike* gold.

Weather: Lightning can *strike* before a storm.

Military: The air *strike* was considered successful.

With good reason, ELLs will be confused by these multiple meanings and usages. You can help them by scanning the text for words that might be confusing or misunderstood because they would be more commonly known with a different meaning in a conversational or social context.

All subject domains have their own set of concept words, many of which fall into the category of familiar words used in new ways. Figure 8.2 lists examples from science, math, and social studies.

Science	energy, mass, matter, force, kingdom
Math	table, round, root, mean, power, expression
Social Studies	river bed, river bank, interest rates, (political) parties, left wing, right wing

Figure 8.2 Domain-Specific Usages of Familiar Words

Figure 8.3   A True Tale of Misunderstanding

A second-grade teacher of a self-contained ESL class was
teaching a unit on Christopher Columbus and how he explored
the Caribbean Islands and conquered the native Indian populations living there. She asked her class why they thought that
Columbus, with so few men, was able to conquer the many
thousands of native Indians who lived there. When none of
them answered, she explained: "It's because Christopher
Columbus and his men had arms, and the native Indians didn't
have any."

Not yet realizing any misunderstanding, she continued the
discussion by asking about the kind of life the Caribbean
Indians had before being conquered by Columbus. One student
answered, "Very hard," as all the others nodded their heads in
agreement.

Surprised by this response, she asked, "How could it have
been a hard life? They had beautiful warm weather, lots of food
to eat—especially fruits and vegetables. They didn't need to
wear a lot of clothing or build strong houses to keep out the
cold. Why do you think they had a hard life?"

One student timidly offered an explanation: "Because they
had no arms! How could they do anything?"

Imagine a student's puzzlement about how Sunday mass at church fits into science.
Can you visualize the mental images that ELLs might form from the expressions *river bed*
and *river bank?* Who got invited to those political parties? And what about those wings
in government—where did they come from? Add to this the further complication of a single word used to represent unrelated concepts in separate domains, as, for example, the
word *root* in science and math.

It's easy to see why such words create confusion for ELLs. Figure 8.3 is a true story
of a near perfect misunderstanding resulting from students knowing only the common
usage of a word.

Just Plain New Words

This is the catchall category—the least well defined, the most individualized, and the
most challenging for the teacher. Words in this category are unknown to the learner and
do not fit easily into the other categories. These are the words that are most often overlooked in vocabulary development. Following are some ideas to help you and your students determine and define words that may need some extra attention.

TEACHING AND LEARNING VOCABULARY

The Objective: Use Meaningful Strategies for Teaching and Learning Vocabulary.

The Rationale

Knowing which words to teach is not the same as knowing how to teach them.
Methodologies for teaching and learning vocabulary are often old-fashioned, uncreative,
and unproductive.

The most widely used strategies for teaching vocabulary result in little long-term retention because they teach words in isolation. The traditional assignment of "Look the words up in a dictionary and use each in an original sentence" is rarely an effective approach. Students remember the words only as long as they must to pass a test. Similarly, activities such as word searches, scrambled words, matching tasks, or crossword puzzles do little to add to students' long-term retention and usage of new words, again because the words are used in isolation. Vocabulary teaching and learning strategies that approach words as they are used in context and are meaningful to students will result in more authentic and effective learning.

 ## STRATEGY 51   SELECT STUDENTS TO BE YOUR VOCABULARY HELPERS

IN CONCEPT

Teachers can help their ELLs by asking the more advanced students to preview text chapters for ELLs, looking for potentially confusing vocabulary.

IN PRACTICE

Designated or volunteer students scan text looking for words and phrases used synonymously to refer to one or several central concepts or ideas, as well as for idiomatic usages and references. The resulting lists help to lighten the vocabulary load for ELLs as they read the chapter. Additionally, the students making the lists reinforce their vocabulary knowledge and can receive extra credit or bonus points for their efforts.

Although this strategy may at first seem to limit ELLs' vocabulary development, bear in mind that scaffolding strategies are used only until the learner no longer needs them. In this case, you are decreasing the language load so that ELLs can access the content in the textbook. During class instruction and discussion, however, you can feel comfortable using synonyms and idioms freely, pairing them with their more widely known word (see Strategy 56, later in this chapter).

 ## STRATEGY 52   TURN YOUR STUDENTS INTO "LANGUAGE DETECTIVES"

IN CONCEPT

This is a wonderful strategy for students whose native language is Spanish or one of the other Latin root languages. This strategy works because of an event that took place in the year 1066.

In that year, the Normans from France conquered the Angles and Saxons living in what is now England. The conquerors' language, an early version of today's French, became the language of position and power. It also became the language of academia and the educated. The conquered Anglo-Saxons continued using their own language in everyday life, and a duality was created that still exists in the English that we use today.

Many academic words in English—the words that cut across all academic disciplines—come from the old Norman French, which has its roots in ancient Greek and Latin. The common words used in social, spoken English derive from Anglo-Saxon roots. So, we often speak and hear different words in conversation than we read and write in school, as illustrated in Figure 8.4.

Conversational English	Academic English
Did you *meet* anyone at the store today?	The troops *encountered* no resistance.
Get in *line*.	Arrange the numbers in *sequence*.
Let's *build* a castle.	The troops planned to *construct* a bridge.
The vacation *lasted* two full weeks.	The people *endured* two centuries of tyranny.
The salad was *enough* for two people.	The supplies were *sufficient* for only a week.

Figure 8.4 Comparing Conversational and Academic English

IN PRACTICE

You can use this information to help your Spanish speakers, whose language is also based on Latin–Greek roots, to become *language detectives*. Spanish speakers can apply the database of their native language to textbook vocabulary by scanning texts for academic words with Spanish cognates, some examples of which are shown in Figure 8.5. They can even share their discoveries with the rest of the class. It becomes a win–win situation.

STRATEGY 53 HAVE STUDENTS DEVELOP A PERSONAL DICTIONARY

IN CONCEPT

Personal dictionaries benefit all students. They are valuable, easy-to-use tools for building vocabulary.

Personal dictionaries can be formatted in a variety of ways. No matter their form, they help students remember words that they find academically useful and/or personally meaningful or interesting.

IN PRACTICE

You or the students can select an organizing principle: subject specific, alphabetical, general/technical, or social/academic. Dictionaries can be written in English only or can include notations in students' native languages. ELLs at the beginner's level can use the format shown in Figure 8.6, the Vocabulary Circle. Additional possibilities for inclusion in

Figure 8.5 Turn Your Spanish Speakers into Language Detectives

Academic Word	Spanish Word	Common Word
encounter	*encontrar*	meet
observe	*observar*	watch
maintain	*mantener*	keep
ultimate	*último*	last
equal	*igual*	same
entire	*entero*	whole
quantity	*cantidad*	amount

Figure 8.6 Vocabulary Circle

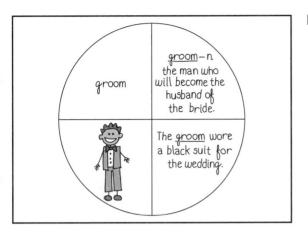

the circle or as a column entry in personal dictionaries are native language translation, synonyms, or antonyms.

It may also be helpful to include a section for collocations: words that commonly appear in combination with the entry word. ELLs must learn these high-frequency word associations that come so naturally to native speakers who know, for example, that air can be heavy with humidity but thick with smoke, and thin, never slim or skinny, at high altitudes. Figure 8.7 offers additional examples of collocated usages in a format suitable for students to use.

STRATEGY 54   DEMONSTRATE THE VALUE OF A STUDENT-FRIENDLY DICTIONARY

IN CONCEPT

Have you ever looked up a word in the dictionary and, after reading the definition, found you still had no idea of what the word meant? If that can happen to an educated native English language speaker, imagine what a challenge it would be for an ELL!

Dictionaries, which all students need, are essential for ELLs. Student dictionaries are available at beginner, intermediate, and advanced levels. In the Longman series of dictionaries, the vocabulary used in the definitions is based on the 2,000 most commonly used words in the English language. A side-by-side comparison of the definitions shown in Figure 8.8 leaves little doubt about which one is easier to understand.

Figure 8.7 Examples of Collocations

New Word	Goes with . . .	But not . . .
bargain	fair bargain hard bargain	balanced, just firm, stiff, rigid
trick	clever trick dirty trick	bright, smart, intelligent dishonest, crooked
truce	uneasy truce	worried, nervous
rhetoric	empty rhetoric	vacant, blank, unoccupied
famine	severe famine	rigid, stern, strict, heavy
oath	solemn oath	serious, grave, somber

Longman's Basic Dictionary	*Webster's Ninth Collegiate Dictionary*
landlady	**landlady**
"A woman who owns a building and rents it to others."	"A woman who is a landlord."
landlord	**landlord**
"Someone who owns a building and rents it to others."	"The owner of property (as land, houses or apartments) that is leased or rented to another; the master of an inn or lodging house (innkeeper)."

Longman's Advanced American Dictionary	*Oxford American Dictionary and Language Guide*
spurious 1 a spurious statement, argument, etc. is not based on facts or good reasoning and is likely to be incorrect: *A jury rejected the spurious claim that the police created evidence.* **2** insincere: *a spurious smile.*	**spurious 1** not genuine; not being what it purports to be; not proceeding from the pretended source *(a spurious excuse).* **2** having an outward similarity of form or function only.

Figure 8.8 Two Comparisons of Dictionary Definitions

Longman's Advanced American Dictionary (2000), p. 1408. Essex, England: Pearson Education Limited.

Longman Basic Dictionary of American English (1999), p. 162. Essex, England: Pearson Education Limited.

Merriam-Webster's Collegiate Dictionary, Eleventh Edition (2003), p. 699. Springfield, MA: Merriam-Webster.

Oxford American Dictionary and Language Guide (1999), p. 978. New York: Oxford University Press.

Student dictionaries list multiple meanings of words as separate entries and use words in sentences. Additionally, they offer usage notes, synonyms, antonyms, examples, illustrations, and photographs. At the more advanced level, student dictionaries label words as approving or disapproving (think about the subtle differences between the words *thin/slim/skinny* or *childish/childlike,* for example), formal, literary or old-fashioned, informal, humorous, slang or nonstandard, and even offensive or taboo. Idiomatic expressions, collocations, usage notes, and frequency information for spoken and written words are also presented.

Students must become familiar with using the dictionary so that the task of finding a word definition no longer appears formidable. Dictionaries are wonderful resources but only if students feel confident enough to use them.

IN PRACTICE

Technique I

Play dictionary games to accustom your students to working with a dictionary. Figure 8.9 gives examples of items that might be included in this type of activity. Make the activity feel like a game by setting it up as a timed competition. Group students by tables or set one-half of the room against the other. Activities that are gamelike in nature get students instantly involved and motivated.

Technique II

While student dictionaries are valuable to students, they are perhaps even more valuable as aids to teachers. Use a student dictionary to make your vocabulary teaching clearer and more complete.

Find synonyms for the word _____.
Find the first and last word in the dictionary.
Find a word on page _____ that means _____.
Find the first adjective on page _____.
Find an informal word on page _____.
Find the third word on the page with the guide words _____ and
_____.
Find a word with more than one meaning on page _____.

Figure 8.9 *Find It Fast!* The Dictionary Game

In teaching, a word often comes up that requires some explanation. Keep a student dictionary at hand on your desk to take advantage of that teachable vocabulary moment. Using one will help you give your students a better definition of the word. Each time you reach for the dictionary, you are modeling an effective vocabulary strategy.

Every classroom should have at least one student dictionary. You and your students will find yourselves reaching for one on a regular basis.

STRATEGY 55   USE AN INTERNET WEB SITE TO DETERMINE WHICH WORDS TO TEACH

IN CONCEPT

A text analysis Web site can help you decide which words, of all the many in a text passage, you really need to teach. It is an awesome tool.

One such Web site, *The Compleat Lexical Tutor*, has been developed by the Université de Québec à Montréal. It is designed to create a vocabulary profile of any text you input. You can find it at this Web address: *http://www.lextutor.ca/vp/eng*. You can also use a search engine to find The Compleat Lexical Tutor by name.

The Lexical Tutor Web site presents you with a box to type or paste in the desired text. When you have completed inputting the text, click on the | Submit-window | button, and in a matter of seconds a color-coded vocabulary profile of the text appears on your computer screen. The color coding represents words of four different frequency types:

K1 (blue): the most frequent 1,000 word families

K2 (green): the second 1,000 most frequent word families

AWL (yellow): Academic Word List, or words that are common across all subject domains

Off-List Words (red): topic-specific, technical, and/or infrequently used words; also dates, place names, and names of people

IN PRACTICE

The easiest way to understand the wonders of this Web tool is to look at an actual example from a middle school social studies textbook, *World Explorer: People, Places, and Cultures* (Kracht, 2003, p. 35). Figure 8.10 shows the original passage as it appears in the textbook. After typing or pasting it into the Web page's textbox, the black-typed passage is returned, in a matter of seconds, color coded with a complete analysis of word counts and other linguistic data. Accompanying the passage is a vocabulary profile showing the actual listings of words in each of the four frequency categories. This vocabulary profile, summarized in Figure 8.11, gives you systematic information to help you locate specific words that your ELLs may find difficult.

The first piece of valuable information is that almost 78% of the words (184 of the 239) are in the K1 category. You can reasonably assume that these words are currently part of your ELL students' working vocabularies.

Figure 8.10   Original text passage.

From *Prentice Hall World Explorer: People, Places, and Cultures* by James B. Kracht © 2003 by Pearson Education, Inc., publishing as Pearson Prentice Hall, p. 35. Used by permission.

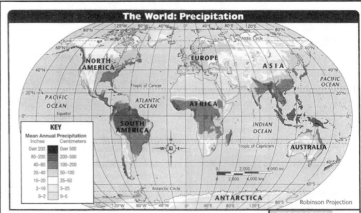

The World: Precipitation

The Impact of Wind and Water

Without wind and water, the Earth would overheat. Together, wind and water moderate the effect of the sun's heat. Heat causes air to rise, especially near the Equator and over warm ocean water. Cold air sinks towards the surface away from the Equator. Wind blows from places where air is sinking towards places where air is rising. The Earth's rotation bends this flow to create circular wind patterns. So, depending on where you are in a circling weather system, the wind may be blowing north, south, east, or west.

The Earth's rotation also creates ocean currents, which are like rivers in the oceans. Some currents carry warm water from near the Equator toward the north and the south. Other currents carry cold water from the poles toward the Equator. Oceans also moderate the climate of nearby land just by their presence. Water takes longer to heat and cool than land. As a result, when the land has warmed during the summer, the nearby ocean remains cooler. Air blowing over the ocean becomes cool and then cools the land. In the winter, the opposite occurs.

Raging Storms   Wind and water can make climates milder, but they also create storms. Hurricanes are storms that form over the ocean in the tropics. Hurricanes rotate in a counter-clockwise direction around an "eye." They have winds of at least 74 miles (124 km) per hour and usually involve heavy rainfall. Tornadoes are just as dangerous, but they affect smaller areas. Their wind can range from 40 miles (67 km) per hour to over 300 miles (501 km) per hour and wreck anything in their path.

GEOGRAPHY   The mean annual precipitation is the amount of rain or snow that falls in a region in an average year.   **Map Study**   Which areas get the most precipitation? Which get the least?

LINKS TO Science

Smog   Normally, air is cooler at higher altitudes. During a temperature inversion, however, a layer of warm air sits on top of the cooler air. The warm air traps pollution near the ground. This mixture of dangerous smoke and fog is called *smog*. The brown air seen in cities such as Los Angeles and Denver is smog caused by car exhaust.

CHAPTER 2   EARTH'S PHYSICAL GEOGRAPHY   **35**

Examine next the words that fall into the other three categories, as listed in Figure 8.12. Of the 13 words listed in the K2 category, students may already know some words, such as *bend, cool, during, especially, ocean, storm, warm,* and *weather.* Now 5 words remain.

The Off-List category contains 12 words. This list, too, can be reduced by removing words such as *climate, Equator, hurricane, km,* and *tropics,* which will have been either included in the preselected vocabulary for the chapter or previously learned. Add the 7 words remaining in the Off-List category to the 5 K2 word families and the 4 academic word families (AWL), and the grand total of potentially unknown words for your ELLs is 16, listed in Figure 8.13, or less than 7% of the original 239 in the passage.

Category	Word Families	Tokens (Words)	Percentage (%)
K1 Words (1–1,000)	81	184	77.99
K2 Words (1,001–2,000)	13	28	11.72
AWL Words (academic)	4	6	2.51
Off-List Words	12	21	8.79
TOTALS	98	239	100.00

Figure 8.11   Vocabulary Profile Summary

K2 Words	Academic Words	Off-List Words
bends	create	climate
cool	impact	clockwise
during	involve	counter
especially	occurs	currents
milder		Equator
moderate		hurricanes
ocean		km
opposite		overheat
patterns		poles
sinking		raging
storms		rotate/rotation
warm		tropics
weather		

Figure 8.12 K2, Academic, and Off-List Words

K2 Words	Academic Words (AWL)	Off-List Words
Teach:	Teach:	Teach:
milder	create	clockwise
moderate	impact	counter
opposite	involve	currents
patterns	occur	overheat
sink		poles
		raging
		rotate/rotation
Review:		Review:
bends		climate
		Equator
		hurricanes
		km
		tropics

Figure 8.13 Which Words to Teach?

It should come as a comforting thought to know that your ELLs can handle over 90% of the words in this passage. Only the small number of remaining words are the ones you and your students need to focus on to increase their understanding of concepts. Vocabulary tools such as this Web site help you, the content teacher, narrow the challenge of "So many words, so little time." Try it—it's amazing.

TEACHING AND LEARNING VOCABULARY

The Objective: Integrate Vocabulary Development into Daily Instruction.

The Rationale

Just as words do not appear in isolation in the environment, so too should it be with vocabulary development. Substitute the once-a-week vocabulary lesson followed by a quiz with strategies that integrate vocabulary into every lesson you teach. Finding words in context and using them repeatedly in authentic applications aid long-term retention.

STRATEGY 56   GET INTO A PAIR–DEFINE–EXPLAIN ROUTINE

IN CONCEPT

Young children acquire words from the environment at a staggering rate. Classroom strategies to expand vocabulary in ways similar to the natural acquisition of children are effective for long-term retention.

IN PRACTICE

As you teach, advance students' vocabulary development by sprinkling your instruction with interesting words and phrases, but *pair* the word or phrase with a high-frequency synonym, a definition or explanation, or a visual depiction. Students will learn new words naturally if you repeat them frequently, pairing them every time with an explanatory source. The more naturally you can work this pairing into your speech patterns, as in the examples in Figure 8.14, the more effective this technique will be.

STRATEGY 57   SET UP A WORD OF THE WEEK PROGRAM

IN CONCEPT

Learning new words involves more than just knowing their meaning; students also must be able to use words appropriately in authentic contexts. This is a fun strategy that promotes natural usage as it extends students' knowledge of vocabulary.

IN PRACTICE

Technique I

An entire school can make vocabulary growth a long-term goal. Each Monday morning, a word, along with its definition and several examples of usage, is announced as the Word of the Week. Words selected for this honor should be academic words that cross many disciplines. Students receive bonus points for using the word appropriately in any of their classes. Teachers, too, make every effort to use the word daily in natural and meaningful academic contexts. Students can show by a predesignated nonverbal signal that they recognize the word.

Figure 8.14 Extend Students' Vocabulary through the Pair–Define–Explain Routine

> "He committed an egregious error—a *very* bad mistake."
>
> "The liquid becomes effervescent—bubbly, full of bubbles—when we stir it."
>
> "The Pilgrims embarked on a long journey. They began . . . they started on a long trip."
>
> "She was motivated by vengeance—she wanted to punish him, sort of get back or get even with him."

Technique II

As an individual class strategy, teachers can do a Word of the Day, choosing new and interesting words or recycling previously used words for reinforcement. Students try to use the day's word, orally and in written form, in class activities and homework assignments. Daily or weekly, students record the words in their personal dictionaries. You may also make it a practice to give extra bonus points to students who manage to use a former Word of the Day in class.

STRATEGY 58 MAKE YOUR STUDENTS INTO WORD WIZARDS

IN CONCEPT

Make vocabulary growth an ongoing objective in your classroom. Develop practices that encourage your students to become Word Wizards by using interesting words in class.

IN PRACTICE

Create a "word wall" board upon which students can write new words they come across in any form of media. Motivate students by making an ongoing game of it: Students win points for using a new word orally or in writing. Be ready to verbally recognize unusual vocabulary during class Q and A sessions, discussions, and conversations. Show your appreciation of uncommon or interesting words with comments that praise their usage. Ask students how they know the word. Make vocabulary one-upmanship work to everyone's advantage.

STRATEGY 59 PLAY VOCABULARY BINGO

IN CONCEPT

Bingo is a game that has been enjoyed by every generation of children. Many adults still like it. Make learning new vocabulary fun with a strategy that gives Bingo a twist.

IN PRACTICE

After handing out preprinted blank Bingo grids, tell your students to fill in the week's vocabulary words in any pattern on their papers. As caller, you randomly select words, but instead of saying the word, you pantomime, show or draw a visual, or give a verbal description, example, synonym, antonym, or—occasionally—the definition. By filling in their own grids, students cannot sulk over bad card choices or an unfair caller.

An additional twist to *Vocabulary Bingo* is that the winner must not just say the winning words but also may use them in a sentence. You can increase motivation and participation by using a team approach that invites team members to create the sentences.

IN SUMMARY: TEACHING AND LEARNING VOCABULARY

True vocabulary growth is a long-term process. Students need a variety of approaches to develop the vocabulary that they need for academic success.

Students don't have to know the meaning of every word before they read a text passage. A great deal of vocabulary learning occurs as students engage in the reading process and afterward in discussion and assignments, especially when teachers make vocabulary learning a routine part of their classrooms.

QUESTIONS FOR DISCUSSION

1. How do the strategies for teaching and learning vocabulary reflect the *Guidelines for Practice* presented at the beginning of this chapter?
2. Research the strategies for teaching vocabulary most commonly practiced in today's classrooms. Evaluate their effectiveness.
3. Prepare a list of additional domain-specific usages of familiar words, similar to the examples illustrated in Figure 8.2.
4. What strategies did you use in your years of schooling to learn vocabulary? How would you evaluate them? Do you believe you might have benefited from any of the vocabulary strategies discussed in this chapter?
5. What do you currently do when you find an unfamiliar word in a book you are reading? How often do you look it up in a dictionary? Do you remember the word and its meaning after you have looked it up? What strategies could you use if you really wanted to remember the word?
6. How often have you used a thesaurus? When was the last time you referred to one? What are the advantages and disadvantages of using a thesaurus?

REFERENCES AND RESOURCES

Cobb, T. (n. d.). Why & how to use frequency lists to learn words. Retrieved August 9, 2006, from *www.lextutor.ca/research/rationale.htm*.

Folse, K. (2004). *Vocabulary myths: Applying second language research to classroom teaching*. Ann Arbor: The University of Michigan Press.

Kracht, J. B. (2003). *Prentice Hall world explorer: People, places, and cultures*. Upper Saddle River, NJ: Pearson Education.

Nation, P. (2001). *Learning vocabulary in another language*. New York: Cambridge University Press.

English Language Resources for Students and Teachers

For Beginners

Student Dictionaries

Oxford picture dictionary for the content areas. (2000). Oxford, England: Oxford University Press. Also available in English/Spanish version.

Vox Spanish and English student dictionary. (1999). Columbus, OH: McGraw-Hill, 1999.

Word by word picture dictionary. (1993). White Plains, NY: Pearson Longman. Also available in eight bilingual versions: English + Chinese, Haitian Kreyol, Japanese, Korean, Portuguese, Russian, Spanish, Vietnamese.

For High Beginners and Low Intermediates

Student Dictionary

Longman basic dictionary of American English. (1999). White Plains, NY: Pearson Longman.
> The three levels of the *Longman Student Dictionary* series use the Longman Defining Vocabulary, the 2,000 most common English words, to ensure that all definitions and sentence examples are easy to understand.

For Intermediates

Student Dictionary

Longman dictionary of American English (3rd ed.). (2002). White Plains, NY: Pearson Longman.

Thesaurus

Longman essential activator (2nd ed.). (2002). White Plains, NY: Pearson Longman.

Dictionary of Idioms

Longman pocket idioms dictionary. (2002). White Plains, NY: Pearson Longman.

For High Intermediates and Advanced

Student Dictionary

Longman advanced American dictionary. (2001). White Plains, NY: Pearson Longman.

Thesaurus

Longman language activator. (2002). White Plains, NY: Pearson Longman.

Dictionaries of Idioms

Longman American idioms dictionary. (2000). White Plains, NY: Pearson Longman.
Oxford idioms. (2001). Oxford: Oxford University Press.

Collocation Dictionaries

BBI dictionary of English word combinations. (1997). Amsterdam, The Netherlands: John Benjamins Publishing.
LTP dictionary of selected collocations. (1999). Hove, England: Language Teaching Publications.
Oxford collocations dictionary for students of English. (2002). Oxford: Oxford University Press.

The TechConnection

http://www.wordcentral.com
> An online all-purpose dictionary.

http://www.math.com/students/references.html#dictionaries
> An online reference for math words and more.

http://www.clichesite.com/index.asp
> An online source for idioms, sayings, and proverbs.

CHAPTER 9

EXTENDING COMPREHENSION: TEXTBOOK READING STRATEGIES

THEORY TO APPLICATION: GUIDELINES FOR PRACTICE

- Use scaffolding strategies to challenge ELLs to advance beyond their present state of independent activity, into the areas of potential learning in which content is learnable with the assistance of teachers and peers.
- Use scaffolding strategies that embed the oral and written language of content material in a context-rich environment to facilitate learning for ELLs.
- Use scaffolding strategies with ELLs to facilitate comprehension of the specialized academic language of content classrooms.
- Use scaffolding strategies that maintain a high level of cognitive challenge, but lower the language demand by embedding it in context.
- Actively teach learning strategies to give students a "menu" of ways to process and learn new information.
- Provide opportunities for ELLs to negotiate conceptual understandings and to explore language usage through classroom interaction.
- Lower learner anxiety in the classroom to create students who are more willing to participate in class, to become risk takers in the learning process, and ultimately to become more successful learners.
- Provide opportunities for students to experience success in the classroom: Success in learning promotes more success by increasing learner motivation, interest, and self-confidence.

Teachers often have little control over which textbooks they use in their classrooms. In most school districts, teachers simply use the ones they are given and generally find them acceptable, as today's textbooks and ancillary materials tend to be user-friendly and engaging for students. ELLs, however, may view their texts with apprehension. Their English reading skills are not yet sufficiently developed to comprehend grade-level textbook materials. For them, reading content-area textbooks is often a frustrating experience. The amount of information may appear overwhelming. The time and effort they spend trying to make it understandable often bring few rewards and little satisfaction. Incorporating some of the strategies that follow will help make reading the class textbook more comprehensible for ELLs.

WORKING WITH YOUR TEXTBOOK

The Objective: Show Students How to Get the Most out of Their Textbooks.

The Rationale

The shift from learning to read to reading to learn occurs in third grade. From that point-on, teachers instruct students in learning the information within their textbooks but rarely in *using* their textbooks to make that learning easier. Few students instinctively develop the skills to use their textbooks in ways that could facilitate their comprehension.

 ## STRATEGY 60   TEACH TEXTBOOK AIDS

IN CONCEPT

Textbook aids embed the written word in context. Hard as it may be to believe, however, students do not make the connection between textbook aids and the surrounding text. One student actually came to her teacher in mid-January and said, "Our textbook has a bilingual dictionary in the back! Did you know that?" There is no doubt that this student would have benefited had she been able to use this resource during the first half of the year.

Teachers must make students aware that textbook aids are included not to make the page look pretty (or, as one student suggested, so the author didn't have to write so many words) but to support students' efforts to understand the ideas that the printed words convey.

IN PRACTICE

Using textbook aids to facilitate comprehension is an important learning strategy and should be taught actively and explicitly at the beginning of the school year or whenever a new textbook is introduced. Use a class session to teach about the aids that your particular textbook offers (types of aids and their uses are described in the following paragraphs). Give explicit instruction or try a discovery approach: Give your students a list of aids and have them work in groups to identify and locate examples of each item in their textbooks. In either case, explain the purpose of each aid and how to use it to support students' understanding of the text. You can use the activity described in Figure 9.1 as an introduction to the lesson and, later, at the beginning of each new chapter. Or try a more radical approach, described in Figure 9.2, that one teacher used.

Figure 9.1   An Activity to Demonstrate the Value of Textbook Aids

Write:	chapter title, headings, and subheadings on board
Ask:	"What is chapter about?"
Make:	brainstorming graphic
Tell:	students to open textbook to that chapter
Allot:	3 minutes to look over other textbook aids
Add:	more ideas to graphic
Use:	graphic as review at end of reading

On the first day of school, Ms. Molvick, a middle-school science teacher, spent the period talking about the course that lay ahead. The class ended with a homework assignment to "Familiarize yourselves with your textbook." What the students heard, of course, was "No homework."

The next day as class began, Ms. Molvick told the students to clear their desks, take out a piece of paper, write their names at the top, and number a list 1 through 10. The students gave each other puzzled looks. A quiz? How could they have a quiz when they hadn't had any homework?

The first question on the quiz was "What is the name of your textbook?" Other questions followed:

What information is given at the beginning of each chapter?

What information is given at the end of each chapter?

How is new vocabulary presented in the text?

Does the text use margin notes or footnotes?

Does your textbook have a glossary?

Are any appendices included?

Ms. Molvick created the opportunity to teach a lesson on textbook aids when she corrected the quiz with the class. It was her way of ensuring that the students became well acquainted with their textbooks. The students in this science class learned a valuable lesson in class that day—about their textbook *and* about their teacher.

Figure 9.2   True Tale: One Way to Teach Textbook Aids

Remind students frequently to use textbooks aids as a *pre-reading* activity each time they encounter the text. The more students use textbook aids, the more they will recognize how valuable the aids are to text comprehension.

Table of Contents and Index. The table of contents and the index serve as shortcuts for locating specific information contained in a text. A simple technique to teach the usefulness of these aids is to give grouped students a list of topics and have them note the page number(s) in the text where information is given. They might also note whether they used the index or the table of contents to find the information. Try turning this practice activity into a game: Give it an intriguing name, like *Textbook Sleuths*, add a time limit, and make it a competition.

Chapter Titles, Section Headings, and Subsection Headings. Titles and headings should be considered *clues* to help students organize their thinking about the type of information that follows. Section and subsection headings usually contain key words or phrases that highlight important facts or concepts. Teach students to scan headings and make associations as a regular *pre-reading* activity.

Outlines and Questions. Content outlines or focus questions at the beginning of each chapter highlight forthcoming information. As a *pre-reading* activity, use these outlines and questions to direct students' attention to important concepts, ideas, and details presented in the chapter. Students can use outlines and questions during the reading to organize information and then as a *post-reading* strategy to check their comprehension and to engage in critical thinking.

Summaries and Reviews. The summaries and reviews at the ends of sections and chapters highlight the key concepts presented in the body of the text. ELLs should know that the language used in reviews and summaries is generally more readable because the sentences are shorter and more concise. Teach your ELLs to read summaries and reviews *before* reading a textbook section or chapter. Pre-reading the summary/review sections helps all students organize their thinking about the content they are about to read in the text. It allows them to form a foundation that facilitates comprehension of the concepts and supporting details presented in the body of the text.

Glossaries. Textbook glossaries are a bonus feature for all students. For ELLs, they can be a lifeline. Make your students aware that the words or phrases highlighted by color or bolding in the body of the text are important to understanding the concepts. Show how these key words are explained in their textbooks: In a glossary at the end of the textbook, or written as notations in margins, or listed at the beginning or end of each chapter. Some textbooks include a bilingual glossary, but if yours does not, encourage your ELLs to make liberal use of *bilingual dictionaries* for additional clarification.

Text Organizers. Text organizers, and the aids that follow, are particularly valuable to ELLs because they offer a great deal of information in the fewest number of words. Text organizers call attention to key concepts by showcasing them in boxes, bulleted or numbered lists, and sentences written in bold or different colored ink. Students should be made aware that these elements indicate important information.

Graphics. Textbook graphics present information in chart, table, or diagram formats. They increase comprehensibility by visually contextualizing the printed words. ELLs can derive a great deal of information by learning to analyze the information displayed in these graphics.

Visuals. Visuals in textbooks are designed to appeal to students, to capture their attention, to offer them contextual support, and to enrich their understanding of concepts presented in the text. As with graphics, students should understand that they are not decoration or page fillers—indeed, real information is offered in the maps, pictures, and illustrations included in the text. ELLs and below grade-level readers should be encouraged first to scan visuals and graphics to activate or build background knowledge and then to use these features as an adjunct to the written text to help clarify meaning.

STRATEGY 61   TEACH READING IN REVERSE

IN CONCEPT

Reading in reverse is a scaffolding strategy that previews concepts to prepare students to mentally organize a forthcoming reading. It literally reverses the order of the traditional approach to an assigned textbook reading.

The standard pattern for reading generally looks like this:

- Teacher activates background knowledge.
- Students read the text.
- Students answer the questions in the text.
- Teacher discusses information in the text.
- Teacher applies information to real-life and/or past learning.

This widely practiced model, shown graphically in Figure 9.3, asks students to do the more difficult, dense part of the lesson first, before enough scaffolding is in place to support their attempts to read the text. Assigning students the text reading before the activities that embed the information in context means that students lack the strong foundational base to support their comprehension. There is a better way to do it.

The strategy of reading in reverse places the hardest part of the task at the end of the activity, rather than at the beginning. Students who complete these pre-reading steps have in place a strong scaffold for learning.

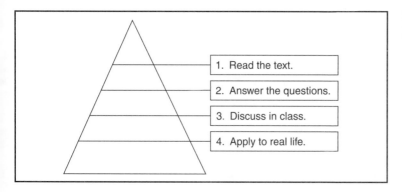

Figure 9.3 The Traditional Model for Reading a Textbook

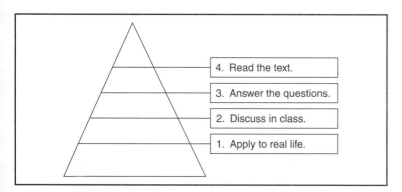

Figure 9.4 A New Model for Reading a Textbook : Reading in Reverse

IN PRACTICE

Reverse the order of the reading, as illustrated in Figure 9.4. Step 1 is application: Relate the reading to real-life experiences or do something concrete to make it meaningful. Ideas to help you can often be found by looking at the application and extension sections at the end of the text chapter or in your teacher guide.

In Step 2, use discussion to introduce the topic and key concepts. This is the time to use the new vocabulary that will appear in the reading. Hearing new words spoken in authentic contexts (using the Pair–Define–Explain routine described in Strategy 56) prepares students for understanding when they encounter them in their written form.

Step 3 involves reading the summary and questions at the end of the chapter to focus student attention on "the big picture"—the main ideas and purpose of the reading. This is also the time to focus on the textbook aids. Preview the subheadings as a guide to the chapter's organization and the pictures and graphics for information.

In Step 4, students do the actual reading. At this point you return to the traditional model, following the reading sequentially with questions, class discussion, and real-life application. The strategy of reverse reading supports students' efforts and facilitates their comprehension of concepts as they read the textbook.

To demonstrate how this works with an actual reading, look now at the short reading "Nomads" in Figure 9.5.

As you read, think about the four-step process by focusing on these questions:

1. How would you introduce the topic of nomads? How would you relate this material to concrete, real-life experiences?
2. How would you apply these ideas to a class discussion of nomads?
3. How would you preview the reading?
4. How would you go about the reading itself?

Figure 9.6 offers ideas for each of the pre-reading steps. How do they compare with yours?

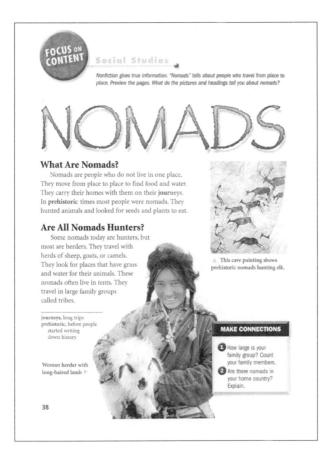

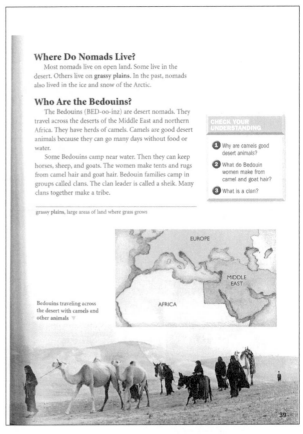

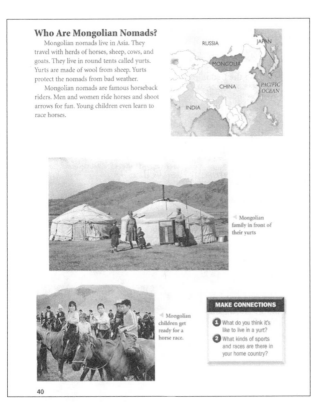

Figure 9.5   "Nomads," excerpted from *Shining Star*, Introductory Level.

Source: Excerpt pp. 38–41 from SHINING STAR Introductory Level by Kaye Wiley. Copyright © 2004 by Pearson Education, Inc. Reprinted by permission.

Step 1. Apply to real life.

Talk about:

- personal experience with moving.
- immigration experiences.
- experiences with frequent moves to seek employment, other reasons.
- migrant worker experiences.

Step 2. Discuss in class.

Talk about the following:

- Is moving from place to place "fun?" Why/why not?
- Does it feel different if the move is voluntary or forced?
- Compare leaving school, friends, and family behind to taking it all with you. (This is the time to introduce the word and the concept of *nomads*.)
- Look at pictures in the text to compare differences among nomad homes and students' homes.

Step 3. Read the questions—and the section and subsection headers.

Ask the following:

- What is this section about?
- What information will this section focus on?
- What is the main idea of this section?

Step 4. Read the text.

- Read one section at a time.
- Follow each section reading by discussing the questions in Step 3.

Figure 9.6   Reading "Nomads" in Reverse

STRATEGY 62   READ TEXT IN SMALL SEGMENTS AND HIGHLIGHT MAIN IDEAS

IN CONCEPT

Today's textbooks are impressive in the amount of information they present, as well as in their size and weight. It is quite likely that, for students, they are intimidating. Students need strategies to break long text passages into smaller learnable segments. Techniques to do this can be used individually or in combination with each other and with reverse reading.

IN PRACTICE

Technique I

T-Notes, shown in Figure 9.7, are really a simplified form of an outline that ELLs can use as a reference while they are reading. The left column represents a main idea, and the right column lists supporting details and/or examples. You can ask for volunteers among your more advanced students to make and share sets of T-Notes. Everyone benefits from this technique: The ELLs have a clear outline to guide their reading, and the volunteers get extra credit while reinforcing their own understandings.

Figure 9.8 shows T-Notes for the first sections of the "Nomads" reading. For ELLs, the task of comprehending these concepts is facilitated by following the organized presentation and concise language of the outline as they read.

Figure 9.7 T-Note Format

Main Ideas	Details/Examples
1. _____	1. _____ 2. _____ 3. _____
2. _____	1. _____ 2. _____ 3. _____
3. _____	1. _____ 2. _____ 3. _____

The T-Note format is user-friendly, easy to learn, and readily adaptable to multiple tasks. Figure 9.9 uses this format to outline a segment on water quality from the textbook *Focus on Earth Science* (Pearson Prentice Hall, 2001, pp. 333–336).

T-Notes serve as a reference and aid to learning not only during the reading process but also later as a review. Students can use them individually, in pairs, or in small groups to study for exams. T-Notes are a powerful strategy that helps to streamline the reading and learning process for ELLs and perhaps for other students in your classes.

Technique II

Learning logs are structured content journals based on reading assignments from the text-book. Students use them while they are attempting to complete assigned pages. Figure 9.10 shows two variations of a format for learning logs. The positive phrasing of the last columns—phrases such as "Questions I Have," "Things I Want to Know," and "Clueless"—are more student friendly and less self-stigmatizing than the more traditional "What I Didn't Understand."

Figure 9.8 T-Notes for Reading: "Nomads"

Main Ideas	Details/Examples
1. Nomads are groups of people who . . .	1. move from place to place. 2. take homes with them. 3. move to find food and water.
2. Nomads are hunters or herders . . .	1. now most are herders. 2. travel with sheep, goats, camels. 3. look for grass and water for the animals. 4. travel in large family groups (tribes).
3. Nomads are people who live . . .	1. in the desert. 2. on grassy plains. 3. in ice and snow (long ago).
4. Bedouins are . . .	1. desert nomads. 2. travel across the Middle Last and northern Africa deserts. 3. herd camels. 4. family groups called clans. 5. sheik is leader of clan. 6. many clans make a tribe.

Main Ideas	Details/Examples
1. Appearance and taste	1. cloudiness 2. odor 3. color 4. minerals and chemicals
2. Acidity	1. measured in pH—0 to 14 2. pure water is neutral—pH of 7 3. lower pH = more acid 4. higher pH = more base
3. Hardness	1. based on 2 minerals—calcium and magnesium 2. hard water doesn't make suds 3. deposits from hard water clog water pipes and machines
4. Disease-causing agents	1. contamination from E. coli bacteria 2. comes from human and animal wastes
5. Standards of quality	1. set by the EPA 2. standards set concentration limits 3 concentration = amount of 1 substance in a certain amount of another substance 4. example: alphabet soup—number of letters per liter of soup

Figure 9.9 T-Notes for Science: Factors Affecting Water Quality

Text Pages	What I Understood	New or Difficult Vocabulary	Questions I Want to Know

Text Pages	I Get It	I Think I Get It	I Don't Have a Clue

Figure 9.10 Two Formats for Learning Logs

Because of the way that learning logs are structured, it is important to set aside a few minutes of class time to address the issues, questions, or difficulties that the students have noted in their logs. Students can meet in small groups to discuss their entries. They can help each other by exchanging understandings, answering each other's questions, and clarifying vocabulary. Encourage their independence, but offer your support as needed. Students should note in their logs the new understandings that result from these discussions.

Learning logs give language learners another way to become engaged in the process of negotiating knowledge and increasing their understanding of the text. The entries in students' learning logs also provide an excellent source of information for ongoing or summary review of the material. They can also serve teachers as an additional source of input for student assessment.

Learning logs, like T-Notes, are highly adaptable and can be used by students for a range of activities that go beyond text readings. In science, for example, the first column could be adapted for use with in-class experiments or demonstrations. In math, learning logs may be useful during lessons in which new concepts or applications are presented. In literature, learning logs can record characters as they are introduced or reactions to plot developments. In all subject areas, learning logs can be used when videos or other media are used to contextualize or enrich understandings. The uses of learning logs are limited only by the imagination and creativity of the teacher.

Technique III

Grouping students heterogeneously to discuss a text is another effective means to help ELLs understand main ideas and important concepts. (Rules for successful group work are addressed in Strategy 72 in Chapter 10.) The benefits of small group discussion of text are many.

Group work facilitates reading comprehension because the give and take of peer discussion embed the written words in context. ELLs—actually, *all* students—have the opportunity to clarify difficult or confusing concepts as they negotiate meaning. Working in groups lowers students' affective filters, allowing more learning to occur. Group discussion supports ELLs' language development by providing an authentic context to hear and use new vocabulary, and it readies students to participate in class discussion.

Technique IV

It has been well established that reading comprehension and retention rise when readers simultaneously see and hear information. Closed-captioned video has proven an effective technique for developing reading skills both for nonnative speakers and for preliterate native-speaking adults (Bean & Wilson, 1989; Goldman & Goldman, 1988; Neuman & Koskinen, 1992). Interestingly, one way that a good reader attempts to comprehend a difficult text is by reading the passage aloud. Hearing the printed words, even when reading them to yourself, assists in producing meaning.

ELLs also benefit from seeing and hearing text in other ways. They learn pronunciation of unfamiliar words. They may make new associations of words in their oral and written forms, words that they may know in spoken form but may not recognize in writing because they are spelled so differently from the way they are pronounced, like those in Figure 6.6 in Chapter 6. A final advantage concerns *homophones,* words that are pronounced the same but are spelled differently and have different meanings—*there, their,* and *they're,* for example—and homographs, words that are spelled the same but pronounced differently and have different meanings, as in *wind, lead,* and *bow.* Simultaneously seeing and hearing words like these in context may help students to understand and retain meanings and usages.

Again for extra credit, students in your class can read into a tape recorder entire chapters or important segments of the textbook. The bonus here again is that the readers are reinforcing their own learning while helping others (and helping themselves, too, with extra credit). Language learners can listen to the tape while reading the text, at home if possible or, if not, in school. Using this multimedia approach facilitates comprehension and offers ELLs greater access to important content concepts.

WORKING WITH YOUR TEXTBOOK

The Objective: Help Students to Become Competent Note Takers.

The Rationale

Few students are offered direct instruction in how to take notes. It is a skill students simply acquire and refine during their academic years. In today's educational environment, note-taking skills, like learning strategies, must become a part of classroom instruction. Like learning strategies, they are an essential key to academic success.

STRATEGY 63   TEACH NOTE-TAKING SKILLS

IN CONCEPT

As students advance through the grades, the importance of taking good notes intensifies. Students must take notes in an increasingly efficient and automatic manner. ELLs, in particular, need formats and techniques that put the most information into the fewest number of words. Explicit instruction in note-taking skills will help students become good note takers.

IN PRACTICE

Technique I

T-Notes are a useful format for teaching students the basics of note-taking skills. Prepare a set of T-Notes in which main ideas have already been listed in the left column as shown in Figure 9.11. Give your students an in-class or home assignment of completing the

Main Ideas	Details/Examples
1. Nomads are groups of people who	1. move from place to place 2. _____ 3. _____
2. Nomads are hunters or herders . . .	1. _____ 2. _____ 3. _____ 4. _____
3. Nomads are people who live (where?)	1. in the desert 2. _____ 3. _____
4. Bedouins	1. are _____ 2. travel _____ 3. herd _____ 4. _____ 5. _____ 6. _____

Figure 9.11   Use T-Notes to Teach Note-Taking skills

Details/Examples column. Students who are new to the use of T-Notes or those with low-level note-taking skills will benefit from seeing one or two items included in the Details/Examples column as a model of the type of information to look for. Once learned, T-Notes are an ideal format to record information from class instruction and text readings.

T-Notes can also be used to teach the concept of getting the main idea. In this instance, students' T-Notes show items in the Details column, and students must find the main idea that the details represent.

Technique II

Graphic organizers (discussed at length in Chapter 10) are an excellent device for note-taking because they visually convey large amounts of information in the fewest number of words. ELLs can use a web (see Figure 10.12 in Chapter 10) or a matrix (see Figure 10.18) to record the main ideas and supporting details of a reading. Other graphics that work well for note taking are graphs, charts, maps, diagrams, timelines, and sequenced pictures, all illustrated in Chapter 10.

Technique III

Early in the school year, try teaching a lesson with the combined objectives of finding important information and taking notes. Start by photocopying a section of several pages from the students' textbook. Distribute the passage in class and read it with the students, section by section.

Start by asking the students to read only the first subsection. When students have finished their individual reading, re-read it aloud to them, stopping to explain your reasoning about what is important: how you recognize the details from the main ideas. Be sure to explain the *why* and *why not* behind your thinking.

As you finish discussing each subsection, show students how to highlight key words, phrases, and sentences from the photocopied passage with a highlighter pen. Repeat this read–discuss–highlight procedure with each successive subsection, encouraging greater student input as the lesson continues.

The next step in effective note taking is to teach students to condense the highlighted segments into a set of notes. Depending on the type of information, students can use T-Notes or any appropriate graphic. Model the wording of the notes you would make from the highlighted segments of the first subsection, demonstrating which words and phrases to omit or shorten. Be sure students understand the concept of *condensing:* Effective note takers do not copy each phrase or sentence from the text in its entirety.

Teach students that using abbreviations is another element of effective note taking. Explain to students the art of abbreviating commonly used words—*because, therefore, leading to, compared to*, for example. You can create a class set of abbreviations, and can encourage students to create their own—a practice they may not know is acceptable.

WORKING WITH YOUR TEXTBOOK

The Objective: Use Alternative Resources for True ELL Beginners.

The Rationale

Teachers often ask what to do in class with the true ELL beginner. How can a grade-level textbook be used by a newcomer who has just begun to learn English? The answer is as obvious as it is unsatisfying: An ELL at the earliest stage of language development cannot successfully use a grade-level textbook. Some approaches, however, may help students gain *some* knowledge of content while they are developing their English language skills.

STRATEGY 64 PAIR ELL BEGINNERS WITH VOLUNTEER BUDDIES

IN CONCEPT

In almost every class, certain students are the *nurturers*. These students can often be enlisted to work one on one with ELL beginners in a volunteer buddy system, a win–win situation for both sides. Beginners appreciate the help and support of a peer, and nurturers feel gratified and satisfied.

IN PRACTICE

Volunteer buddies can work together to use some of the strategies presented in previous sections of this chapter. A good place to start is with some of the less linguistically demanding textbook aids. Volunteer buddies can help as ELL beginners focus on getting information from charts, tables, diagrams, maps, pictures, and other illustrations. Buddies can also assist with vocabulary development by discussing cognates in the language detective activity, locating and explaining synonyms and idioms, and prompting generous use of personal and bilingual dictionaries. Most of all, volunteer buddies can offer support, encouragement, and perhaps even friendship.

You may think the buddy system would be most valuable if the buddy is one who is bilingual in English and the beginner's native language, or at least one at a more advanced level of English language development. While this type of pairing can be highly beneficial, it can also be fraught with risk by encouraging overtranslation of concepts and information from the readings. It may place an undue burden on the buddy and lead to the beginner's dependence on the translation and the translator. It can sometimes even slow the language learner's development of English reading skills. In reality, any willing student can offer enough help and support to make a difference.

STRATEGY 65 IN A PINCH, USE ALTERNATIVE TEXTBOOKS

IN CONCEPT

An approach of last resort for students at beginning levels of English language development is to obtain an alternate textbook for them as a supplement to your regular classroom textbook. If your school or district has no objection, you might consider using a text that is written either at a lower reading level or in the students' native languages. While this strategy may offer a small short-term advantage, it has a greater number of both short- and long-term disadvantages.

IN PRACTICE

Using an alternative textbook is stigmatizing, especially one written at a lower level. It sends a subtle, unintended message that those who use it are less capable than the others in the class. Using a native-language textbook may violate state laws concerning classroom use of a language other than English. Even if no legal issues are involved, students using native-language textbooks may become dependent on them to the point of not wanting to make any attempts at using the regular classroom text. Much like using a translator, it may ultimately impede the development of English language skills.

The use of native-language textbooks presents an additional difficulty. Your beginning ELLs may be from several language backgrounds. It is improbable that you could find suitable textbooks in each of the languages spoken by the beginners in your classroom. Is it fair to find native language textbooks only for some?

Despite the disadvantages of using alternative textbooks, however, it is important to note that—in some instances—native language resources can mean the difference between learning some content and learning none for ELLs, particularly for those entering U.S. schools in the middle of a school year and/or at the secondary school level.

There is no magic formula to help the true ELL beginners in your content class. These strategies are probably the best you can use for a while because, at the very least, they allow the student to learn some content and they show that you care.

IN SUMMARY: WORKING WITH YOUR TEXTBOOK

Reading the textbook is a daunting task for many students, ELLs and native speakers alike. Students arrive in your classes with differing levels of reading and language ability and differing sets of reading and literacy skills. They need a variety of strategies that show them how to interact with the text to derive meaning—techniques that embed written words in context and focus thinking on main ideas and supporting details. You can ease the challenge for your students by using the strategies in this chapter to scaffold their content learning as they learn English.

QUESTIONS FOR DISCUSSION

1. How do the strategies for working with your textbook reflect the *Guidelines for Practice* presented at the beginning of this chapter?
2. Examine the textbooks you use in your classes to see which textbooks aids they contain. Plan a lesson to teach students how these aids can facilitate comprehension. How can you determine if students are already using these aids?
3. Using a textbook with which you are *not* familiar, examine a chapter following the steps in Figure 9.1. How successful do you believe you were in getting the gist of the chapter?
4. Read the "Nomads" passage again, this time focusing on the types of problematic vocabulary discussed in Chapter 8. Look for words and phrases that might cause confusion: synonyms, idioms, and familiar words used in new ways.
5. Plan a Reading in Reverse lesson to introduce a reading or a new topic from a textbook. Select a reading or topic and follow the three preliminary steps to reading. Explain the reasoning behind your choices. Work individually if you are now teaching a class, or in pairs if you are not.

REFERENCES AND RESOURCES

Bean, R. M., & Wilson, R. M. (1989). Using closed-captioned television to teach reading to adults. *Reading Research Instruction, 28*(4),27–37.

Bortz, A., Padilla, M. J., Miaoulis, I., & Cyr, M. (2001). *Focus on earth science: Prentice Hall science explorer; California edition.* Upper Saddle River, NJ: Pearson Prentice Hall.

Daniels, H., & Semelman, S. (2004). *Every teacher's guide to content-area reading.* Portsmouth, NH: Heinemann.

Dornan, R., Rosen, L. M., & Wilson, M. (2005). Lesson designs for reading comprehension and vocabulary development. In P. A. Richard-Amato, M. A. & Snow (Eds.), *Academic success for English language learners: Strategies for K–12 mainstream teachers* (pp. 248–274). White Plains, NY: Pearson Education.

Echavarria, J., Vogt, M., & Short, D. J. (2000). *Making content comprehensible for English language learners: The SIOP model.* Needham Heights, MA: Allyn & Bacon.

Goldman, M., & Goldman, S. (1988). Reading with closed captioned TV. *Journal of Reading, 31*(5), 458.

National Captioning Institute (2003). *Using captioned television in reading and literacy instruction.* Retrieved March 20, 2006, from *http://www.ncicap.org/classroom.asp.*

Neuman, S., & Koskinen, P. (1992). Captioned television as comprehensible input: Effects of incidental word learning from context for language minority students. *Reading Research Quarterly, 27*(1), 95–106.

Peregoy, S. F., & Boyle, O. F. (2001). *Reading, writing, and learning in ESL: A resource book for K–12 teachers* (pp. 257–411). New York: Addison Wesley Longman.

The TechConnection

www.ncela.gwu.edu/practice/itc

The "In the Classroom" section of the National Clearinghouse for English Language Acquisition brings research and practice together for teachers of culturally and linguistically diverse learners, offering teaching tools and strategies that reflect principles of effective practice.

CHAPTER 10

REINFORCING LEARNING: ACTIVITIES AND ASSIGNMENTS

THEORY TO APPLICATION: GUIDELINES FOR PRACTICE

- Use scaffolding strategies to challenge ELLs to advance beyond their present state of independent activity, into the areas of potential learning in which content is learnable with the assistance of teachers and peers.
- Use scaffolding strategies that embed the oral and written language of content material in a context-rich environment to facilitate learning for ELLs.
- Use scaffolding strategies that maintain a high level of cognitive challenge, but lower the language demand by embedding it in context.
- Provide opportunities for ELLs to negotiate conceptual understandings and to explore language usage through classroom interaction.
- Lower learner anxiety in the classroom to create students who are more willing to participate in class, to become risk takers in the learning process, and ultimately to become more successful learners.
- Provide opportunities for students to experience success in the classroom: Success in learning promotes more success by increasing learner motivation, interest, and self-confidence.

After the lesson is taught and the textbook is read, teachers assign in-class and at-home activities to reinforce and extend learning. For ELLs, these activities may present a challenge. For teachers, planning activities that are cognitively complex but linguistically simplified may present an equal challenge. Content teachers must look beyond the traditional activity types—question and answer, research reports, oral presentations—to strategies that engage ELL students in alternative means and products. The goal is to build rich conceptual understanding of content while keeping the language input and output as streamlined as possible.

ASSIGNMENTS TO PROMOTE STUDENT SUCCESS

The Objective: Good Assignments Begin with Good Directions.

The Rationale

Have you ever been a student in a class where you've been given directions that you didn't understand? You sat there with a growing sense of anxiety because you had absolutely no idea what to do. You looked around—had others already started working? Are you the only one who didn't get it? Perhaps you quietly asked several of your peers if they knew what you were supposed to do, only to discover that they didn't know either. By now you are all feeling considerably less capable than you felt just a few minutes ago. Anxiety is never a good way to begin an assignment.

STRATEGY 66   GIVE CLEAR DIRECTIONS

IN CONCEPT

Successful activities begin with clear directions. Students need to approach each assignment with a complete understanding of process and product. When you follow the simple, five-step plan summarized in Figure 10.1, you can be sure that your instructions will always be clearly understood by all your students.

IN PRACTICE

1. *Say* the directions. Explain them as explicitly as you possibly can. State what you want students to do in a simple, step-by-step manner. If the directions are complex, use the "one-step" approach: Tell students that after they complete the first step, you'll tell them what they'll be doing next.

2. *Write* the directions on the board, on chart paper, or on an overhead transparency. Written words reinforce spoken language and help language learners process what they are being asked to do. Keep the written directions on view so students can refer to them as needed during the assignment.

3. *Model* the process and the product. Demonstrate how to begin, and explain the choices you make to reach the final product. Show students what a finished product should look like. Show several possibilities of product if there will be variations. You may also want to show examples of excellent, acceptable, and poor products. Adding this visual element to your directions is essential for your ELLs because it shortcuts your need for wordy explanation. It also gives all students a clear understanding of your expectations.

4. *Check* comprehension by asking the students to repeat, step by step, what they are expected to do. Start by asking "So, what's the first thing we're going to do?" Go through each step of the activity, adding detail or correcting as needed. Point to each step of the written directions as students review them orally.

It is important for the students themselves to explain each of the steps they are going to take to complete the project. After all, they are the ones who will be doing the activity.

Figure 10.1   Clear Directions in Five
Steps

> 1. *Say* the directions clearly.
> 2. *Write* them and leave them on view.
> 3. *Model* the process and the product.
> 4. *Check* comprehension.
> 5. *Ask* for questions.

5. *Ask* for questions. "Question time. Who's got a question for me?" Most likely they'll have none.

Clear directions start students out right. Using the five-step approach allows students to focus immediately and confidently on the work to be done—no lost time, no unnecessary anxiety. Students benefit from hearing detailed directions before every assignment, including homework. Good instructions give students the best chance of producing a satisfying result.

ASSIGNMENTS TO PROMOTE STUDENT SUCCESS

The Objective: Modify Whole Class Assignments to Make Language Comprehensible.

The Rationale

ELLs will be able to demonstrate that they understand content when the output required for the assignment matches their level of English language development. Modifying ELLs' assignments by lowering language demand does not mean that you are lowering your expectations.

Modifying assignments recognizes the difficulties that ELLs face in developing English language competency at the same time they are attempting to learn content in English. The types of modifications you choose should consistently challenge your ELLs with incrementally complex language. The strategies that follow are widely adaptable and can be applied to many homework tasks and in-class activities.

 STRATEGY 67   OFFER A WORD BANK

IN CONCEPT

For assignments that require simple, short answers to a series of questions, consider using a word bank, especially with students who are in the early stages of English language development. Word banks are lists of content-related word or phrase choices. To correctly answer the assigned questions, students select items from the list. Including at least three extra words or phrases that relate closely to the topic encourages thoughtful consideration of answer choices and promotes critical thinking.

IN PRACTICE

Word banks work well with many straightforward questions used to check comprehension after textbook readings. They are also well suited to assignments that ask students to label, for example, parts of a diagram in science, such as that of the eye in Figure 10.2, or specific items on maps in social studies.

Word banks can be used as an additional support in combination with many of the following strategies. They allow ELLs to focus their attention on content by lowering the language demand.

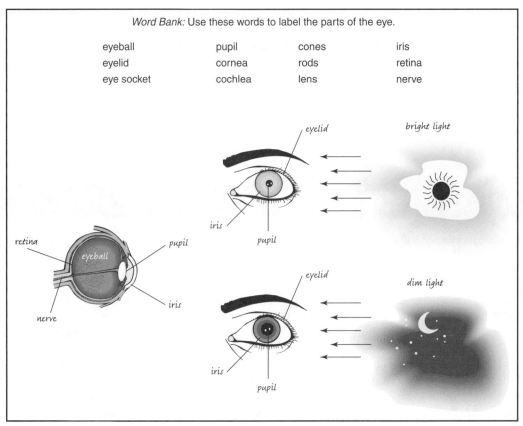

Figure 10.2   Diagram of the Eye

STRATEGY 68   ASSIGN FEWER QUESTIONS

IN CONCEPT

Textbook chapters usually have a set of summary questions to check comprehension and to encourage students to think critically about the topic. An assignment that seems reasonable for your native English-speaking students may feel overwhelming to your ELLs. They will be able to respond better if you assign fewer questions, focusing on those that are either more conceptually important or less linguistically complex.

IN PRACTICE

Technique I

Textbook comprehension questions are written to check students' understanding of broad concepts and specific facts. Some questions are conceptually more central to the topic than others. By assigning only the more important questions, especially in combination with one or more other strategies presented in this chapter, your ELLs can focus their efforts on those that are most critical to their understanding.

Technique II

The second approach is to select questions that are linguistically easier to complete. Questions vary in the amount and type of information required to answer them. Some questions can be answered adequately with a single word or short phrase while others require much longer, more linguistically complex responses. Again, especially for students in early stages of English language development, consider requiring written responses to only those questions that are linguistically simple to answer (perhaps even in combination with a word bank) and use one of the alternative assignments described later in this chapter for questions involving a longer, more complicated written answer.

STRATEGY 69   ALLOT EXTRA TIME

IN CONCEPT

Every assignment is twofold for ELLs: They must first decode the language and then deliver the content. They clearly need more time to get their work done.

IN PRACTICE

With this extra burden in mind, allow additional time for ELLs to complete readings and assignments. Remember that they are learning English at the same time that they are learning *in* English. More time makes content more learnable for them.

STRATEGY 70   SEPARATE CONTENT FROM LANGUAGE

IN CONCEPT

While you probably require the use of good grammar and complete sentences as a normal part of your regular assignments, remember that if your ELLs could write that way, they wouldn't be classified as ELLs. Separating content from language allows teachers to make more effective assessments of ELLs' understanding of content.

IN PRACTICE

Evaluate student assignments for accuracy of content information only. Look for key content words or phrases that signify some grasp of the topic under study and give credit for those. Accept grammar and spelling errors as long as the content is correct. Look for the positive—even by trying to pronounce an unreadable word phonetically to see if you can bring meaning to it. Using a simple rubric, such as the one discussed in Chapter 11 (see Strategy 88), helps keep the focus on content. It's important to think about the *message* being sent, not about the *means* by which it is being sent.

STRATEGY 71   OFFER MODELS AND OUTLINES

IN CONCEPT

Many written assignments follow a relatively standardized type of paragraph structure. For these, consider giving the ELLs a model, an outline, or a preformatted page to follow. This strategy also appeals to native English-speaking students who find written work, in general,

- Describe the process by which _____ causes _____.
- Describe the factors that affect _____.
- Describe the characteristics of _____.
- Describe how _____ (changes) (uses) _____.
- Describe conditions that cause _____.
- Describe how _____ form _____.
- Name and describe (two) kinds of _____.
- List factors that affect _____.
- List and explain the main types of _____.
- Identify and explain the effects of _____.
- Explain why _____ is important to _____.
- Give examples of how _____ uses _____.

Figure 10.3   Typical Writing Assignments that Can Be Modeled

a challenge. Students—English speakers and learners alike—often feel more able to tackle an assignment when they don't have to begin with a completely blank page.

IN PRACTICE

Think about the kinds of written assignments you give. Most assignments ask students to classify, identify, list, explain, describe, predict, and compare and contrast in language much like that in Figure 10.3. For tasks such as these, student responses follow a basic pattern that can be modeled to lighten the linguistic burden. Figures 10.4 and 10.5 illustrate response models for questions in science and social studies, respectively.

Many types of written assignments lend themselves to modeled formatting. In science classes, for example, students often are required to write up experiments, demonstrations, or activities done in class. Figure 10.6 shows a format that students can use for this purpose. When the language and pattern of reports like these are prestructured, ELLs can concentrate on cognitively processing the content required for the response instead of first having to focus on creating the language to convey that content. Of equal importance, repeated exposure to formatted patterns teaches ELLs how to formulate appropriate responses when this scaffolding strategy is removed.

Figure 10.4   Modeled Response to a Comprehension Question: An Example from Earth Science

Question

Name and define the three major types of interactions among organisms.

Modeled Response

The first type of interaction is called _____.
This means _____.

The second type of interaction is called _____.
This means _____.

The third type of interaction is called _____.
This means _____.

Figure 10.5   Modeled Response to a Comprehension Question: An Example from Social Studies

Question

What was the goal of the Open Door Policy in China? Did it succeed?

Modeled Response

The goal of the Open Door Policy in China was to _____

_____. It (was, was not)

successful because _____

_____.

Name of Experiment: _____

We wanted to show that _____

_____.

We used (materials) _____, _____, _____

_____, _____, _____, _____.

The first thing we did was _____

_____.

The second thing we did was _____

_____.

The third thing we did was _____

_____.

What happened was _____

_____.

This happened because _____

_____.

This shows that _____

_____.

Figure 10.6   Model for Write-up of Science Demonstration

STRATEGY 72   DO MORE SMALL GROUP WORK

IN CONCEPT

ELLs can often do assignments in pairs or small groups that they would be unable to do individually. Group work is beneficial for many reasons.

Working in pairs or groups of three to four students promotes concept acquisition through social interaction. Small groups create a natural setting that encourages the negotiation of meaning in a nonthreatening environment. For ELLs especially, small groups offer the opportunity to use academic language in a meaningful way. ELLs can explore new vocabulary, attempt oral communication, and clarify knowledge through the exchange of information, examples, and comparisons with native English-speaking peers. Many students learn better by negotiating meaning with peers within the safety of small groups.

Figure 10.7 Rules for Successful Group work

> 1. Select an appropriate task.
> 2. Establish ground rules for group work.
> 3. Group students heterogeneously.
> 4. Give clear directions.
> 5. Announce a time frame for completion.
> 6. Monitor the groups as they work.
> 7. End with a whole-class sharing.

Partners or buddies act as resources for each other by enhancing each other's understanding. ELLs can work together to produce a pair product while other students work individually. Students may be able to accomplish together an assignment that neither could complete alone. Think of it as an equation: *1 + 1 > 2*.

IN PRACTICE

Many teachers are reluctant to engage in frequent group work because they worry about loss of control. Following the set of basic rules in Figure 10.7 will maximize your chances for successful shared activities in your classroom.

1. Good group work starts with *selecting an appropriate task*. And what exactly is an appropriate task? It is one in which students must work together because each student in the group has only *part* of the information needed to reach the final product. Students must interact in a cooperative manner to figure out how to make all the pieces work together as a whole.

A good way to understand the concept of *appropriate task* is to examine a task that is definitely *not* appropriate. In this example of an unsuccessful group experience, the teacher tells the students that they are going to work in groups to review material from a content reading. Each student in the group gets a copy of a worksheet with five questions on it, along with directions to work together to answer the questions.

After several minutes of silence, one student asks the others in the group, "So what did you put for Question 1?"

As one student offers an answer, the others quickly write it down. Done this way, the task itself necessitates no negotiation of meaning, no communication or cooperation, no need to exchange any information. This is not group work; it is simply an individual task with students sitting in a group.

In good group work, students must rely on other group members' input and information to complete the task. Such tasks are challenging, creative, interesting, and widely adaptable for use in content classrooms.

Figure 10.8 illustrates an example of an appropriate task to review content information, about forest biomes in this instance. Students in each group receive individual envelopes containing information printed on slips of paper. In this type of group review, students work together to categorize items based on qualities or characteristics, arrange items sequentially, or classify items by types and subtypes.

Group tasks can also promote critical thinking, as shown in Figure 10.9. For this type of task, students use the items in their envelopes to make groupings based on as many different sets of similarities as they can think of. One student lists the groupings on paper so that items can be reused. During class discussion, students share lists and explain the basis for each set of groupings.

2. Good group work follows *a set of class rules* that have been generated through class discussion before the first group work session takes place. Students can be directed to offer

Students sit in groups of three. Each student receives an envelope containing slips of papers with details about forest biomes. Together they work to sort them into their appropriate categories.

Group A
Student 1

Coniferous Forests

Location: temperate zone

Poor acidic soil

Examples: spruce, cedar

Trees shed leaves seasonally.

Examples: hickory, ash

Trees have buttressed trunks.

Located in climates with four different seasons

Examples: teak, mahogany

Group A
Student 2

Deciduous Forests

Trees produce cones.

Examples: maple, oak

Thin, nutrient-poor soil

Trees have shallow root systems.

Location: tropical zone

Biome with the greatest diversity

Examples: cypress, balsa

Group A
Student 3

Rain Forests

Examples: fir, hemlock

Location: subarctic regions

Trees have needles.

Examples: beech, birch

Triangular-shaped trees

Rich, fertile soil

Trees produce seeds.

Figure 10.8   Group Task: Review the Characteristics of Forest Biomes

Directions: Classify these animals into different groups based on common features or behaviors. How many different classifications can your group think of? Keep a list of the animals in each grouping, and specify what they have in common. Then reuse the animals to make another grouping.

The group receives this envelope:

Group A

ape   dog   rabbit
mouse   cat   whale
mole   zebra   horse
giraffe   anteater   goat
monkey   kangaroo
koala   elephant
human being

Figure 10.9   Group Task: Stretch Your Thinking to Classify These Mammals

rules that include these, among others: (1) Stay in your seat. (2) Use conversational voices. (3) Disagree politely. (4) Stay on task.

Rules should be displayed prominently and permanently for teachers to direct students' attention to if needed during group sessions. Some strange quirk of human nature makes students less likely to argue with the statement "You're not following rule number two about using conversational voices" than with the perceived accusation "Your voices are way too loud."

3. Divide the class into *heterogeneous groupings*. All groups should reflect the general mix in your classroom. Each group should include diversity of gender, ability, language, and ethnicity. ELLs extend their zone of proximal development (see Chapter 1) by working with more advanced peers, who themselves have the opportunity to reinforce and extend their own understandings.

4. Introduce the topic and task, and give *explicit directions*. Follow up with a *clarification check* to make sure students know exactly what to do. Use the five-step approach outlined in Strategy 68 in this chapter.

5. Give students a *time frame* for completing the task. People of all ages seem to focus better under the pressure of a deadline. Allocate the minimum amount of time you think the task will take, and announce frequently how many minutes remain to complete the work. If students groan about not being able to finish, you can always extend the time as needed.

6. *Monitor the task* by walking around the room as students work. Many students are more willing to seek clarification from their teachers in the security of small group settings. Consider this your golden opportunity to answer student questions and offer individual help.

7. Bring *closure* to group work through whole class sharing. Even if the group work is ongoing, students should report how the session went and where their groups are now. This rewards students' natural curiosity to see the progress and products of the other groups.

If you'd like to do more group work in your classroom, follow these rules and start small. Start with paired assignments, such as grouping students to discuss answers to homework questions during the first few minutes of class, and build up to big group projects over time. You'll see that even small group activities bring big results.

 ## STRATEGY 73   TRY PEER TUTORING

IN CONCEPT

ELLs can often complete an assignment with a little individualized assistance, and in every class certain students enjoy the role of peer tutor or peer coach. Peer tutoring pairs willing students with ELLs who can use a little extra help on an as-needed basis.

Peer tutoring—and group work in general—promotes language development, concept acquisition, and cognitive growth. It offers an opportunity for students to use academic language in a meaningful way in an authentic situation. It allows exchange of questions and clarification of knowledge in a lowered risk environment. It personalizes and adds a social element to learning and instruction. It can change students' attitudes toward content and to school in general. It ultimately raises students' feelings of self-confidence. In pair and small group work, one plus one really does add up to more than two.

IN PRACTICE

Peer tutoring helps in your classroom in several ways. First, pairing ELLs (and other students, too) who need extra help with peer coaches gives ELLs an opportunity for personalized attention from a more advanced student who is not the teacher.

Second, this strategy may also offer a rewarding solution for students who consistently complete individual assignments early and wait for others in the class to finish. Explaining concepts to others clarifies and expands tutors' conceptual knowledge and acts as a strong aid to retention.

A final benefit of peer tutoring is that you, the teacher, benefit from your small cadre of assistants who give you more flexibility to monitor all your students' understanding and progress.

ASSIGNMENTS TO PROMOTE STUDENT SUCCESS

The Objective: Develop Alternative Assignments.

The Rationale

Academic assignments must promote cognitive challenge. To meet the needs of ELLs' linguistic and conceptual development, teachers need to offer parallel, alternative assignments.

Alternative assignments engage ELLs in activities that maintain a high level of cognitive challenge and, at the same time, lower language demand. These assignments should be viewed as stepping stones on the path toward academic success in an English language environment. The goal is to move ELLs toward full participation in the mainstream assessments required of all students.

STRATEGY 74   USE DIAGRAMS, MAPS, AND CHARTS AS ASSIGNMENTS

IN CONCEPT

Students are often required to engage in factual descriptive content writing. ELLs can convey much of the same information alternatively through graphic or visual means.

IN PRACTICE

ELLs can label a diagram, map, chart, or drawing in place of expository writing. In subsequent assignments, they can add supplementary information in the form of more detailed descriptive words and explanatory phrases. Students can expand the drawings of the eye shown in Figure 10.2, for example, to include additional functional or descriptive data. For other types of diagrams, students can classify items by color coding or can indicate relationships among elements by adding arrows. Figure 10.10 uses separate drawings to label and explain a type of ocean movement.

STRATEGY 75   USE SEQUENCED PICTURES AS ASSIGNMENTS

IN CONCEPT

ELLs can show their understanding by drawing or arranging a set of pictures. While other students are completing an assignment in standard paragraph form, language learners can be doing the same assignment through graphics.

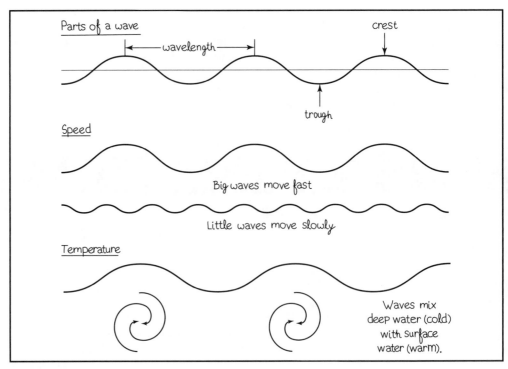

Figure 10.10 All About Waves

IN PRACTICE

Sequenced pictures can depict steps or stages, or they can be as simple as *before* and *after*. After the pictures have been drawn or arranged, students can supplement the pictures with additional appropriate information.

Look at Figure 10.11, an assignment done as a series of sequenced pictures showing the process and results of an in-class science experiment. The student who did these drawings demonstrated a clear understanding of the experiment in a way that would have been unattainable in a written report.

Students whose English language skills are at the beginner level can label parts of each picture, with or without a word bank. Students at higher levels can add descriptive and explanatory words, phrases, and sentences.

Figure 10.11 Sequence Pictures of a Science Experiment

STRATEGY 76   USE GRAPHIC ORGANIZERS AS ASSIGNMENTS

IN CONCEPT

It is likely that you make frequent use of graphic organizers as a routine part of your teaching. Now consider using them as alternative assignments for your ELLs.

Certain graphic organizers are widely adaptable, while others are more tightly structured. It is important to predetermine the most appropriate graphic format to convey the information that your other students will be expressing in written form.

Graphic organizers are interesting and easy for ELLs to work with. As an alternative assignment, they allow ELLs to convey a large amount of content information in a linguistically simplified form.

IN PRACTICE

Technique I

The graphic organizer with the widest application and greatest flexibility uses the concept of clustering or webbing, as illustrated in Figure 10.12. Students are able to give a maximum amount of information with only a minimum amount of language.

Cluster or web organizers are useful for explaining topics with multiple elements and for showing relationships among elements. Figure 10.13 uses a web to show details about the groups described in the "Nomads" passage in Chapter 9 (Figure 9.5).

Web organizers would work well in social studies, for example, to show the complex causes of World War II or factors influencing immigration to the United States in the early 1900s. In science, the web would be appropriate to categorize, classify, and describe types and subtypes of substances and structures.

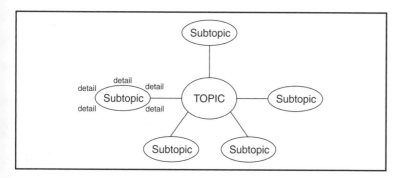

Figure 10.12 The Cluster or Web

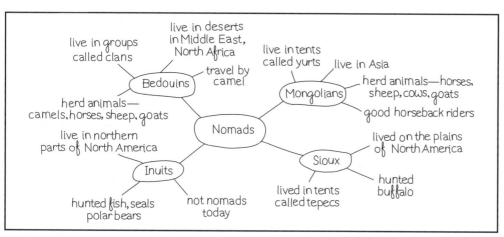

Figure 10.13 The Web in Action: Nomads

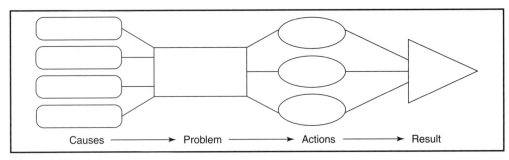

Figure 10.14   The Problem-Solving Organizer

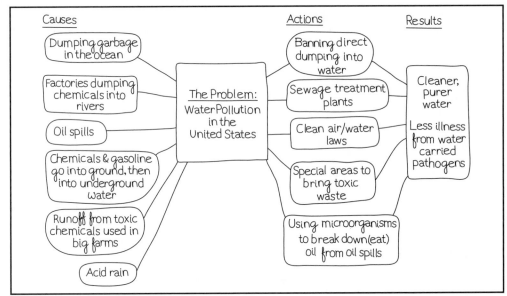

Figure 10.15   The Problem-Solving Organizer in Action: Water Pollution in the United States

Technique II

A more tightly controlled form of clustering is the problem-solving organizer, shown in Figure 10.14. It is a concept map designed to show multiple and sequential cause and effect. It is an effective graphic to explain more direct relationships and linear patterns.

The problem-solving organizer is structured around a central issue or problem. Figure 10.15 uses this format to graphically depict some causes of water pollution in the United States, the actions taken to deal with the problem, and the effects of these actions.

Language learners can use this type of organizer in science and social studies classes as an alternative to written reports on environmental and societal issues, such as those listed in Figure 10.16. The problem-solving organizer is an ideal way for students to express complex ideas and relationships in a linguistically simplified manner.

Figure 10.16   Some Topics for Using Problem-Solving Organizers in Science and Social Studies

Environmental Issues	Societal Issues
Global warming	Slavery
Air or water pollution	Reconstruction of post-Civil
Recycling	War South
Endangered species	Rise of labor unions
Depletion of tropical rain forests	The Cold War
	Terrorism

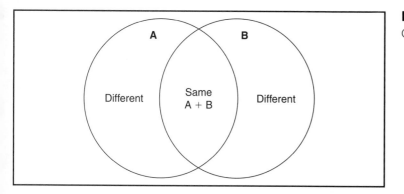

Figure 10.17 Venn Diagram Comparing Two Things

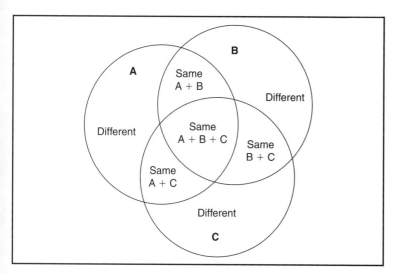

Figure 10.18 Venn Diagram Comparing Three Things

Technique III

Venn diagrams are familiar to most teachers and students. They are used to show similarities and differences among concepts, events, people, or things. Figure 10.17 illustrates the Venn diagram in its most common form, comparing and contrasting two elements. Because students seem to enjoy expressing information in this graphic format, you may want to challenge them with a triple Venn diagram, as shown in Figure 10.18. Like other graphic organizers, Venn diagrams reduce language demand to single words and short phrases and allow ELLs to focus on the content.

Technique IV

Timelines show chronological sequences and temporal relationships graphically. Timelines can be drawn to record developments over periods of time as short as seconds or as long as many millennia. They can, for example, illustrate chemical change of matter within seconds, depict historical development over a single century, or show the evolution of man over hundreds of thousands of years. The timeline in Figure 10.19 shows the year that each department in the executive branch of U.S. government was created. In subsequent assignments, students can add additional information to explain the function and focus of each department.

Students can draw *parallel timelines* to compare two or more chains of related activity over simultaneous time periods, as in a timeline representing developments in land, sea, and air transportation from 1800 to 2000. Or students can expand a segment of a timeline to add greater detail to a short period within the longer timeline. Timelines are readily adaptable and simple to create. They convey a great deal of information in very few words, which makes them a valuable combination of qualities for language learning students.

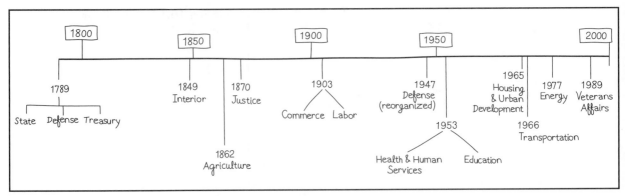

Figure 10.19 The Executive Branch: Executive Departments Timeline

Technique V

The *matrix*, as shown in Figure 10.20, is a form of attribute charting. It is a grid that visually compares key variables of a set of related items. Figure 10.21 shows a matrix that could be used in science lab to compare the characteristics and qualities of five different mineral substances. In social studies, the matrix is useful to compare, for example, the character and achievements of selected presidents, or demographic, geographic, and economic data of several countries or regions. Figure 10.22 illustrates the matrix used to graphically represent key information in the "Nomads" passage in Chapter 9 (Figure 9.5).

Qualities → Items to Compare ↓	1	2	3	4	5
A					
B					
C					
D					
E					

Figure 10.20 The Matrix

Specimen ↓	Luster	Cleavage	Hardness	Color	Other
A					
B					
C					
D					
E					

Figure 10.21   The Matrix in Science: Comparing Minerals

Information in the matrix grids can take a variety of forms. Students can fill boxes with a plus or minus sign to denote presence or absence of something, or insert a number to specify an exact amount or percentage. They can write in descriptive words or short phrases or can give specific representative names. The matrix is versatile and widely adaptable.

Nomads	Hunter/ Herder	Country/ Area	Type of Land	Animals	Tents	Other
Bedouins						
Mongolians						
Sioux						
Inuits						

Figure 10.22   The Matrix in Social Studies: Nomads

STRATEGY 77   BUILD LANGUAGE FROM GRAPHICS

IN CONCEPT

Graphic organizers and other alternative assignments are productive means for ELLs, especially those in the early stages of English language development, to show what they know. However, if ELLs do only this type of written assignment, they will make slow progress in developing the language and literacy skills they need for academic success. Language learners must move from relying on graphics to building language by developing models, outlines, or formatted sentences to take them beyond graphics.

IN PRACTICE

All graphic organizers can be formatted to build language. Figure 10.23 presents examples of formatted models that students can use to convert information from their timelines to complete sentences. Figure 10.24 does the same for Venn diagrams.

Although the complexity of the problem-solving organizer requires a bit more ingenuity to create a simple format, Figure 10.25 shows a generic model that teachers can tailor to fit specific topics. Additionally, consider using the T-Notes discussed in Strategy 63 (Figure 9.7, Chapter 9) or the formatted models or outlines discussed in Strategy 71 in this chapter (Figures 10.4 to 10.6).

Using formats as an intermediary stage helps ELLs transition to more complex written expression at the same time that it offers models of good ways to do so. With enough practice and repetition, students can move from the model to effective independent writing. At this stage, they may still need assistance with certain academic

Figure 10.23 Using Timelines to Build Language

The First Step

In _____, _____ occurred.
    year   event
        _____ was invented by _____.
    product
    _____ was born.
    person
    _____ gained independence.
    country

The Next Step

_____ began in ____ and ended in ____.
Event   year   year

The Final Step

_____ began in the _____
Trend or movement   ordinal number (first/third/middle)

_____ of the _____.
period (decade/quarter/half)   _____century

First Steps

To Compare:
(X) were _____, and (Y) were, too.
(X) were _____, and (Y) were _____, too.

To Contrast
(X) were _____, but (Y) were _____.

The Next Step

When we compare _____ to _____, we can
see that some things are the same and some things are different.
The things that are the same are _____
_____
_____.

The things that are different are _____
_____
_____.

Figure 10.24 Using Venn Diagrams to Build Language

words and phrases to write a complete answer. Posters on a bulletin board listing common words and phrases associated with writing in your discipline will be helpful to *all* students. Additionally, phrases to make writing more cohesive—for example, the lists of transition words shown in Figure 10.26—will provide support and help students become better writers.

First Steps
The problem was _____.
The causes were _____, _____,
and _____.
The actions taken were _____, _____,
and _____.
The result is _____.

The Next Step

The issue (problem) of _____
has (several, four, many, etc.) causes. The causes are _____
_____
_____.

People (agencies, the government, etc.) have tried to deal
with this issue (problem) by _____
_____
_____.

These actions have (helped, not helped) because _____
_____
_____.

The issue (problem) of _____ (has
been resolved, needs more action, is unchanged, is growing, etc.).

Figure 10.25 Using the Problem-Solving Organizer to Build Language

Showing Addition	Showing Chronological Order
First, first of all	First (second, etc.)
Additionally, in addition	Next
Also	Then
Another reason	After that
The most important reason	Finally
Finally	

Showing Contrast	Showing Similarity
On the other hand	Likewise
In contrast	Similarly
However	In a similar way
But	
Rather than	

Giving Examples
For example
For instance
One example of this is _____.
Another example is _____.

Showing Cause and Effect

Cause	→→→	Effect
X _____.	So,	Y _____.
X _____.	Consequently,	Y _____.
X _____.	As a result,	Y _____.
X _____.	Therefore,	Y _____.

Figure 10.26 Transition Words for Writing Assignments

IN SUMMARY: ASSIGNMENTS THAT PROMOTE STUDENT SUCCESS

The assignment strategies you choose for your ELLs will depend on the combination of the content itself and the students' level of language development. Students need to start with simple tasks that are highly context-embedded before moving on to more complex ones. Remember that academic language develops slowly over a long period of time.

Modified and alternative assignment strategies allow students to demonstrate their understanding of content while they are building language skills. These assignments balance high levels of cognitive challenge with low levels of language demand so that language learners can begin to experience academic success. Even minimal changes, such as the inclusion of a word bank, can mean the difference between feelings of frustration and feelings of success.

Try to view assignments as your ELLs learners might see them. Anticipating areas of language difficulty and making appropriate modifications will go a long way in helping your language learners demonstrate their comprehension of the content you teach. The small investment of time and effort to put these ideas to work in your classroom will yield big returns for you and your students.

QUESTIONS FOR DISCUSSION

1. How do the strategies dealing with assignments reflect the *Guidelines for Practice* presented at the beginning of this chapter?

2. All of the assignment strategies presented in this chapter encourage students to extend their understanding by maintaining high cognitive challenge while lowering linguistic demand. Many of them also support ELLs in other areas. Which of the assignment strategies do you think specifically raise learner self-confidence? Which raise student motivation? Which lower anxiety?

3. Choose an appropriate graphic organizer and use it to depict concepts presented in this chapter.

4. Working individually if you are now teaching or in pairs if you are not, choose an assignment and modify it for ELLs. Create several levels of modifications for beginners, intermediates, and advanced ELL students.

REFERENCES AND RESOURCES

Brinton, D. M., & Master, P. (Eds.) (1997). *New ways in content-based instruction.* Alexandria, VA: TESOL (Teachers of English to Speakers of Other Languages), Inc.

Bromley, K., Irwin-De Vitis, L., & Modlo, M. (1995). *Graphic organizers: Visual strategies for active learning.* New York: Scholastic Professional Books.

Forte, I., Pangle, M. A., & Drayton, A. (2001). *ESL content-based language games, puzzles, and inventive exercises.* Nashville, TN: Incentive Publications.

The TechConnection

www.inspiration.com

An interactive site for grade-level graphic organizers, with common topics listed for the subject areas. You select the topic, and the program creates colorful graphic organizers.

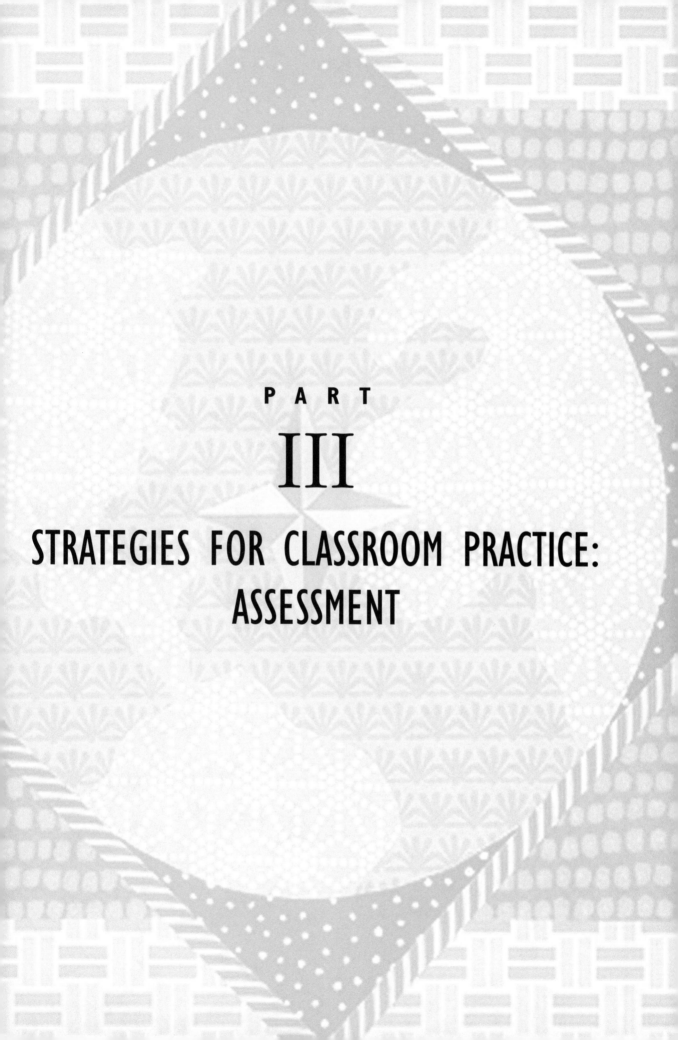

PART

III

STRATEGIES FOR CLASSROOM PRACTICE: ASSESSMENT

CHAPTER 11

CLASSROOM ASSESSMENTS: DID THEY LEARN WHAT YOU TAUGHT?

THEORY TO APPLICATION: GUIDELINES FOR PRACTICE

- Use scaffolding strategies to assess content knowledge separate from English language knowledge so students can show what they know.
- Actively teach learning strategies to give students a "menu" of ways to process and learn new information.
- Provide opportunities for students to experience success in the classroom: Success in learning promotes more success by increasing learner motivation, interest, and self-confidence.

MEASURING ACHIEVEMENT THROUGH TESTS

Increased emphasis on school accountability has turned the spotlight on student assessment. The attention of all shareholders—students, teachers, administrators, and parents—is now focused on annual standardized tests that determine whether students have met state and local standards. The importance of classroom assessment practices, however, should not be overlooked.

The true purpose of assessment is to inform teachers about the progress and achievement of their students: where they are now and what they need next. State assessments do not produce their results in a manner timely enough to meet this need. Well-written teacher-made tests can provide this information. They can maximize learning and ultimately raise performance levels on high-stakes tests.

Good classroom tests assess students' understanding of key concepts the teacher has taught. Good tests contain questions that do not come as a surprise to students. Good tests are made up of items that vary in type and content demand, balancing basic, factual questions that evaluate surface level topic knowledge with questions that elicit higher level reasoning skills and critical thinking. Good tests differentiate among students' varying levels of understanding and depth of knowledge. Classroom tests that meet these criteria are not easy to create under the best of circumstances. In classes with ELLs, the challenge is even greater.

Creating classroom tests that allow ELLs to show what they really know puts teachers on the horns of a dilemma: Essay questions require high-level *writing* skills and multiple-choice questions require high-level *reading* skills. The question for teachers, then, is twofold: How can teachers create good tests that, first, meet the criteria set out here and, second, evaluate ELLs' mastery of subject matter in a way that separates content knowledge from English language knowledge? This important question is best answered after a brief exploration of the types of difficulties that essay questions and multiple-choice questions create for ELLs and the pitfalls of writing good multiple-choice questions.

ESSAY QUESTIONS, MULTIPLE-CHOICE QUESTIONS, AND LANGUAGE DEMAND

Formulating responses to essay questions is a multistep process combining content knowledge and English language *writing* skills. In the first step, students need to decode what the question is asking. The next step involves sorting through mental files to retrieve appropriate content information and organizing it to address the question. The final step, and perhaps the most difficult for ELLs, is to structure that content information into a cohesively written answer. The fact that some native English-speaking students struggle with essay responses offers an insight into the degree of challenge this format presents to ELLs.

The multiple-choice question format requires English language *reading* skills that are generally beyond the level of ELL students. Multiple-choice questions are usually constructed using more complex sentences structures and synonyms other than those that appear in the original text.

Well-written multiple-choice questions demand critical analysis of four or more options for selection of the best answer. Options that are long or worded with subtle distinctions, such as the examples in Figure 11.1 cause language confusion that prevents ELLs from demonstrating their content knowledge. For ELLs, a test of several pages of multiple-choice questions presents a formidable reading task.

Multiple-choice tests that offer students combinations of option choices, such as those shown in Figure 11.2, increase the reading load even further. Questions like these require students to first read and comprehend the information presented in the options, then to match the correct facts to the question, and finally to weed out the one, two, three, or

---

1. The Battle of Antietam was important because
   a. the South regained all of Virginia but Stonewall Jackson was killed.
   b. Confederate troops abandoned Kentucky and increased Grant's determination to win.
   c. Richmond was saved from capture and Northern forces retreated.
   d. the Confederate retreat gave Lincoln the occasion to issue the Emancipation Proclamation.
2. The people known as "Copperheads" were
   a. policemen exempt from fighting to maintain order in Northern cities.
   b. miners from the North who formed a fighting unit in the Union Army.
   c. men who deserted shortly after being paid for enlisting in the Confederate Army.
   d. Democrats demanding an immediate armistice and peaceful settlement of the war.
3. The North and South had different opinions about tariffs. Choose the statement that is true:
   a. The North wanted high tariffs because it helped sell tobacco and cotton in foreign countries.
   b. The South wanted high tariffs because it helped factories make better goods.
   c. The North wanted high tariffs because it made the price of foreign goods higher.
   d. The South wanted high tariffs because it was good for foreign trade.

Figure 11.1   Typical Multiple-Choice Questions About the American Civil War

Figure 11.2 Combining Option
Choices Is Confusing

Changes in energy consumption in the United States during the
past 100 years is due to
   (a) population growth.
   (b) industrialization.
   (c) modernization.
   (d) medical advances.
A. Both (a) and (b)
B. Both (b) and (c)
C. All but (d)
D. None of the above
E. All of the above

even all four incorrect choices. Combining option choices in multiple-choice questions simply adds an additional level of confusion for many students, not only the ELLs.

Multiple-choice tests are challenging for ELLs for still another reason: The format is unique to the American school system. The majority of students from other countries have had no experience with this common type of test before their arrival in U.S. classrooms. Lack of familiarity with the format makes multiple-choice tests even more difficult for ELLs.

The Pitfalls of Multiple-Choice Tests

Multiple-choice question tests have become the preferred test format for one reason: They are easy to score. It is their primary advantage, and with so many demands on teachers' time, it is an important one. This type of test, however, has many inherent disadvantages and pitfalls. While there are only a few rules for writing good multiple-choice questions, bad ones can be written in an almost infinite number of ways.

High-stakes standardized tests generally avoid many common pitfalls because they are created, field-tested, and analyzed by professional test makers. Classroom teachers have neither the time nor the expertise to create tests at the same level of sophistication. Multiple-choice tests created by teachers for classroom use are often flawed.

Making up a set of good multiple-choice questions is difficult and time consuming. The foremost problem with teacher-made multiple-choice tests lies in writing questions that assess students' deep conceptual understandings. It is easy to create items that check basic lower order knowledge of factual information such as names, dates, and definitions. However, trying to write higher order questions—those involving critical thinking and problem solving skills—may produce options that are overly long, confusing, silly, or illogical. (*Options* and other terminology for the multiple-choice question format is shown in Figure 11.3.) The question in Figure 11.4, for example, seeks an inferential judgment. Not

STEM   1. A glacier may be defined as
       a. turbulent water moving down a river.
       b. a huge mass of ice or snow that moves slowly over land.
OPTIONS
       c. small particles of material moved by water or wind.
       d. the process of moving particles of rock grinding away other rock.
CORRECT RESPONSE   = b
DISTRACTORS   = a, c, and d

Figure 11.3   Parts of a Multiple-Choice Question

Figure 11.4 It's Difficult to Assess Critical Thinking with Multiple-Choice Questions

> Based on the past relationship between Shoshanah and her mother, we could predict that the years to come would find them
>   a.   distant but with episodes of closeness.
>   b.   close but with episodes of distance.
>   c.   in a generally unsatisfying relationship.
>   d.   in a generally satisfying relationship.

only is the stem wordy and complicated, but the options are indistinct and confusing. The difference between option a, "distant with episodes of closeness," and option b, "close with episodes of distance," is nothing more than a matter of interpretation. And what distinguishes option a from option c "in a generally unsatisfying relationship"? Lacking any way of supporting one's choice of answer, this can only be viewed as an unfairly subjective question.

In addition to unclear choices, distractors must seem like reasonable choices with appeal to those who don't know the correct answer. To be a true test of students' knowledge, questions must have distractors that are chosen by at least some of the test takers, unlike those in Figure 11.5. For questions that test factual knowledge, teachers have available an abundance of good option choices. There is never a shortage of dates, names, places, and definitions to serve as distractors to the correct answer. Testing the type of knowledge shown in Figure 11.6 is using the multiple-choice format to its best advantage.

However, even in its best application, the issue of backwash—the effect that tests have on actual learning—remains. A perennial question from students is "Is this going to be on the test?" The answer to that question determines whether or not they make the effort to learn that particular set of data.

Even without this question, students quickly perceive what they actually need to study for classroom tests. If teachers discuss concepts, relationships, and implications in class but test just the facts, students know that it's just the facts that really count, and those are what they study. That is backwash: The effect that tests have on actual learning.

Multiple-choice questions also cause negative backwash on the way students process information. The multiple-choice format requires students simply to recognize and select the correct option when they read it. In the world outside the classroom, those who are asked a question (other than "May I take your order?") are not often given choices from

Figure 11.5 Unreasonable Distractors Don't Distract

> Wild animals are considered domesticated when they
>   a.   enjoy being with people.
>   b.   are toilet trained.
>   c.   eat burgers and fries.
>   d.   are taught to work for human beings.

Figure 11.6 Multiple-Choice Questions Best Assess Factual Knowledge

> A nation with a population that is not increasing is
>   a.   Peru.
>   b.   Guatemala.
>   c.   Sweden.
>   d.   Kenya.

A network of all the feeding relationships in an ecosystem is called a

  a.   ecological pyramid.

  b.   energy chain.

  c.   food web.

  d.   energy web.

Options a, b, and d can be eliminated because they would require the stem to end with *an* instead of *a,* leaving *c. food web* as the only grammatically correct choice.

Figure 11.7   Wording in the Stem May Point to the Correct Answer

Of the following, the factor most likely to result in a decrease in the size of a specific population is

  a.   improved medical care.

  b.   increased food availability.

  c.   famine.

  d.   industrialization.

The three distractors—*a, b,* and *d*—are all positive factors. Only the correct choice— *c. famine*—is negative.

Figure 11.8   Options Can Highlight the Correct Choice

which to select a correct response. They are expected to *produce* an answer. In real life, people need to engage in high-level cognitive processing to become effective and creative problem solvers. Multiple-choice testing does not give them much practice toward this end.

Teacher-made multiple-choice questions present additional pitfalls. The wording of the stem may point to the correct option, as shown in Figure 11.7, or the options themselves may point to the correct choice, as in Figure 11.8.

Questions that include the words *never* or *always* may penalize the more knowledgeable students who think of exceptions that mislead them from selecting the intended choice. Information in one test question may inadvertently offer a clue that helps answer another question on the test. Guessing and cheating are factors as well. In sum, multiple-choice tests may not be the best indicator of students'—*all* students'—true knowledge.

SEPARATING LANGUAGE FROM CONTENT IN ASSESSMENTS

The Objective: Modify Testing Techniques.

The Rationale

To assess ELLs' real understanding of content, teachers must create tests that assess content knowledge separate from English language knowledge. This means finding formats for assessment that go beyond essay and multiple-choice questions. One approach involves modifying testing techniques. Simple changes can make big differences in student performance on tests.

Original Multiple-Choice Question

A network of all the feeding relationships in an ecosystem is called a

  e. ecological pyramid.

  f. energy chain.

  g. food web.

  h. energy web.

Substitute True–False Question: *a food web.*

T (F) A network of all the feeding relationships in an ecosystem is called ~~an energy web~~

Figure 11.9   Substitute True–False Questions for Multiple Choice

STRATEGY 78   OFFER TRUE–FALSE QUESTIONS

IN CONCEPT

The ELLs in your class will be more able to demonstrate their content knowledge when you create a parallel test for them by replacing the stem and options of multiple-choice questions with a linguistically simplified format. True–False questions are one way to do this.

IN PRACTICE

For each multiple-choice question, substitute a complete sentence using the multiple-choice stem plus any one of the options, as shown in the example in Figure 11.9. To ensure that these questions are not just random guesses, for every question marked false, students must cross out the part that makes it incorrect and write in its place the word or phrase that corrects it.

STRATEGY 79   USE IDENTIFICATION QUESTIONS

IN CONCEPT

Identification questions can assess knowledge of a large amount of information while significantly lowering the amount of reading involved. This format offers teachers the additional advantages of being easy to write and simple to score.

IN PRACTICE

For tests that assess the learning about two or more contrastive concepts, as in Figure 11.10, you can use a format in which a series of simple statements must be labeled with the concept

---

Forest Biomes

Write the letter of the forest biome to which each statement below applies.

C = Coniferous Forests

D = Deciduous Forests

R = Rain Forests

_____ 1. Location: temperate zone

_____ 2. Location: subarctic regions of North America, Europe, Asia

_____ 3. Location: tropical zone

_____ 4. Location: climate with four different seasons

_____ 5. Trees have buttressed trunks

_____ 6. Trees are triangular shaped

_____ 7. Trees produce seeds

_____ 8. Trees shed leaves seasonally

_____ 9. Trees have needles

_____10. Trees have shallow root systems

_____11. Soil: poor, acidic

_____12. Soil: thin, nutrient poor, nutrients recycled back into trees

_____13. Soil: rich fertile

_____14. Examples: cypress, balsa, teak, mahogany

_____15. Examples: maple, oak, beech, ash, hickory, birch

_____16. Examples: hemlock, fir, spruce, cedar

_____17. Biome with the greatest biodiversity

Figure 11.10   Identification Questions Lower the Amount of Reading

they describe in place of the usual set of individual multiple-choice questions. The identification question format reduces reading to a minimum as it allows students to demonstrate knowledge of a large body of simple factual information.

 STRATEGY 80   GIVE COMPLETION QUESTIONS

IN CONCEPT

Completion questions, using the multiple-choice stem but replacing the options with a space or blank lines, are another means of linguistically simplifying multiple-choice tests. Completion questions offer several advantages. They lower the reading and language demand, allowing ELLs to focus on content. They avoid the negative backwash of multiple-choice questions by having students actually *produce* an answer rather than just recognize it. And, completion questions can be used in conjunction with a content word or phrase bank as a supplementary aid for students in the early stages of English language development.

Figure 11.11 Completion Questions
Put the Focus on Content

> 1. The Battle of Antietam was important because _____
> _____ .
>
> 2. "Copperheads" were people who _____
> _____ .
>
> 3. The North wanted _____(high or low?) tariffs because
> _____ .

IN PRACTICE

Technique I

ELLs will respond more easily to the three questions from Figure 11.1 when they are changed to the completion format shown in Figure 11.11. In these questions, the blanks all intentionally appear at the end of the stem. Filling in blanks that appear at the beginning or end, rather than in the middle, are easier to process both linguistically and cognitively.

Technique II

The *cloze* technique extends and interrelates a series of completion type questions. In the content cloze format, the teacher composes a series of paragraphs on a topic and then systematically deletes key content words or phrases, replacing them with blanks for the student to fill in. Figure 11.12 shows the use of a cloze passage to assess knowledge of the circulatory system in the human body. Again, beginner and low intermediate-level ELLs could use a word bank to assist them.

Giving ELLs true–false, identification, and completion questions in place of multiple-choice puts the focus where it belongs: on content, not on reading ability. These types of questions offer the additional benefit of avoiding many of the pitfalls of multiple-choice testing. And, from the teacher's perspective, they are easier to write than multiple-choice questions and almost as fast to score.

Circulation

  Circulation is the pumping of blood around the body. The _____ is the main organ of the circulatory system. It never rests. It _____ and _____ in a regular, even motion, about _____ times a minute. It makes the blood travel around your body bringing _____ to muscles and other parts of the body.

  Tubes that carry blood around the body are called _____. There are three types of tubes that carry blood—arteries, veins, and capillaries. Each type has a different job to do. Arteries _____ (what do they do?). Veins _____ (what do they do?). And capillaries _____ (what do they do?).

  Blood is made of four main parts. The largest part of blood is called _____. Its job is to _____ . The three other parts of the blood are (1)_____ whose job is to _____ ; (2) _____ whose job is to _____ _____ ; and (3) _____ whose job is to _____ _____ .

Figure 11.12 The Cloze Technique Takes Completion Questions to the Next Level

STRATEGY 81 USE GRAPHICS TO EXPRESS KNOWLEDGE

IN CONCEPT

Essay questions also work better when they are linguistically simplified. In place of sentences and paragraphs, ELLs can use visuals and graphics for their responses.

IN PRACTICE

ELLs can demonstrate their understanding of complex concepts and relationships with graphic organizers, T-lists, sequenced pictures, and labeled diagrams and maps. The strategies for activities presented in Chapter 10 can be used effectively for assessment.

STRATEGY 82 BEND THE RULES

IN CONCEPT

Teachers seldom give much thought to the standard rules of testing. After all, these rules have been around for decades, perhaps even centuries. There are, however, some rules concerning communication while testing that you may want to consider modifying.

IN PRACTICE

Technique I

Make some small changes in the way students interact with the test itself and in the way you interact with students as they are taking a test. Start with allowing ELLs to use a *bilingual dictionary* to clarify words they may be unsure of in English. Encourage ELLs to seek clarification of specific test parts they don't understand. *Answer questions* that don't influence or give away content. *Substitute a synonym* for an unknown word. *Paraphrase directions* that ELLs don't understand. For a complicated test, consider having a bilingual student, parent, or volunteer *translate the directions* into the students' native language. It might even be feasible to *translate the questions* themselves. In addition to any of these modifications, you could also *allow rewrites and test corrections* to improve grades and demonstrate more complete understanding.

Technique II

Shorter tests feel more doable for ELLs. Try using *flexible timing*. Think about dividing the test into several shorter sections and giving each section separately. Consider *shortening the test* by selecting only concepts of primary importance. The second question in Figure 11.1 is an example of a question that could be comfortably eliminated.

Another means to shorten the test and decrease the reading load is to *reduce the number of options* offered as choices to each multiple-choice question. This has the additional advantage of giving ELLs practice with this question type without overwhelming them. In combination with any of these other strategies, you could also allow ELLs to use their textbooks during the test. For beginners, you might even consider noting a page number next to each question.

Technique III

A seemingly radical idea is to *pair* two ELL students to take a test. Working together may allow them to complete more of an exam than either one of them could do individually.

In this case, the test is actually helping them learn. It may also be possible for you to give sections of a test as an *individual oral exam,* if time allows. Oral language is often an easier modality for ELLs to convey content knowledge.

Technique IV

Finally, consider adding a section at the end of all classroom multiple-choice tests called *Explain Yourself.* Here students can offer explanations to justify the choice of an answer—perhaps a question for which two options seemed equally true, or one in which none of the choices seemed right. For ELLs whose language development is at a stage that prevents them from explaining themselves, you can substitute an "I need to talk to you about question number _____." The explanation, written or oral, may be good enough for you to give partial or even full credit.

SEPARATING LANGUAGE FROM CONTENT IN ASSESSMENTS

The Objective: Don't Test at All!

The Rationale

"Not testing at all" doesn't *really* mean not giving any tests. It means using alternative assessment techniques and measures in place of, or as a complement to, more traditional forms of tests. It is a productive way of evaluating ELLs' content knowledge.

A caveat to alternative testing is that the alternative formats themselves may present their own sets of language demands for ELLs. And, because they don't necessarily look or feel like tests, students and their parents may need an explanation to understand how these techniques are being used for assessment.

STRATEGY 83   USE PERFORMANCE-BASED ASSESSMENT

IN CONCEPT

Performance-based assessments allow students to demonstrate their content knowledge through concrete examples ranging from writing samples, projects, visuals and graphics to oral reports, presentations, and portfolios. All performance-based assessments are based on a set of criteria that teachers make clear to students in advance of assignments.

IN PRACTICE

To increase students' ability to produce high-quality results, explain the standards—scoring rubric, checklist, point distribution, for example—that will be used for assessment. Show examples of work that meets those standards. ELLs, in particular, benefit from seeing models, knowing the teacher's expectations, and understanding the criteria used for evaluation.

STRATEGY 84   USE PORTFOLIOS FOR ASSESSMENT

IN CONCEPT

Portfolio assessment has gained popularity among teachers and school administrators in recent years. Used in conjunction with other forms of evaluation, portfolio assessment offers students an alternative means of demonstrating their developing understanding. Portfolio evaluation involves a process of shared responsibility and participation for students and teachers. It is an approach to classroom assessment that feels almost "democratic."

IN PRACTICE

In class discussion, students and teachers make decisions about standards for selection of portfolio items and about criteria for evaluation. Throughout the grading period, students discuss and choose the pieces of work that will go into their portfolio collections as evidence of their achievements.

Portfolios invite students to become active participants in their own evaluations. They empower students as well by enabling them to demonstrate mastery of content through a wider range of measures than paper and pencil tests provide. Portfolio collections document growth of both content knowledge and language skills over a period of time.

STRATEGY 85   USE INFORMATION JOURNALS FOR ASSESSMENT

IN CONCEPT

Like portfolios, *information journals* (also called *content journals* or *learning logs*) can be used as a valid means of evaluation. For ELL students who keep them on a regular basis, information journals will show progress over time.

IN PRACTICE

Students use information journals to keep records of information from all content areas. Depending on the content learning in your classroom, entries could include problem solving in math, observations and conclusions in science, historical and geographical information in social studies, and character and plot developments in literature.

Evaluating information journals is simplified by using a format that is structured, concise, and objective. One such example is the learning logs shown in Chapter 9, Figure 9.10. An even more highly structured format is the K–W–L chart shown in Chapter 5, Figures 5.2–5.4. Students may be extra motivated to work on their information journals knowing that they are being used for assessment purposes.

STRATEGY 86   TRY SELF-ASSESSMENT AND PEER ASSESSMENT

IN CONCEPT

Self-assessment and peer-assessments are useful to supplement and complement other types of evaluation. Their advantages are many.

Students develop an understanding that it is normal to find some concepts easier to learn than others, and it is also normal for even quick learners to still have questions. Students feel empowered by contributing to their own evaluations, and they often assess themselves more rigorously than their teachers might.

Teachers who routinely use self- and peer-assessment at the end of each chapter or unit, or at the end of each week, month, or grading period, find that it helps to open and maintain a line of communication with their students whose insightful input can often help teachers find more effective techniques and approaches to facilitate comprehension. Few assessment techniques are as positive as this one.

IN PRACTICE

Teachers can create individual *checklists* that students complete to reflect their personal feelings about comprehension of text or topic, contributions to class or group work, and areas of strength, weakness, and/or improvement. Figures 11.13 and 11.14 show examples of checklists to which items can be changed or added as needed. Teachers can get additional feedback from student self-assessments by including an area for extra explanation and input, either at the bottom, as in Figure 11.14, or in a fourth column, as in Figure 11.15. An even more individually expressive format for self- and peer-assessment involves completing a set of *open-ended questions,* as shown in Figure 11.16.

Textbook: Chapter 12	😦	😐	😊
WEEK OF _____ I understood the reading. I highlighted the text. I used a dictionary. I worked with a friend.			

Figure 11.13   Self-Assessment Checklist I

Textbook: Chapter 12	Usually Not	Sometimes	Almost Always
WEEK OF _____ I understood the assigned reading. I highlighted the text. I made note cards. I made vocabulary cards. I participated in class discussions. I asked for help when I was unsure.			
I also want to tell you that _____ _____ _____			

Figure 11.14   Self-Assessment Checklist II

Textbook: Chapter 12	Usually Not	Sometimes	Almost Always	And I want to tell you . . .
WEEK OF _____ I understood the assigned reading. I highlighted the text. I made note cards. I made vocabulary cards. I participated in class discussions. I asked for help when I was unsure.				

Figure 11.15 Self-Assessment Checklist III

1. The concepts I understood were _____.
2. The concepts I didn't understand were _____.
3. I think I improved in _____.
4. I think I need more improvement in _____.
5. I need special help with _____.
6. The kind of help I need is _____.

Figure 11.16 Open-Ended Self Assessment

SEPARATING LANGUAGE FROM CONTENT IN ASSESSMENTS

The Objective: Grade English Language Learners to Promote Success.

The Rationale

The issue of grading ELLs is a complex one. It seems like a double penalty to give ELLs a low grade in social studies, math, science, or literature because they lack the English language skills to express their knowledge. It is well-known that students who regularly get low grades see themselves as failures and, as such, make even less effort to achieve. On the other hand, is it fair to your native English-speaking students who have worked hard to earn high grades if you use a different system to grade your ELLs?

Grading ELLs requires a delicate balance. It makes little sense to grade down ELLs who, based on their language proficiency level, have no chance of completing an assignment to "acceptable standards." Neither does it make sense to accept lower-level work from ELLs who are capable of producing a better product. Teachers need to be clear about their goals for instruction and the academic and linguistic level of their students; then, based on the instruction provided and the students' backgrounds, they need to give grades that reflect standards that students have a reasonable chance of achieving.

Grading issues can be reduced, at least to some degree, when you modify your regular tests and use alternative means of assessment. Because these assessment strategies offer more opportunity and wider means for ELLs to show what they know, you will have more accurate feedback to use in grading them. Beyond this are several other ways to make grading fairer for your ELLs.

STRATEGY 87 FOCUS ON CONTENT ONLY

IN CONCEPT

As in the strategies in previous chapters that dealt with ELLs' oral participation and written assignments (Strategies 49 and 70), it is equally important to focus on content in all forms of assessment. Separating content knowledge from the language used to express that knowledge may allow you to give more credit for student effort and achievement.

IN PRACTICE

When you evaluate students' written work, look closely for key content words in short answers. You may find enough there to give at least partial credit, even if the whole answer is not completely comprehensible to you.

STRATEGY 88 GRADE WRITTEN WORK WITH A RUBRIC

IN CONCEPT

Rubric scoring can make grading easier for you and fairer for your students. You are probably familiar with state- or districtwide rubrics. Unlike rubrics for your own personal use in the classroom, these are designed to assess all levels of writing skills, from virtual perfection to near total lack of skills.

IN PRACTICE

A rubric designed for daily classroom use must more narrowly reflect the highest to lowest expectations *for your student population*. The simple rubric shown in Figure 11.17 challenges students to do their best, and, at the same time, rewards them for their efforts at their current level of ability.

Figure 11.17 A Usable Rubric

3	Meaningful content on assigned topic Errors do not interfere with reader comprehension
2	Some meaningful content on assigned topic Errors require some rereading for reader comprehension
1	Little meaningful content on assigned topic Errors require frequent or constant rereading for reader comprehension

Rubrics such as these have many benefits. They allow students to experience success by evaluating their written product against reasonable standards, not against perfection. For the teacher, one single rubric can be used with all types of writing, from daily homework questions to research reports. Rubrics evaluate writing with an expectation of excellence and can change to reflect higher expectations as students progress in their English language development. Last but certainly not least, rubrics make scoring quick and easy.

ELLs struggle with written work. Teachers who use rubrics to evaluate writing find that they focus on what is there, rather than what is not there. Teachers like them because they decrease the time needed to read and grade sets of papers. Using the same rubric for all writing assignments gives teachers a comfort level that speeds the process of evaluation.

Rubric scoring also has the advantage of setting and maintaining high expectations without measuring work against the standard of perfection. With teacher-made rubrics, students understand the expectation of excellence, but within the boundaries of *realistic achievement* for the group. As expectations rise, teachers can include additional elements for evaluation, as shown in Figure 11.18. It is easy to design rubrics that keep pace with progressively higher standards.

A rubric makes scoring a set of papers easy and efficient for the teacher. Start by scanning student papers rapidly to separate them into two piles—the betters and the "worsers." Read the *worsers* first. This group will receive scores of 1 or 2, or perhaps 1+ if you feel a paper is better than a 1 but not quite a 2. When you finish reading the papers in the first group, move on to the second set, scoring those 2, 2+, or 3. You need not correct anything on any paper. As you read it, simply focus on the two qualities of the rubric: the amount of meaningful content and the readability of what is written there.

3	Meaningful content on assigned topic **+ with many supporting details** Errors do not interfere with reader comprehension
2	Some meaningful content on assigned topic **+ with some supporting details** Errors require some rereading for reader comprehension
1	Little meaningful content on assigned topic **+ with few or no supporting details** Errors require frequent or constant rereading for reader comprehension

3	Meaningful content on assigned topic **+ with many supporting details** **+ presented in an organized manner** Errors do not interfere with reader comprehension
2	Some meaningful content on assigned topic **+ with some supporting details** **+ presented in a loosely organized manner** Errors require some rereading for reader comprehension
1	Little meaningful content on assigned topic **+ with few or no supporting details** **+ presented in an unorganized manner** Errors require frequent or constant rereading for reader comprehension

Figure 11.18 Rubrics Can Reflect Rising Expectations

STRATEGY 89 WRITE INTERACTIVE COMMENTS

IN CONCEPT

Interactive comments, described in Figure 11.19, directly address the content of the writing. They make writers feel their ideas have been read and affirmed, creating an affectively positive writing environment.

Look at the two comments in Figure 11.20. The first is simply the evaluation of a higher authority; the second makes the writer feel good. It's an interactive comment, a personal reaction from the reader that speaks directly to the writer. It makes the writer want to write more just to be rewarded with more comments like it.

IN PRACTICE

Interactive comments written at the end of each student's paper present the reader's overall reaction to the writing. They should be honest reactions, though phrased in a positive manner. Try softening a negative comment with something like one of these:

"I like what you wrote about _____. I wish you had written more."

"I think you may have some good things to say about _____, but I had a hard time reading your handwriting."

Interactive comments, in the form of questions and comments written in the margins of students' work, can develop student writing skills better than all the corrections you might make on those papers. If, as you read, you think to yourself that very little detail is included in the paper, try writing specific questions, such as those shown in Figure 11.21, to guide students toward the kinds of detail they might have included. Most students who read the traditional teacher comment "Needs more detail" have no idea what they omitted and which additional details they might have written. Similarly, instead of "This doesn't address the topic," try something like "This is interesting. Can you explain how it applies to _____?"

Figure 11.19 What Are Interactive Comments?

> Interactive comments are those in which
> the reader *as a person*
> responds to
> the writer *as a person*
> as if in conversation.

Figure 11.20 How do These Comments Differ?

> "Excellent writing!"
>
> "I loved reading this!"

> *Try these questions instead of "Needs more detail."*
>
> What issues did they disagree on?
>
> Why did they disagree?
>
> How many men were lost in the battle?
>
> How many months did this take?
>
> What types of work were they involved in?
>
> Which materials did we use in the experiment?
>
> Why did we decide not to use other materials?

Figure 11.21 Interactive Comments Promote Writing Skills Development

> **T**   Tell something you liked
>
> **A**   Ask a question
>
> **G**   Give a suggestion

Figure 11.22 TAG: An Interactive Comment Strategy

Write interactive comments in the margins and at the end as you read each paper for rubric scoring. One strategy for writing interactive comments is called TAG. It is outlined in Figure 11.22. It focuses on the positive at the same time that it helps improve student writing skills.

Tune in to the thoughts and reactions that go through your head while you are reading. After a bit of practice, comments will flow quite readily. Combining rubric scoring with interactive comments takes the dread out of scoring a set of papers and creates a powerful evaluation program that is a win–win situation for both students and teachers.

STRATEGY 90   GIVE GRADES FOR PROGRESS AND EFFORT

IN CONCEPT

Progress grades are another grading strategy that should be considered. Using progress grades allows you to focus on the individual growth and development of your ELLs instead of grading them in comparison to expectations set for native English-speaking students.

IN PRACTICE

You can develop a system of using an asterisk following the grade to denote that you are using an alternative grading system. Including some positive comments will make ELLs feel more successful, even if their actual grades are low.

An alternative approach is to give effort grades along with content grades. Effort grades recognize students' persistence, even in the face of less than acceptable grades. If your school has a large number of ELLs, this might be something that the administration could consider adopting as a schoolwide grading system.

STRATEGY 91 OFFER EXTRA CHANCES AND SELF-GRADING OPTIONS

IN CONCEPT

People learn from their mistakes, or at least they try to. Students in classrooms should be allowed to learn from their mistakes, too.

IN PRACTICE

Technique I

Consider allowing ELLs the opportunity to retake a test, to hand in a second draft, or to correct an assignment. Partner or small group editing meetings after papers and tests have been returned will give students ideas for improvement before resubmitting them.

Technique II

ELLs can be offered opportunities to collaborate with peers *before* they submit their work for grading. Partner or small group peer correction and suggestion will have a positive effect on grades.

Technique III

Have your students self-evaluate their work. What grade do they think they *realistically* deserve? Your first thought may be that students will overvalue their products, but in reality many students grade themselves more harshly than you will.

IN SUMMARY: SEPARATING LANGUAGE FROM CONTENT IN ASSESSMENT

Combining strategies that modify grading procedures with those that use scaffolded or alternative assessment approaches will produce a more accurate picture of your ELLs' actual content knowledge. Your students can show what they know and earn grades that better reflect their understanding. They will find themselves motivated to learn when you evaluate them in ways that place success within their reach. You are opening the door to academic achievement.

QUESTIONS FOR DISCUSSION

1. How do the strategies for evaluation reflect the *Guidelines for Practice* presented at the beginning of this chapter?
2. In pairs, examine a teacher-made multiple-choice test. Can you find any pitfalls? How would you eliminate the pitfalls of those you found?
3. In pairs, choose a test that one or both of you have used in your classrooms and analyze it through the eyes of an ELLs. What would have been especially difficult or confusing? Look for specific questions that are high in language demand. What strategies would you use to decrease the linguistic load so that ELLs could more easily demonstrate their understanding of the content?
4. Using a student textbook in a content area of your choice, create a test for a class and then modify it for your ELLs. Pair up with a colleague and critique each other's tests.
5. Obtain a set of student papers containing expository writing. Grade them holistically, using the process explained in Strategy 90, then add interactive comments. (*Note:* Your instructor may want to photocopy a small set of student papers to do this as a whole class assignment.)

6. What are the relative benefits and disadvantages of using modified paper and pencil tests, on the one hand, and alternative assessment techniques on the other? Consider the issues of reliability and validity, structure, and creativity.

REFERENCES AND RESOURCES

Alvermann, D. E., & Phelps, S. F. (2005). Assessment of students. In P. A. Richard-Amato, & M. A. Snow (Eds.), *Academic success for English language learners: Strategies for K–12 mainstream teachers* (pp. 311–341). White Plains, NY: Pearson Education.

De Fina, A. A. (1992). *Portfolio assessment: Getting started.* New York: Scholastic Professional Books.

Gibbons, P. (2005). Writing in a second language across the curriculum. In P. A. Richard-Amato, and M. A. Snow (Eds.), *Academic success for English language learners: Strategies for K–12 mainstream teachers* (pp. 275–310). White Plains, NY: Pearson Education.

Gomez, E. (2000). Assessment portfolios: Including English language learners in large-scale assessments. *CAL Digest,* EDO-FL-00-01. Retrieved March 21, 2006 http://www.cal.org/resources/digest/0010assessment.html from CAL Digests database.

O'Malley, J. M., and Valdez Pierce, L. (1996). *Authentic assessment for English language learners: Practical approaches for teachers.* Reading, MA: Addison-Wesley Publishing Company.

Stiggins, R., Arter, J. A., Chappius, J., & Chappius, S. (2004). *Classroom assessment for student learning: Doing it right—using it well.* Portland, OR: Assessment Training Institute, Inc.

CHAPTER 12

THE BIG ONE: PREPARING FOR HIGH-STAKES TESTS

THEORY TO APPLICATION: GUIDELINES FOR PRACTICE

- Actively teach learning strategies to give students a "menu" of ways to process and learn new information.
- Use scaffolding strategies to assess content knowledge separate from English language knowledge so students can show what they know.
- Lower learner anxiety in the classroom to create students who are more willing to participate in class, to become risk takers in the learning process, and ultimately to become more successful learners.
- Provide opportunities for students to experience success in the classroom: Success in learning promotes more success by increasing learner motivation, interest, and self-confidence.

Teachers in every state of the United States face the twin issues of accountability and high-stakes testing. Performance results on standardized or state-designed assessment instruments affect decisions about promotion, curricular tracking, and graduation for students. In many states, tests results determine teacher, school, and district ratings, often with concomitant differential school or district funding bonuses. Poor showings may result in the imposition of corrective actions ranging from schoolwide restructuring to providing students with alternative school choices. Never before have test stakes been so high.

With accountability and testing as important as they now are, teachers and administrators have become deeply involved in preparing students for successful outcomes. They have developed new programs and innovative approaches for improving the performance levels of their students—their native English-speaking students, that is. For better or worse, however (and there really are two sides to this issue, though that is beyond the scope of this text), ELLs also must face these tests.

In the past, potentially low-scoring ELLs were simply excused from high-stakes testing. Exclusion, at this time, is no longer an option. The provisions of the No Child Left Behind Act (NCLB) of 2001 mandate that virtually all ELLs participate in the statewide assessment instruments along with the native English-speaking students. (Scores of ELLs at early stages of English language development are, however, exempted.)

It seems unrealistically optimistic to expect ELLs to achieve the same level of performance as their English-speaking peers on an exam that is not in their native languages, but it would be equally pessimistic to believe that they are destined to fail. Teachers can maximize the performance potential of their ELLs on yearly state-mandated tests by using a combination of strategic approaches throughout the school year:

- Incorporate into your daily procedures a variety of the instructional strategies presented in Part II of this text to facilitate content comprehension.
- Use the classroom assessment strategies discussed in Chapter 11 to give students ongoing practice in test taking.
- Explicitly teach test-taking skills.
- Ensure that the most appropriate and beneficial test accommodations are being made available to ELLs.

These last two strategic approaches are the subject of this chapter.

MAXIMIZING STUDENT POTENTIAL ON STANDARDIZED TESTS

The Objective: Familiarize Students with the Format and Process of Multiple-choice Testing.

The Rationale

Experience counts in tests, as it does in life. Students become better test takers through repeated exposure. ELLs in particular need practice to become familiar with the format and process of multiple-choice tests, as this test type is not widely used outside the United States.

 STRATEGY 92   TEACH HOW TO APPROACH A MULTIPLE-CHOICE QUESTION

IN CONCEPT

The process of reading the stem and option choices (see Figure 11.3 in Chapter 11 for labels of the parts of multiple-choice questions), eliminating the incorrect options, and then bubbling in the chosen response on a separate answer sheet may completely bewilder ELLs. Frequent practice with this type of test will sharpen students' skills and make them more comfortable with multiple-choice test design.

IN PROCESS

Technique I
Acquaint ELLs with multiple-choice question format by starting small. Offer questions with only two option choices per question. Increase the number of options to three shortly thereafter. Starting small will start the ELLs on a positive testing path.

Technique II
Another way to familiarize ELLs with multiple-choice questions is to give them two parallel tests. Use any of the linguistically simplified question formats discussed in Chapter 11 so that ELLs can demonstrate their actual content knowledge. *At the same time,* give them side-by-side multiple-choice questions that exactly parallel the questions on the first test. For example, students could see a true–false question in tandem with a two-option

T F   A glacier may be defined as a huge mass of ice
        or snow moving slowly over land.

        A glacier may be defined as
            a. turbulent water moving down a river.
            b. a huge mass of ice or snow that moves slowly over
               land.

Figure 12.1 Parallel Test Questions:
True–False with Multiple-Choice

_____ is a nation with a population that is not increasing.

A nation with a population that is not increasing is
    a. Peru
    b. Sweden
    c. Kenya

Figure 12.2 Parallel Test Questions:
Completion with Multiple-Choice

multiple-choice question, as in Figure 12.1, or a completion question with a three-option multiple-choice question, as shown in Figure 12.2. By explicitly demonstrating the correspondence between the parts (stem, options, correct answer) of multiple-choice question and the same question in the simplified format, students will begin to make sense of the multiple-choice process.

Technique III

To clarify students' understanding even further, give them several practice sessions in scrutinizing the distractors. Show students how to analyze and compare each set of distractors. Have them circle the word or phrase that makes it incorrect.

Combining these strategies—distractor analysis, decreased multiple-choice options, and parallel formats—allows ELLs to develop processing skills that increase their chances for success with standard four-option questions. Continued practice will lower students' anxiety and improve their performance on high-stakes tests.

STRATEGY 93   TEACH HOW TO USE THE ANSWER SHEET

IN CONCEPT

ELLs also need to become familiar with the process of using a Scantron sheet for answering multiple-choice questions. Some of you may remember the anxiety these separate answer sheets provoked when they were first introduced. Scantron sheets are a new experience for most ELLs, and, like early users, bubbling-in answers on a separate sheet raises their anxiety levels, too. As with most other aspects of learning, ELLs benefit from the strategy of repeated practice.

IN PRACTICE

Photocopy Scantron sheets and use them in conjunction with classroom tests so ELLs can practice transferring answers from the question page to the answer sheet. Students need to be made aware to check frequently that the numbers they are bubbling-in on the answer sheets match the numbers of the questions, especially if they have skipped a question.

An obvious and simple test-taking strategy is to answer as many questions as possible in the allotted amount of time. ELLs should know to tackle first the questions they find linguistically and conceptually easy and to skip over difficult questions, reserving these for whatever time remains at the end of the test. However, for any question they skip, they need to know how critical it is to skip that number line on the answer sheet. A strategy students can use is to make a light mark in the left margin next to the number of the skipped row as a reminder to return to it at the end.

STRATEGY 94   FAMILIARIZE STUDENTS WITH PREDICTABLE PATTERNS AND PHRASES

IN CONCEPT

When ELLs understand the design of the multiple-choice format and answer sheet, practice sessions can extend to familiarizing them with the common word patterns of test directions.

IN PRACTICE

Written directions on standardized or statewide tests often differ from those that students are accustomed to hearing in class or reading in their textbooks. The wording of directions for a given task can also vary from one test to another. It may not be apparent to ELLs that the two sets of directions in Figure 12.3, for example, are asking them to do the same thing. Practice that familiarizes ELLs with the variations in word patterns will allow them to focus their linguistic efforts on finding answers to the questions instead of trying to figure out what to do with the questions themselves.

STRATEGY 95   TEACH THE FACTS-WITHOUT-FLUFF STRATEGY

IN CONCEPT

Math word problems on standardized tests often present a challenge to ELLs, not because of the math skills involved but because of the vocabulary used as the setting of the problem. The *Facts-Without-Fluff* strategy teaches students to brush away the cumbersome vocabulary to reveal the data needed to solve the problem.

Figure 12.3   Same Task, Different Directions

Directions on a standardized test:

Choose the word or group of words that means the same, or nearly the same, as the underlined word. Then mark the space for the answer you have chosen on your answer sheet.

Directions on a classroom test:

Bubble-in the letter of the word or phrase that is closest to the meaning of the underlined word.

A stable manager had a 78.3-foot length of braided leather line to use to replace the fraying reins on his horse bridles. Which equation could be used to find L, the number of lengths of rein measuring 3.7 feet, that could be cut from the 78.3 feet?

A. $78.3L = 3.7$

B. $78.3 = 3.7L$

C. $L = (3.7)(78.3)$

D. $\dfrac{L}{78.3} = 3.7$

Figure 12.4 Is it the Math or the English that's hard?

Facts with All the Fluff

A stable manager had a 78.3-foot length of braided leather line to use to replace the fraying reins on his horse bridles. Which equation could be used to find L, the number of lengths of rein measuring 3.7 feet, that could be cut from the 78.3 feet?

The Facts Without the Fluff

Someone . . . had 78.3 feet . . . of something.

Which equation to use to find L?

L = the number of 3.7-foot lengths (*pieces, things*) in the 78.3 feet?

Figure 12.5 The Facts-Without-Fluff Strategy

IN PRACTICE

Look at the linguistic complexity of the problem presented in Figure 12.4. It is apparent that the challenge here lies in the English, not in the math. You can help your ELLs show what they know in math by explicitly teaching them how to strip away the fluff to get to the facts they need. Talk them through making word substitutions and deletions, "translating" *stable manager* to *someone,* for example. Figure 12.5 shows the process and results of focusing on the data students must use to solve the problem, a strategy they can practice in pairs or small groups throughout the school year.

STRATEGY 96   TEACH TEST-TAKING SKILLS

IN CONCEPT

At this point, ELLs can join the rest of the class when you teach test-taking skills. All students will benefit from learning testing strategies to "improve the odds."

It should be recognized here that teachers' real goal is to help students become competent in the content of the test and not to become better test takers. However, students can improve their scores by knowing how to take a test.

IN PRACTICE

The first thing students need to know about any test is whether wrong answers are penalized or not. In tests that assess penalties for wrong answers, students should consider guessing only if they can eliminate two of the options. If there are no penalties for guessing, the best strategy is to answer all questions.

Give students demonstrations and practice in looking for clues before guessing an answer. Begin by eliminating any option known to be wrong. Then look at the length of the remaining options. Often the longest is the best choice. Look also for similarities: If two options are close in meaning, it is likely that neither will be the correct choice. Look next for two options that are opposites: Choose one as a guess. Finally, if none of these options result in clues to a choice, students should select the same letter to guess at all unknown questions throughout the test. Consistency offers the best statistical odds for a correct guess.

STRATEGY 97   GIVE SHORTER TESTS MORE FREQUENTLY

IN CONCEPT

ELLs become better test takers through repeated practice. It is a good idea to establish a pattern of twice monthly mini-assessments, rather than saving everything for "the big one."

IN PRACTICE

Shorter tests, given more often, allow ELLs to focus on understanding smaller amounts of material. They also serve as grade indicators: Students know how they are doing at all times throughout the grading period. They prevent the surprise of failure at the end of the grading period. They allow students multiple opportunities to improve their grades. They let teachers know whether students have a good grasp of concepts or whether review, reteaching, and/or additional individual services are needed.

Perhaps most important of all, frequent tests prepare students for bigger exams. Each test and quiz raises students' comfort level with understanding and following directions, choosing correct responses, and using appropriate test-taking strategies. At the same time, repeated exposure to smaller tests lowers students' anxiety levels.

MAXIMIZING STUDENT POTENTIAL ON STANDARDIZED TESTS

The Objective: Use All Reasonable Allowable Accommodations for English Language Learners

The Rationale

High-stakes standardized tests now mandate the inclusion of ELLs. The benefit of including ELLs' test results in school accountability data is that ELLs' instructional needs can no longer be minimized or ignored. However, those test results may more accurately reflect students' English language proficiency than their actual content knowledge. Any time tests employ language, as all high-stakes test do, they cannot help but include some measure of language ability with the content they purport to test (The Joint Committee Standard 9, in TESOL, 2005). To address this very real difficulty, NCLB specifies four types of testing accommodations that may be offered to ELLs: Accommodations in presentation, response, setting, and timing. In each of these areas, modifications in test materials or procedures attempt to ensure that the assessment measures the students' knowledge and skills rather than their English language proficiency. Teachers who are aware of these test accommodations and use them to their best advantage can maximize the performance potential of their ELLs.

STRATEGY 98   USE ACCOMMODATIONS IN PRESENTATION

IN CONCEPT

Modifications in the realm of test presentation involve ways that teachers or test administrators can communicate with students before and during a test. Accommodations of this type are designed to offer clarification for ELLs in several different ways.

IN PRACTICE

Technique I

Prior to test administration and if state law allows, test directions may be translated into students' native languages. They may also be audiotaped in advance by qualified teachers, parents, or other community volunteers.

Again in states that allow it, teachers can make the accommodation of conducting a linguistic preview of test questions to reduce the need for clarification during actual testing sessions. The unusual vocabulary in the math problem shown in Figure 12.4, for example, could be simplified to that shown in Figure 12.6. Nothing mathematical has changed—only the linguistic ability needed to understand what the question is asking.

Linguistic items such as confusing synonyms, unfamiliar terminology or phrasing (the phrase *given that* in math, for example), and questions that are overly long or structurally complex ("One can say that it is generally not true that . . .") can be rewritten in simplified form and included as part of the test, either in the test booklet itself or as a separate handout.

Technique II

During test administration, test directions may be read aloud, repeated, paraphrased, and/or simplified. Students may also request clarification while they are taking the test. Teachers or test administrators can answer questions that enhance ELLs' comprehension of the question, providing the teacher's response will not affect the answer on the test. They could, for example, offer vocabulary assistance with the math problem in Figure 12.4. Test results will more accurately reflect ELLs' content knowledge and skills when teachers explain, rephrase, or simplify vocabulary, synonyms, idiomatic phrases, or cultural references unrelated to content.

Figure 12.6 Now the Focus Is Math

Which equation could be used to find L, the number of lengths of string measuring 3.7 feet, that could be cut from a length of string measuring 78.3 feet?

  a. $78.3L = 3.7$

  b. $78.3 = 3.7L$

  c. $L = (3.7)(78.3)$

  d. $\dfrac{L}{78.3} = 3.7$

STRATEGY 99   USE ACCOMMODATIONS IN RESPONSE

IN CONCEPT

Accommodations in response are those that involve how a student may respond to a test. Accommodations of this type attempt to address potential difficulties that ELLs may encounter in reading and answering test questions.

IN PRACTICE

The most valuable modification in the response category is to allow ELLs to use reference aids, such as bilingual dictionaries and glossaries. Students can use commercially published editions or they can bring to the test preapproved word lists, vocabulary journals, or dictionaries that they have created throughout the school year.

Other suggested modifications in response may be more difficult to implement. For example, ELLs may be offered the option of marking their answers directly in their test booklets. However, this option makes scoring more difficult, time consuming, and costly. Other even less likely modifications are to bring in a qualified interpreter if one is locally available, to allow ELLs to respond in their native language, or—for large language groups—to offer assessments in the students' native language. Realistically, these options present almost as many problems as they attempt to solve.

STRATEGY 100   USE ACCOMMODATIONS IN SETTING

IN CONCEPT

Accommodations in setting are those that involve *where* a test may be given. Accommodations of this type reduce distractions for ELLs and lower their levels of test-related anxiety.

IN PRACTICE

ELLs may be offered the option of taking standardized tests in a separate location, in small groups, or even individually. They may also be given preferential seating, such as facing a teacher or at the front of the room.

Tests may be administered in a classroom that is familiar to them—their own home-room or their English language development classroom. And a teacher whom the students know and feel comfortable with may be chosen as test administrator.

STRATEGY 101   USE ACCOMMODATIONS IN TIMING
AND SCHEDULING

IN CONCEPT

Accommodations in timing and scheduling are those that involve *when* a test is given. Giving ELLs extra time or modifying their schedule to complete tests is a reasonable and workable modification. Because ELLs must spend extra effort and additional time decoding and deciphering the language of a test before they can demonstrate their content knowledge, it seems fair to schedule their tests in a way that extends the time they have to complete them. Accommodations in time and schedule compensate ELLs for the increased language burden and produce a more accurate assessment of their content achievement levels.

IN PRACTICE

Options for scheduling that allow ELLs extra time include extending test time on the same day, offering the test in several shorter sessions over several days, or some combination of the two. Tests can be scheduled at a time of day that is beneficial to the students. Extra breaks or longer breaks can be included in the test schedule.

While all of these options offer ELLs more time to separate language from content on tests, the extra time to focus may also prolong students' feelings of test-related anxiety. It is important to achieve a good balance.

STRATEGY 102 SELECT A COMBINATION OF THE MOST EFFECTIVE ACCOMMODATIONS

IN CONCEPT

Effective accommodations balance the needs of ELLs and the resources of test administrators. Combining modifications that are practical and relatively easy for schools to accommodate with ones that offer ELLs the maximum benefits produces a short list of recommendations.

IN PRACTICE

- Test ELLs separately, in small groups and in a familiar location.
- Schedule a reasonable amount of additional time for ELLs to take the test.
- Allow ELLs use of bilingual reference aids.
- Simplify directions, word usage, and long, complicated questions.
- Encourage ELLs to seek clarification during the test.

These accommodations seem to present a workable combination. School resources will not be unduly burdened, and test outcomes will more accurately reflect ELLs' content knowledge and skills. It is a win–win situation: Students, teachers, and schools will all benefit from the results.

Finally, it should be said that no accommodation, no matter how advantageous to ELLs, should be used if it has not been previously practiced in a classroom test situation. The day of a high-stakes test is not the time to surprise students with new approaches to test taking.

IN SUMMARY: MAXIMIZING STUDENT POTENTIAL ON STANDARDIZED TESTS

Teaching students to perform well on tests starts with sound content instruction. But often, good test takers are made, not born. Students who feel comfortable taking classroom tests may be able to perform better on high-stakes tests by approaching the testing situation with lower anxiety.

ELLs' performance on standardized tests can improve through practicing reading and answering multiple-choice questions, understanding the patterns and phrases used in test directions, and learning test-taking strategies. Before test administration day, teachers and school administrators should work with the district to agree on the best possible combination of accommodations. ELLs should also know the accommodations available to them on test day.

Bringing together the strategies for assessment with the strategies for instruction will help your ELLs reach their fullest potential on their path to academic success.

CONCLUSION

Yes, the challenge is here. Teachers must find ways to effectively teach content to ELLs—first to facilitate their understanding of subject-area content and then to create instruments and opportunities that accurately evaluate the learning that has taken place. The strategies of instruction and assessment detailed in this volume have given you the means to help you meet that challenge.

Start by choosing strategies that appeal to you and are appropriate for your students. Integrate them into your instructional routines. Add more strategies on a regular basis. Experiment with them. Try them out with the whole class, not just the ELLs. Integrate different types of strategies: learning strategies, instructional strategies, textbook strategies, assignment strategies, and assessment strategies. Evaluate those that work well and those that appear less effective. Eliminate the ones that appear less effective with your particular students and content area. Discuss them with your colleagues, and share ideas and applications. Keep trying. You, like your students, will be encouraged by the rewards of success.

And you *will* be rewarded. By choosing to use these strategies, you point your ELLs toward the path of achievement. With each small accomplishment, they begin to build their academic self-confidence and personal self-esteem. To you, their teacher, goes the credit for making the extra effort to help these students become successful participants in the academic environment that is such an important part of their daily lives.

Indeed, it is a challenge. But it is an exciting and rewarding challenge—one that is well worth embracing.

QUESTIONS FOR DISCUSSION

1. How do the strategies for maximizing student potential on standardized tests reflect the *Guidelines for Practice* presented at the beginning of this chapter?
2. How has high-stakes testing affected the education of ELLs? What has changed since implementation of the No Child Left Behind Act (NCLB) of 2001? If you have been teaching since before NCLB was enacted, draw upon your own observations. If you entered the profession since that time, interview several classroom teachers to gain insights in this area.
3. Research and report your state and/or district rules for standardized assessment, test content, and accommodations as they relate to ELLs.
4. Working in small geographically diversified groups of peers, compare the accommodations used in your schools. Do all schools in your district or county use similar sets of accommodations? Are they all used in the same ways? If your comparisons show nonuniform accommodation usage, how do you think the variations might affect test results?
5. Formulate a personal philosophy for testing ELLs. What do you believe would constitute best practices for ELLs taking high-stakes tests? Justify your beliefs.

REFERENCES AND RESOURCES

Cizek, G. J., & Burg, S. S. (2005). *Addressing test anxiety in a high-stakes environment: Strategies for classrooms and schools.* Thousand Oaks, CA: Corwin Press.

Gottlieb, M. (2006). *Assessing English language learners: Bridges from language proficiency to academic achievement.* Thousand Oaks, CA: Corwin Press.

Pearlman, M. (2002). *Measuring and supporting English language learning in schools: Challenges for test makers.* Presentation at National Center for Research on Evaluation, Standards, and Student Testing (CRESST) Conference, Los Angeles, CA.

Teachers of English to Speakers of Other Languages, Inc. (TESOL). (2005). *Position paper on assessment and accountability of English language learners under the No Child Left Behind Act of 2001 (Public law 107-110).* Retrieved March 22, 2006, from http://www.tesol.org/s_tesol/bin.asp?CID=32&DID=4720&DOC=FILE.PDF

The TechConnection

www.cresst.org

The National Center for Research on Evaluation, Standards, and Student Testing Web site has a dedicated section just for teachers, as well as conference abstracts and presentations.

www.ncela.gwu.edu/spotlight/3_assessment.html

The National Clearinghouse for English Language Acquisition (NCELA) Web site provides resources about the assessment of and accountability for English Language Learners.

GLOSSARY OF ACRONYMS

English language learner or *ELL* is the term used consistently in this text. However, many other terms are in general usage. The acronyms listed here are used in various school districts in the United States and by state and federal education agencies. The terms refer to individuals, classes, programs, concepts, and agencies.

Individuals

LEP	Limited English proficient
NEP	Non-English proficient
PEP	Partially English proficient
FEP	Fluent English proficient
NES	Non-English speaker
LES	Limited English speaker (or speaking)
FES	Fluent English speaker (or speaking)
EL	English learner
ELL	English language learner
NNS	Non-native speaker
NS	Native speaker
LMS	Language minority student

Classes and/or Programs

EFL	English as a foreign language
ESL	English as a second language
ESOL	English for speakers of other languages
EAL	English as an additional language
ELD	English language development
ELA	English language arts
SDAIE	Specially designed academic instruction in English
SEI	Structured English immersion
SEIP	Structured English immersion program
SI	Sheltered instruction
ESP	English for specific (or special) purposes
EOP	English for occupational purposes
EAP	English for academic purposes

IEP	Intensive English program
LCD	Linguistically and culturally diverse
CLAD	Cross-cultural, language and academic development

Concepts

BICS	Basic interpersonal communication skills
CALP	Cognitive academic language proficiency
ELP	English language proficiency
L1	First (native) language
L2	Second (target) language
SLA	Second language acquisition

Agencies

CABE	California Association for Bilingual Speakers
CAL	Center for Applied Linguistics
CREDE	Center for Research on Education, Diversity, and Excellence
NABE	National Association for Bilingual Speakers
NAME	National Association for Multicultural Education
NCBE	National Clearinghouse of Bilingual Education
OBEMLA	Office of Bilingual Education and Minority Languages Affairs (*now defunct*)
OELA	Office of English Language Acquisition, Language Enhancement, and Academic Achievement for Limited English Proficient Students
TESOL	Teaching (or Teachers of) English to Speakers of Other Languages

ADDITIONAL RESOURCES FOR TEACHERS

The books on this list make good reading for all aspects of teaching ELLs. They are broad based and simply too good to be listed in just one chapter!

Cary, S. (2000). *Working with second language learners: Answers to teachers' top ten questions.* Portsmouth, NH: Heinemann.

Dong, Y. R. (2004). *Teaching language and content to linguistically and culturally diverse students: Principles, ideas, and materials.* Greenwich, CT: Information Age Publishing.

Freeman, Y. S, Freeman, D. E., & Mercuri, S. (2002). *Closing the achievement gap: How to reach limited-formal schooling and long-term English learners.* Portsmouth, NH: Heinemann.

Herrell, A. L., & Jordan, M. (2005). *Fifty teaching strategies for English language learners* (2nd ed.). Upper Saddle River, NJ: Pearson Education.

Kottler, E., & Kottler, J. (2001). *Children with limited English: Teaching strategies for the regular classroom.* Thousand Oaks, CA: Corwin Press.

Vaughn, S. S., Bos, C. S., & Schumm, J. S. (2007). *Teaching students who are exceptional, diverse, and at-risk in the general education classroom* (4th Ed.). Boston: Allyn & Bacon.

Walter, T. (2004). *Teaching English language learners: The how to handbook.* White Plains, NY: Pearson Education.

The TechConnection

www.ncela.gwu.edu
  National Clearinghouse for English Language Acquisition & Language Instruction Educational Programs (NCELA) collects, analyzes, synthesizes, and disseminates information about language instruction educational programs for ELLs and related programs. It is funded by the U.S. Department of Education's Office of English Language Acquisition, Language Enhancement & Academic Achievement for Limited English Proficient Students (OELA) under Title III of the No Child Left Behind (NCLB) Act of 2001.

http://iteslj.org
  Published since 1995, this monthly Internet journal offers articles, research papers, lesson plans, teaching ideas, and classroom activities of interest to content teachers and teachers of English as a second language.

http://www.cal.org
  The Web site of the Center for Applied Linguistics gives access to topics of interest to secondary school teachers and to many related resources for ELL development.

http://www.ncela.gwu.edu/expert/glossary.html
  Here you will find a resource that explains and defines terms related to all aspects of teaching linguistically and culturally diverse students.

http://www.ncela.gwu.edu/resabout/literacy
  This Web site includes up-to-date research, articles, and information for helping ELLs achieve their fullest potential development in the areas of English language literacy, academic English, and content area literacy.